ANTHEM

Novels by Ayn Rand

We the Living

Anthem

The Fountainhead

Atlas Shrugged

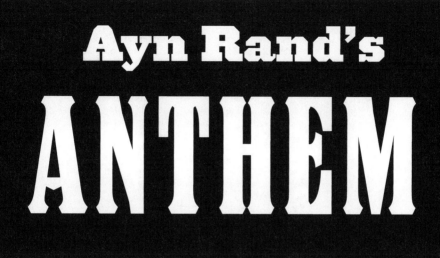

Ayn Rand's ANTHEM

THE GRAPHIC NOVEL

Based on the novella *Anthem* by Ayn Rand

Graphic novel produced by Marshall Holt Entertainment for
New American Library

Production Director: Charles Santino

Script: Charles Santino

Art: Joe Staton

Lettering and Digital Production:
Zachary R. Matheny/Glass House Graphics

 NEW AMERICAN LIBRARY

NEW AMERICAN LIBRARY
Published by New American Library, a division of
Penguin Group (USA) Inc., 375 Hudson Street,
New York, New York 10014, USA
Penguin Group (Canada), 90 Eglinton Avenue East, Suite 700, Toronto,
Ontario M4P 2Y3, Canada (a division of Pearson Penguin Canada Inc.)
Penguin Books Ltd., 80 Strand, London WC2R ORL, England
Penguin Ireland, 25 St. Stephen's Green, Dublin 2,
Ireland (a division of Penguin Books Ltd.)
Penguin Group (Australia), 250 Camberwell Road, Camberwell, Victoria 3124,
Australia (a division of Pearson Australia Group Pty. Ltd.)
Penguin Books India Pvt. Ltd., 11 Community Centre, Panchsheel Park,
New Delhi - 110 017, India
Penguin Group (NZ), 67 Apollo Drive, Rosedale, North Shore 0632,
New Zealand (a division of Pearson New Zealand Ltd.)
Penguin Books (South Africa) (Pty.) Ltd., 24 Sturdee Avenue,
Rosebank, Johannesburg 2196, South Africa

Penguin Books Ltd., Registered Offices:
80 Strand, London WC2R ORL, England

First published by New American Library,
a division of Penguin Group (USA) Inc.

First Printing, February 2011
1 3 5 7 9 10 8 6 4 2

Illustrations copyright © Charles Santino and Joe Staton, 2011
All rights reserved
Permission requests for college or textbook use should be addressed
to the Estate of Ayn Rand, PO Box 51808, Irvine, California 92619-9930.
Information about other books by Ayn Rand and her philosophy, Objectivism, may be
obtained by writing to OBJECTIVISM, PO Box 51808, Irvine, California 92619-9930.

REGISTERED TRADEMARK—MARCA REGISTRADA

Printed in the United States of America

PUBLISHER'S NOTE
This is a work of fiction. Names, characters, places, and incidents either are the product of the author's imagination or are used fictitiously, and any resemblance to actual persons, living or dead, business establishments, events, or locales is entirely coincidental.

The publisher does not have any control over and does not assume any responsibility for author or third-party Web sites or their content.

The scanning, uploading, and distribution of this book via the Internet or via any other means without the permission of the publisher is illegal and punishable by law. Please purchase only authorized electronic editions, and do not participate in or encourage electronic piracy of copyrighted materials. Your support of the author's rights is appreciated.

ANTHEM

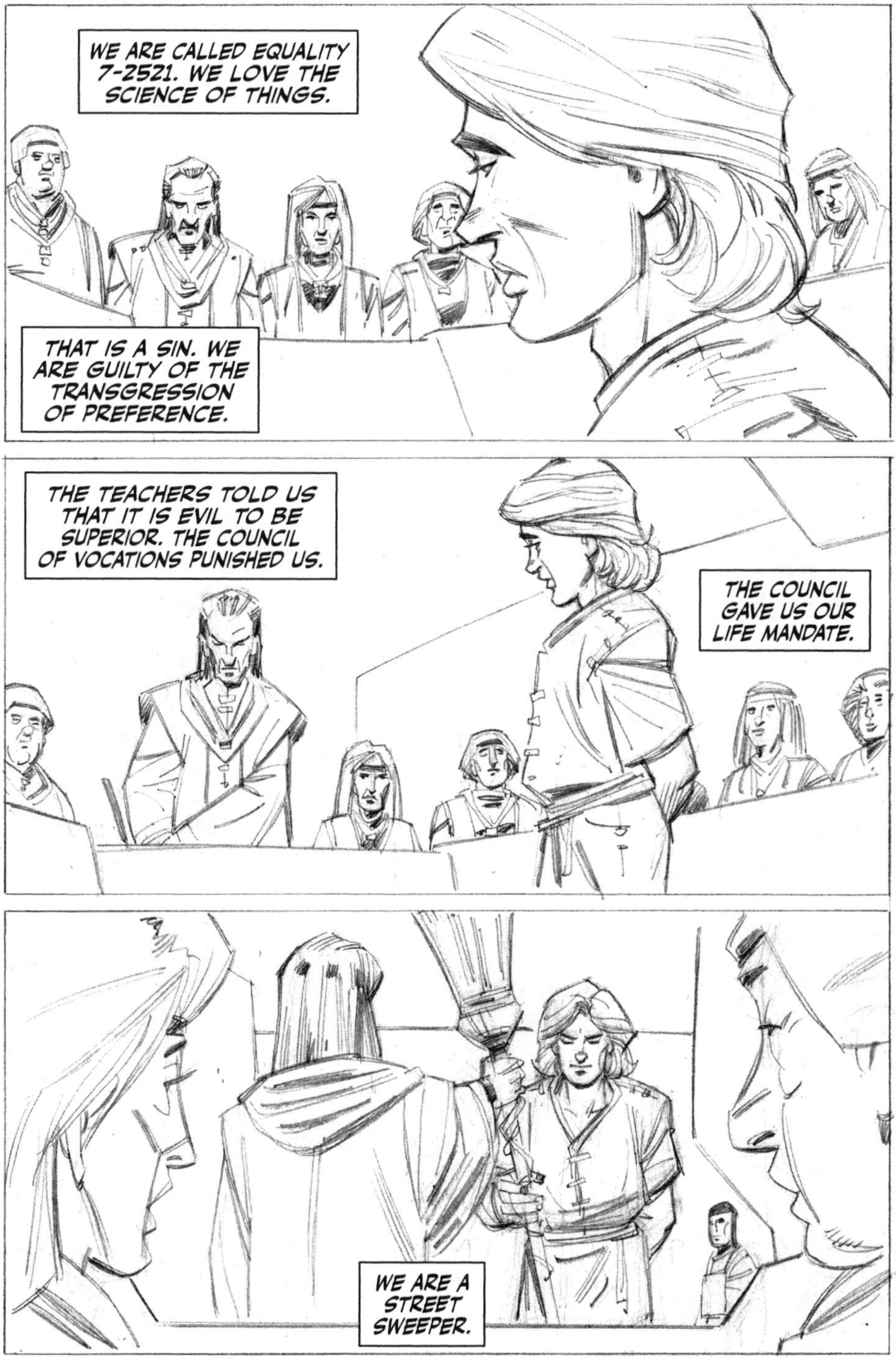
WE ARE CALLED EQUALITY 7-2521. WE LOVE THE SCIENCE OF THINGS.
THAT IS A SIN. WE ARE GUILTY OF THE TRANSGRESSION OF PREFERENCE.
THE TEACHERS TOLD US THAT IT IS EVIL TO BE SUPERIOR. THE COUNCIL OF VOCATIONS PUNISHED US.
THE COUNCIL GAVE US OUR LIFE MANDATE.
WE ARE A STREET SWEEPER.

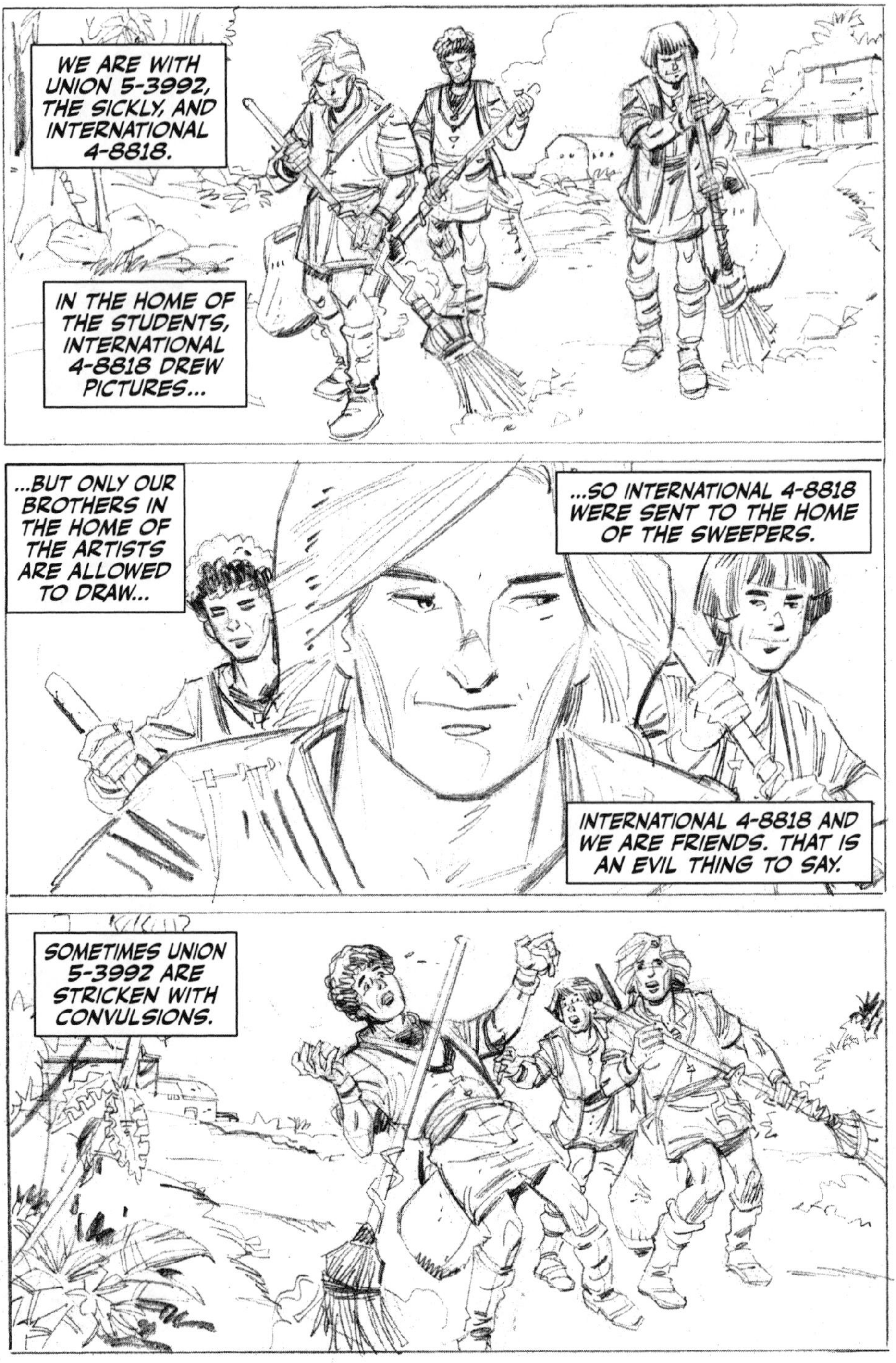
WE ARE WITH UNION 5-3992, THE SICKLY, AND INTERNATIONAL 4-8818.
IN THE HOME OF THE STUDENTS, INTERNATIONAL 4-8818 DREW PICTURES...
...BUT ONLY OUR BROTHERS IN THE HOME OF THE ARTISTS ARE ALLOWED TO DRAW...
...SO INTERNATIONAL 4-8818 WERE SENT TO THE HOME OF THE SWEEPERS.
INTERNATIONAL 4-8818 AND WE ARE FRIENDS. THAT IS AN EVIL THING TO SAY.
SOMETIMES UNION 5-3992 ARE STRICKEN WITH CONVULSIONS.

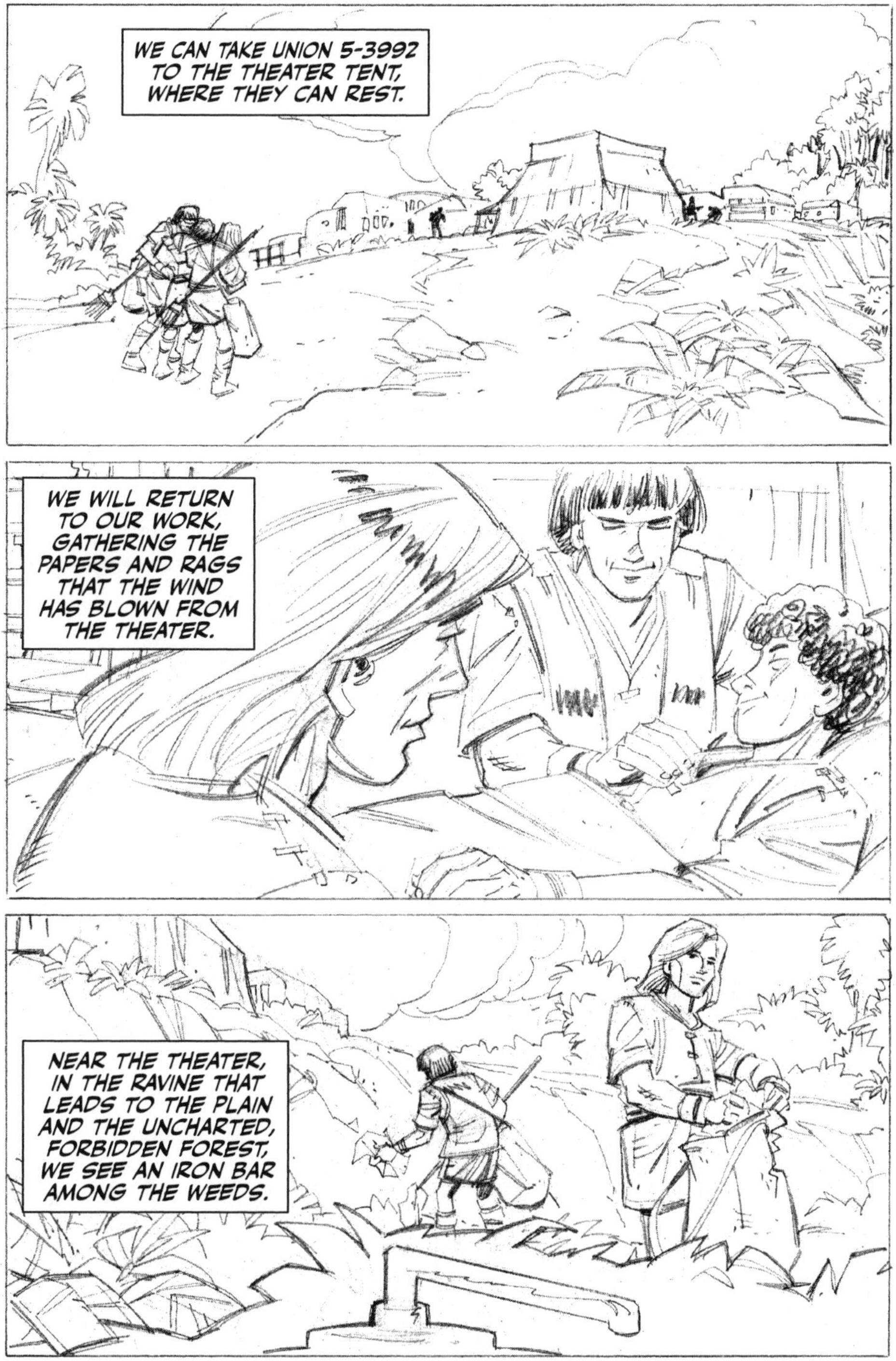
WE CAN TAKE UNION 5-3992 TO THE THEATER TENT, WHERE THEY CAN REST.
WE WILL RETURN TO OUR WORK, GATHERING THE PAPERS AND RAGS THAT THE WIND HAS BLOWN FROM THE THEATER.
NEAR THE THEATER, IN THE RAVINE THAT LEADS TO THE PLAIN AND THE UNCHARTED, FORBIDDEN FOREST, WE SEE AN IRON BAR AMONG THE WEEDS.

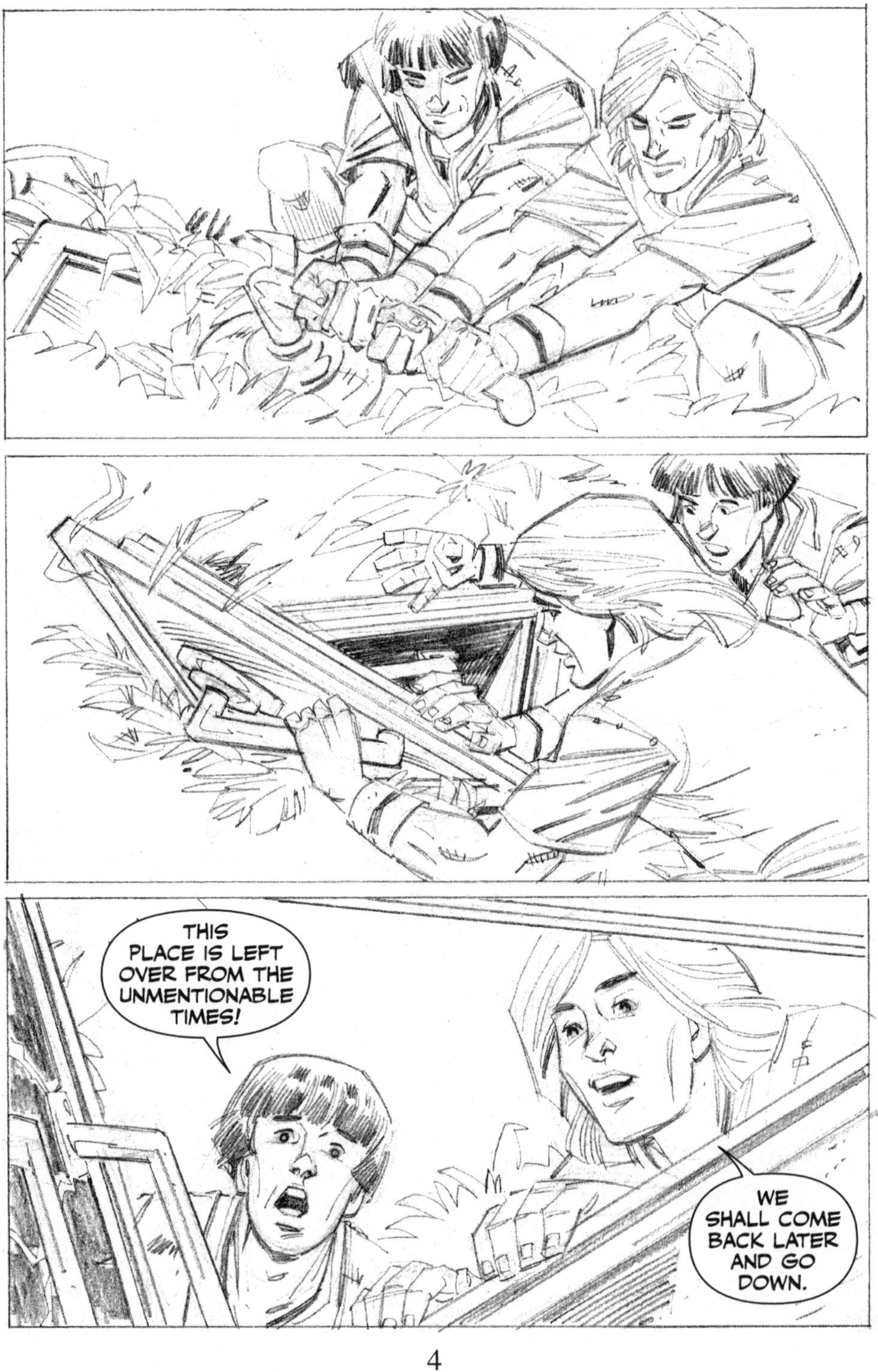
THIS PLACE IS LEFT OVER FROM THE UNMENTIONABLE TIMES!
WE SHALL COME BACK LATER AND GO DOWN.

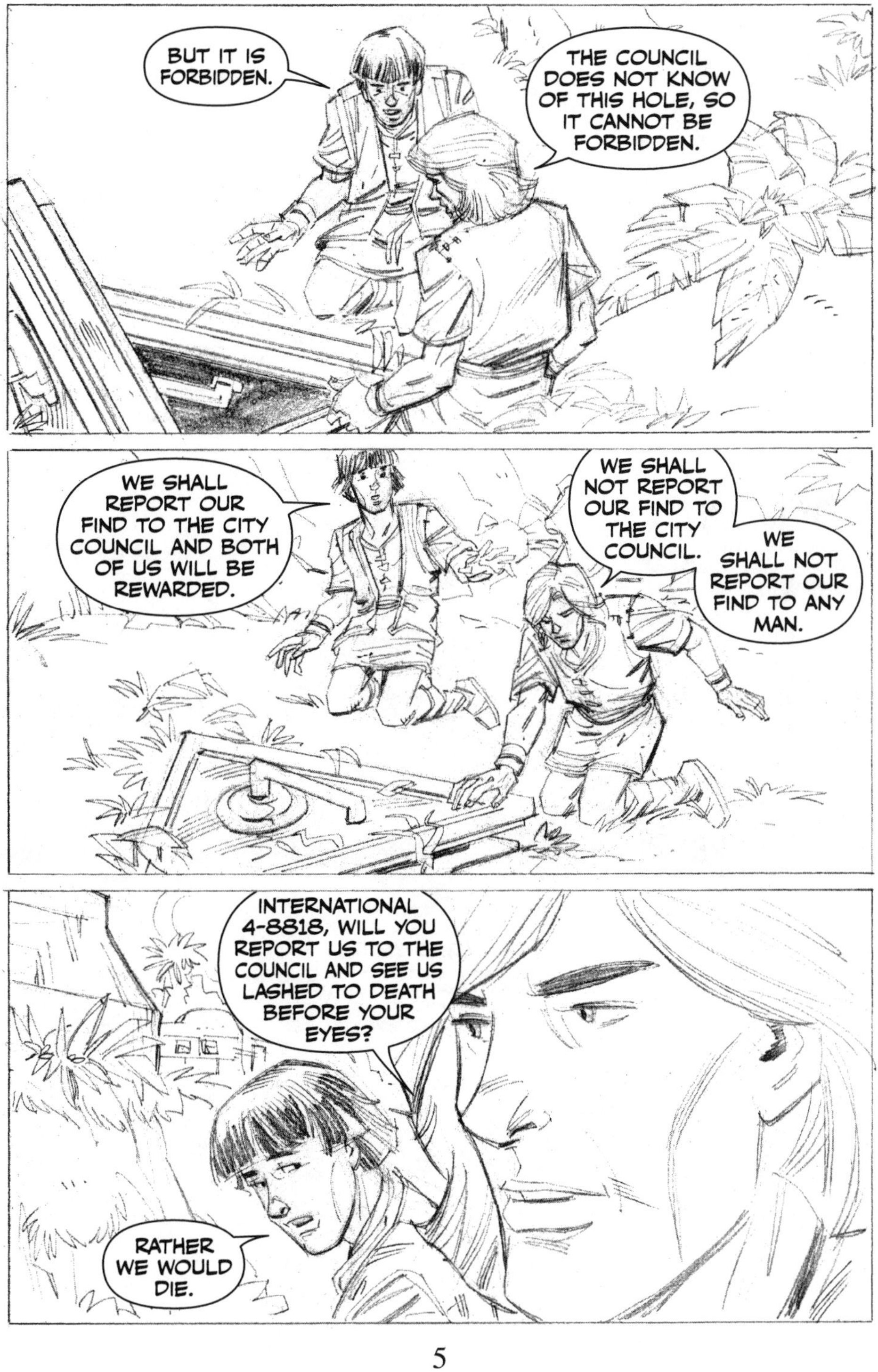
BUT IT IS FORBIDDEN.
THE COUNCIL DOES NOT KNOW OF THIS HOLE, SO IT CANNOT BE FORBIDDEN.
WE SHALL REPORT OUR FIND TO THE CITY COUNCIL AND BOTH OF US WILL BE REWARDED.
WE SHALL NOT REPORT OUR FIND TO THE CITY COUNCIL.
WE SHALL NOT REPORT OUR FIND TO ANY MAN.
INTERNATIONAL 4-8818, WILL YOU REPORT US TO THE COUNCIL AND SEE US LASHED TO DEATH BEFORE YOUR EYES?
RATHER WE WOULD DIE.

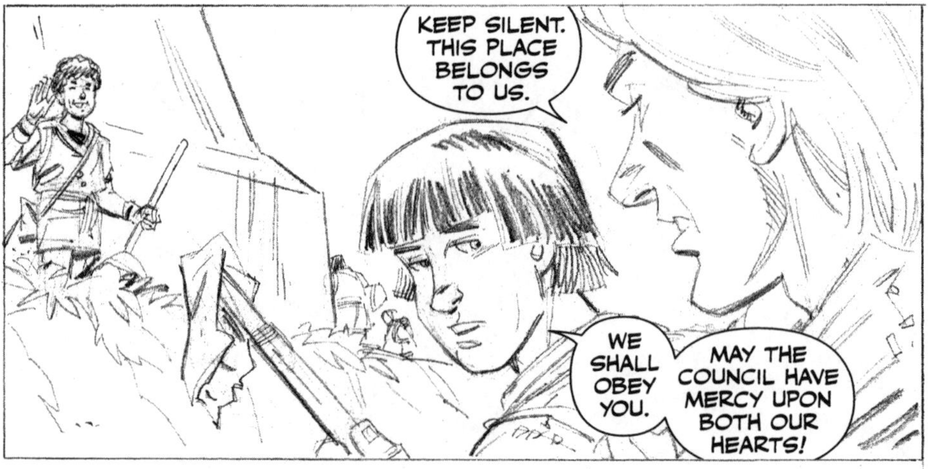
KEEP SILENT. THIS PLACE BELONGS TO US.
WE SHALL OBEY YOU.
MAY THE COUNCIL HAVE MERCY UPON BOTH OUR HEARTS!

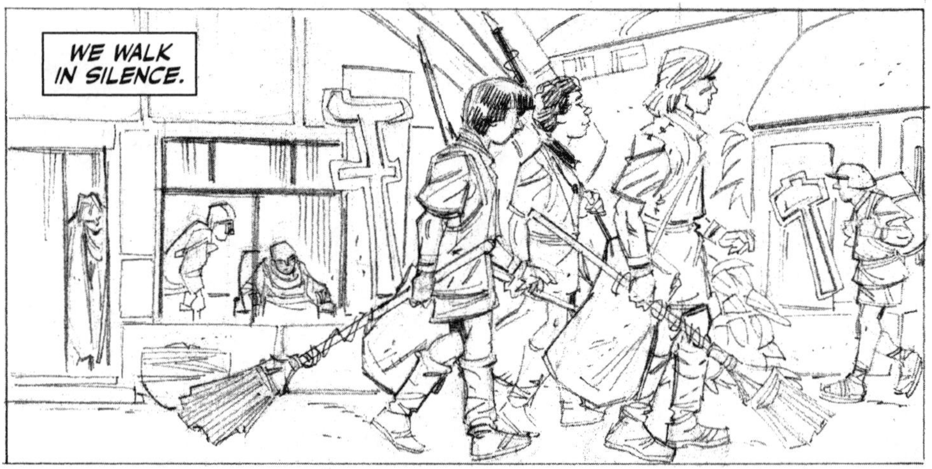
WE WALK IN SILENCE.

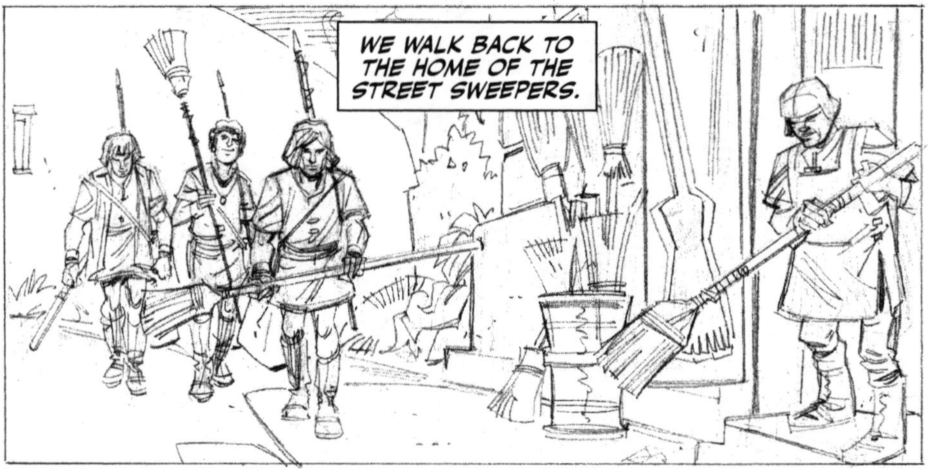
WE WALK BACK TO THE HOME OF THE STREET SWEEPERS.

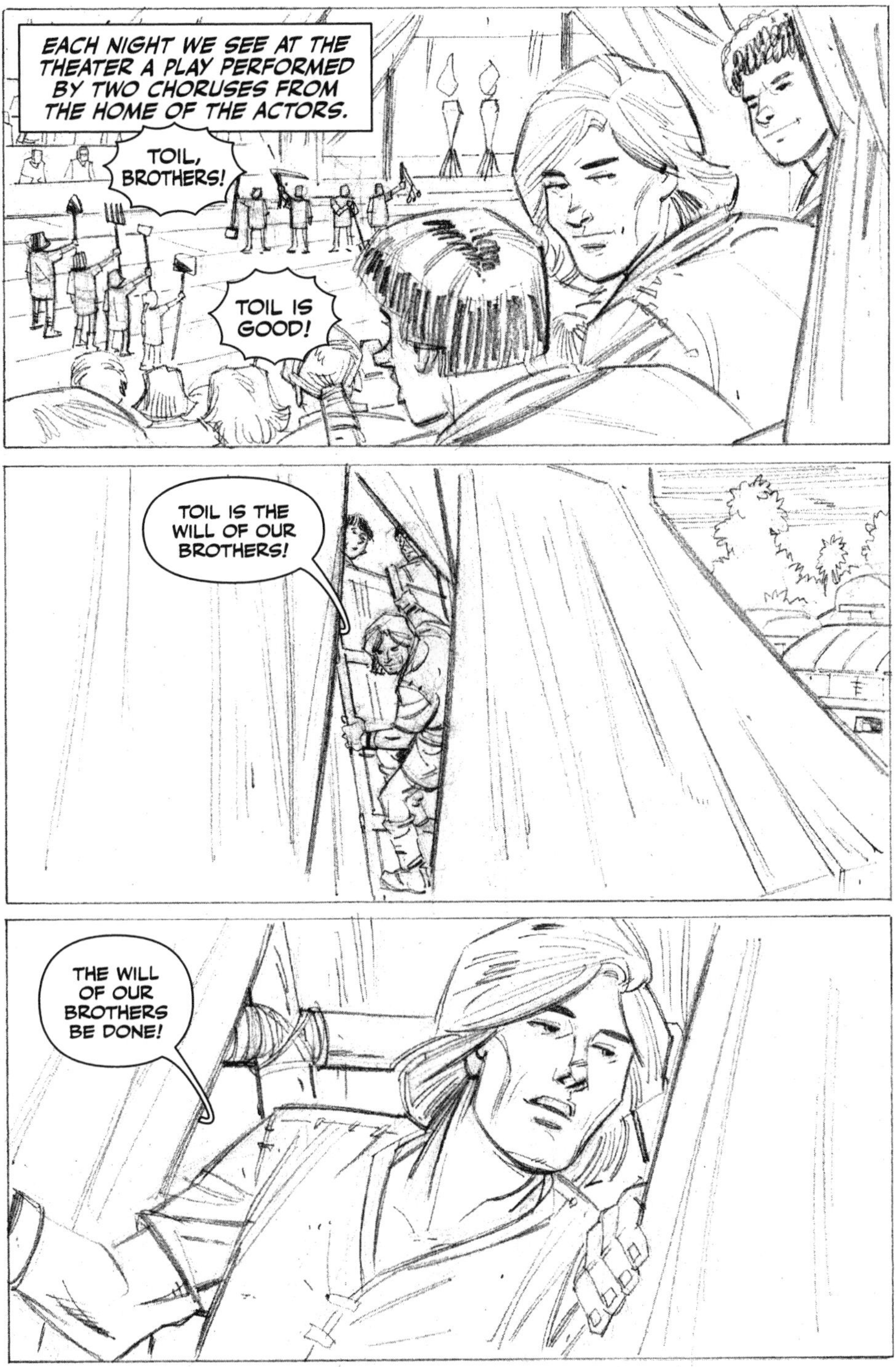
EACH NIGHT WE SEE AT THE THEATER A PLAY PERFORMED BY TWO CHORUSES FROM THE HOME OF THE ACTORS.
TOIL, BROTHERS!
TOIL IS GOOD!
TOIL IS THE WILL OF OUR BROTHERS!
THE WILL OF OUR BROTHERS BE DONE!

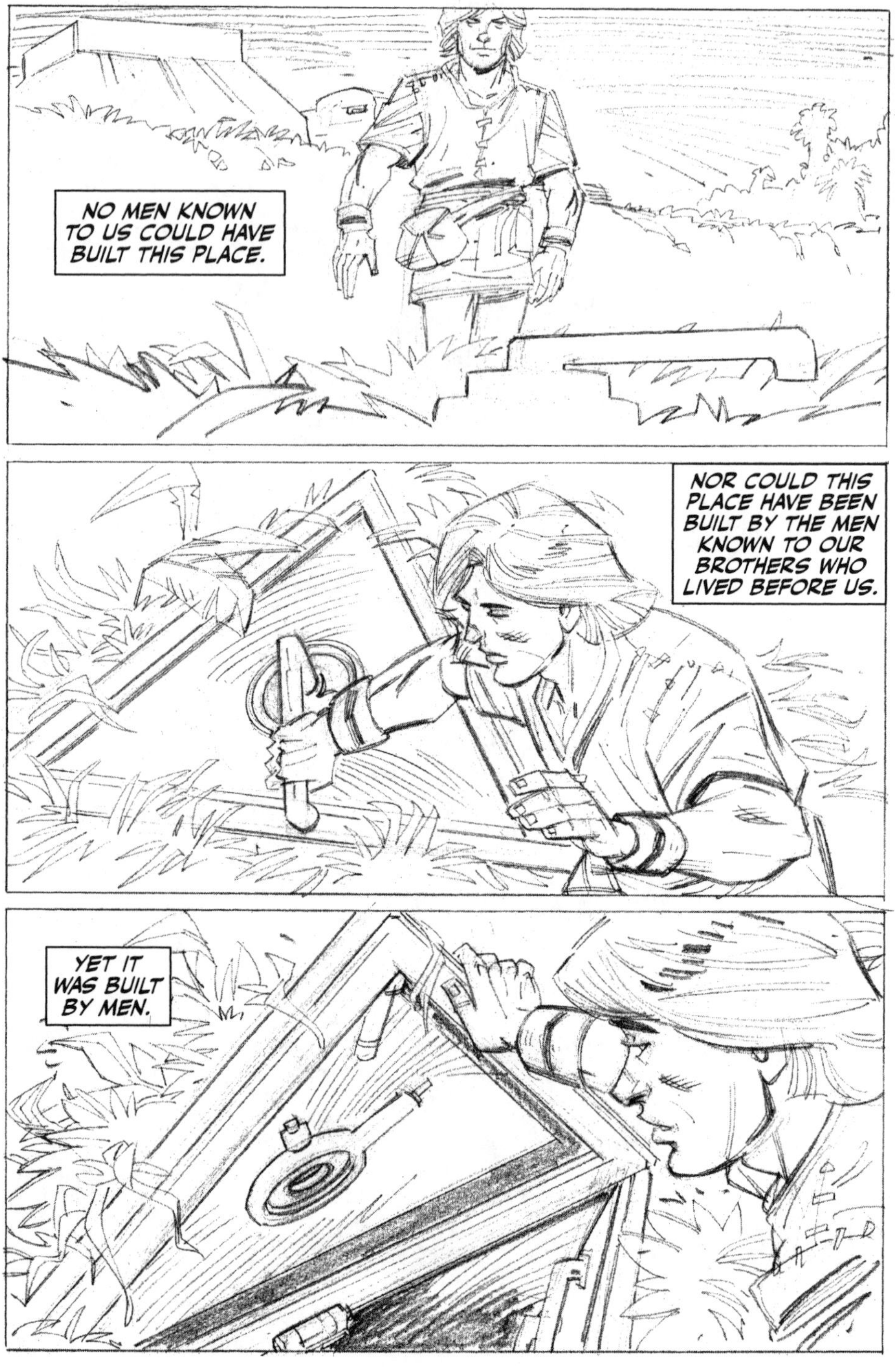
NO MEN KNOWN TO US COULD HAVE BUILT THIS PLACE.
NOR COULD THIS PLACE HAVE BEEN BUILT BY THE MEN KNOWN TO OUR BROTHERS WHO LIVED BEFORE US.
YET IT WAS BUILT BY MEN.

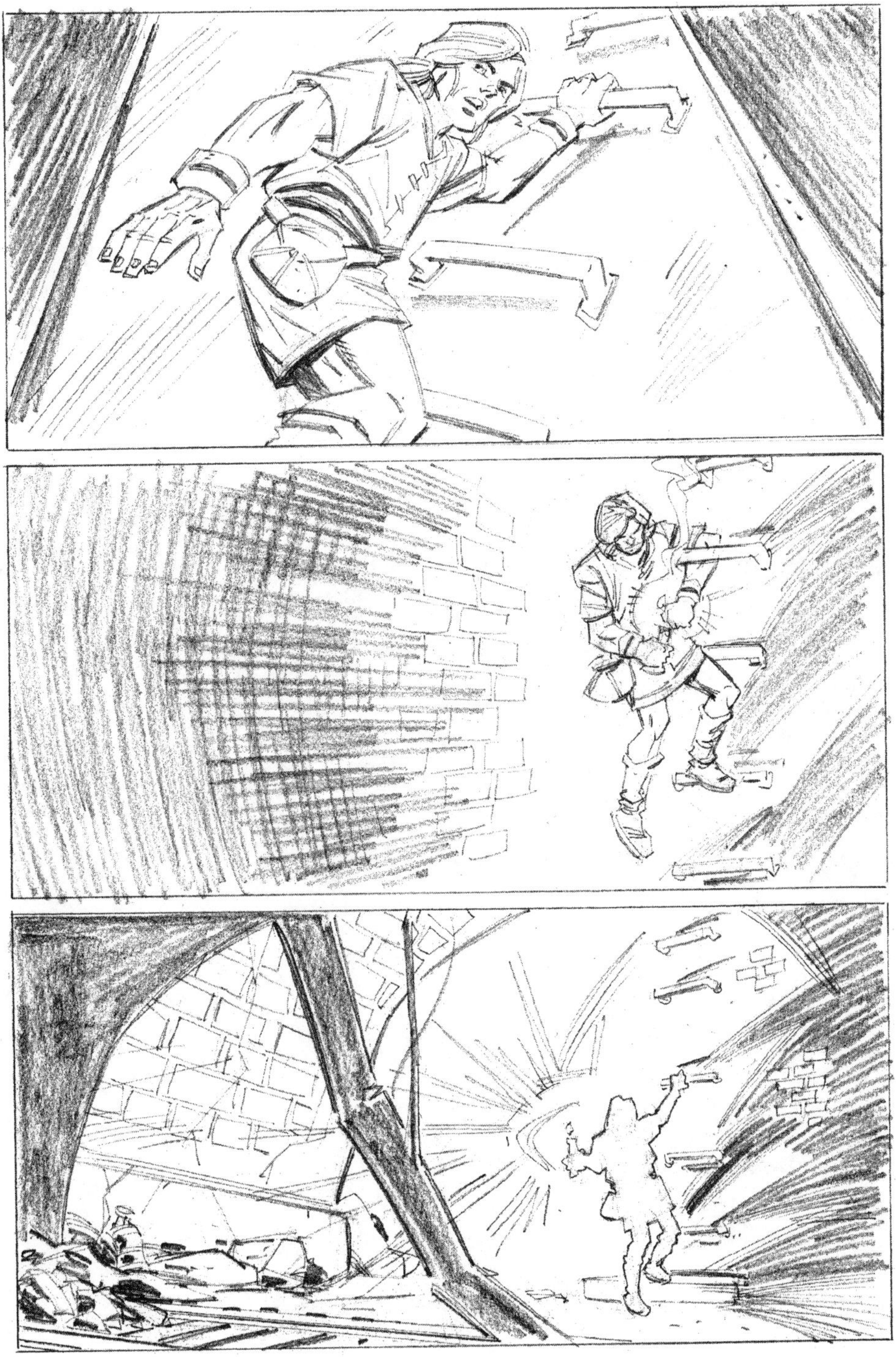

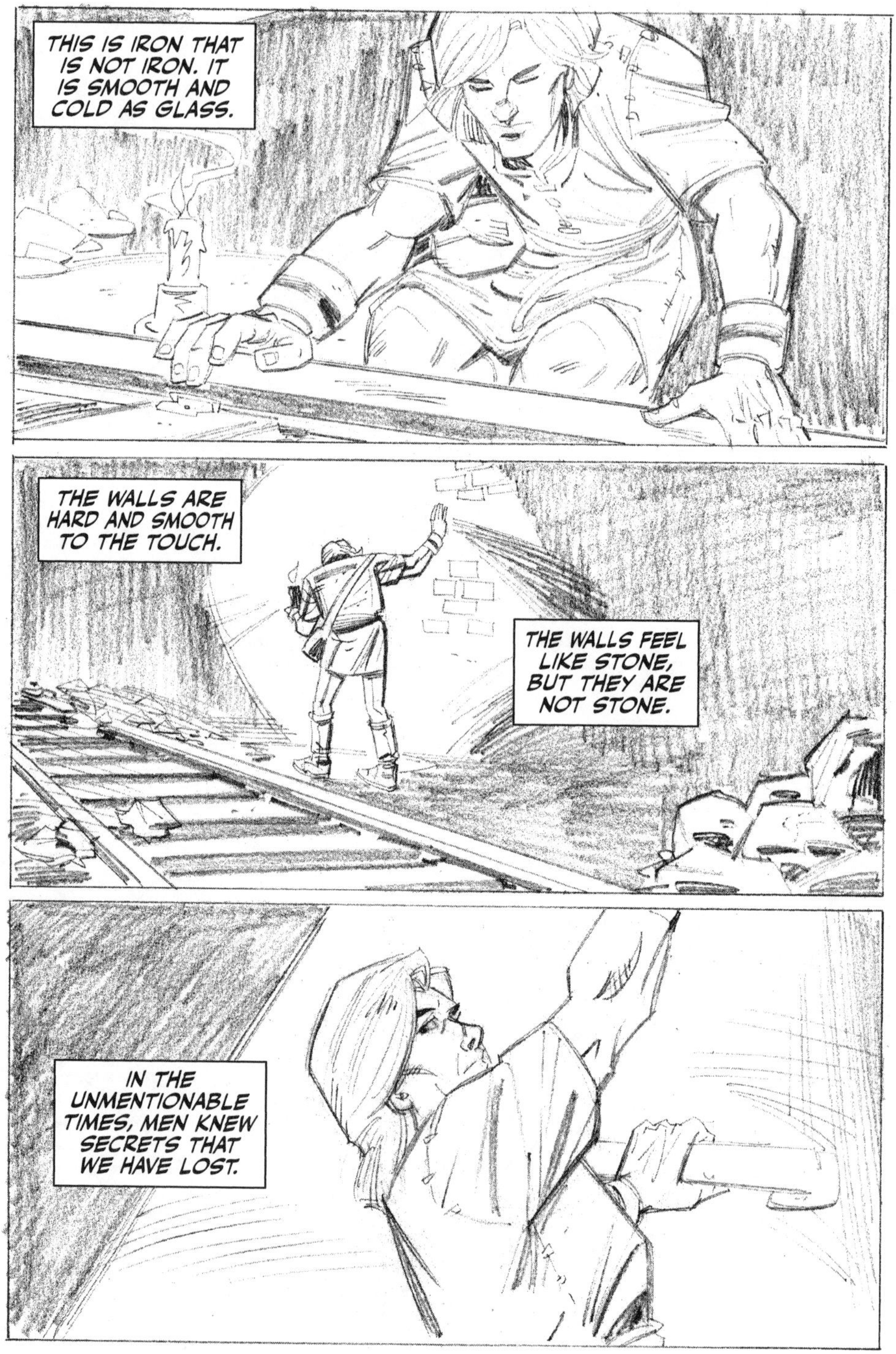
THIS IS IRON THAT IS NOT IRON. IT IS SMOOTH AND COLD AS GLASS.
THE WALLS ARE HARD AND SMOOTH TO THE TOUCH.
THE WALLS FEEL LIKE STONE, BUT THEY ARE NOT STONE.
IN THE UNMENTIONABLE TIMES, MEN KNEW SECRETS THAT WE HAVE LOST.

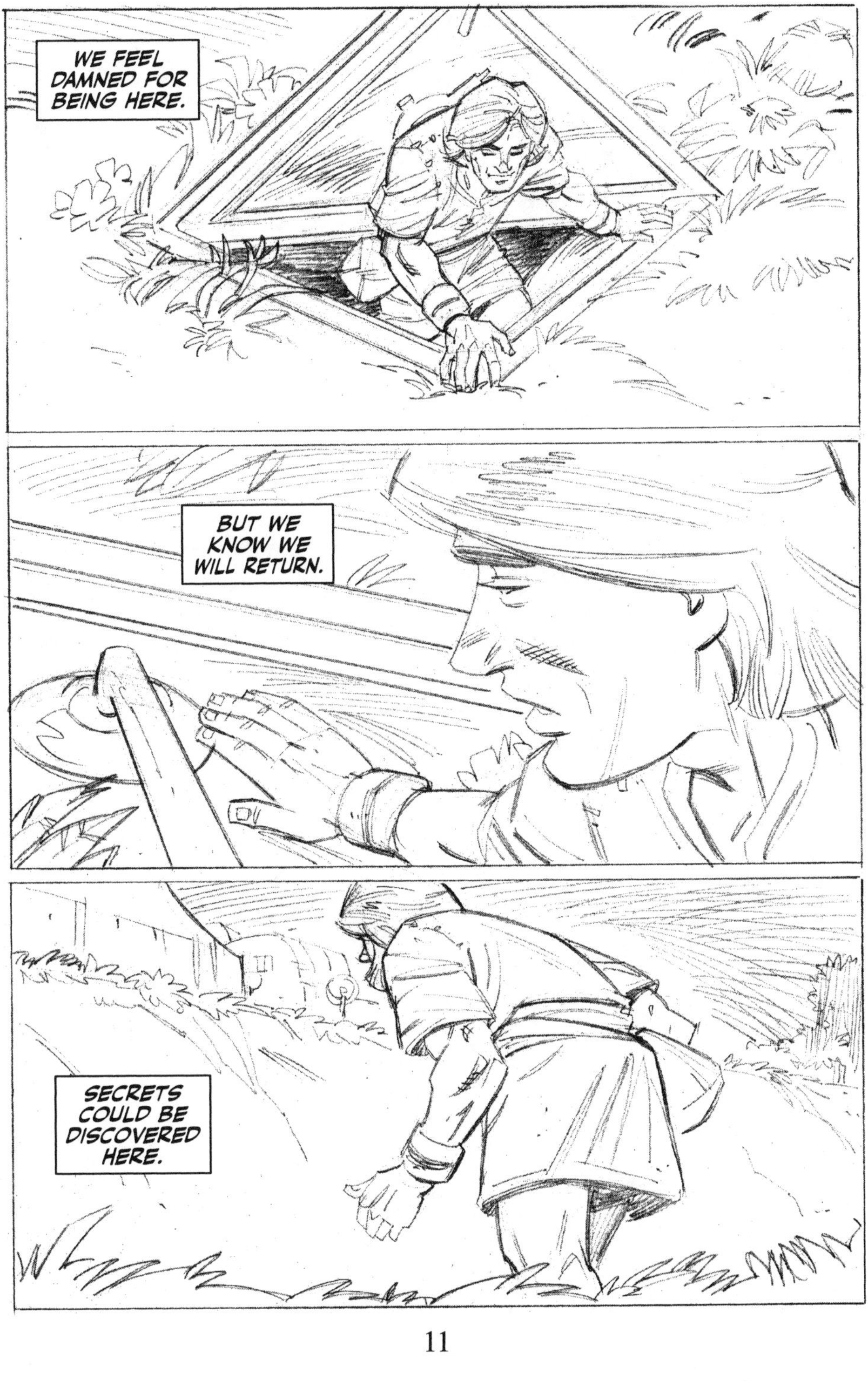
WE FEEL DAMNED FOR BEING HERE.
BUT WE KNOW WE WILL RETURN.
SECRETS COULD BE DISCOVERED HERE.

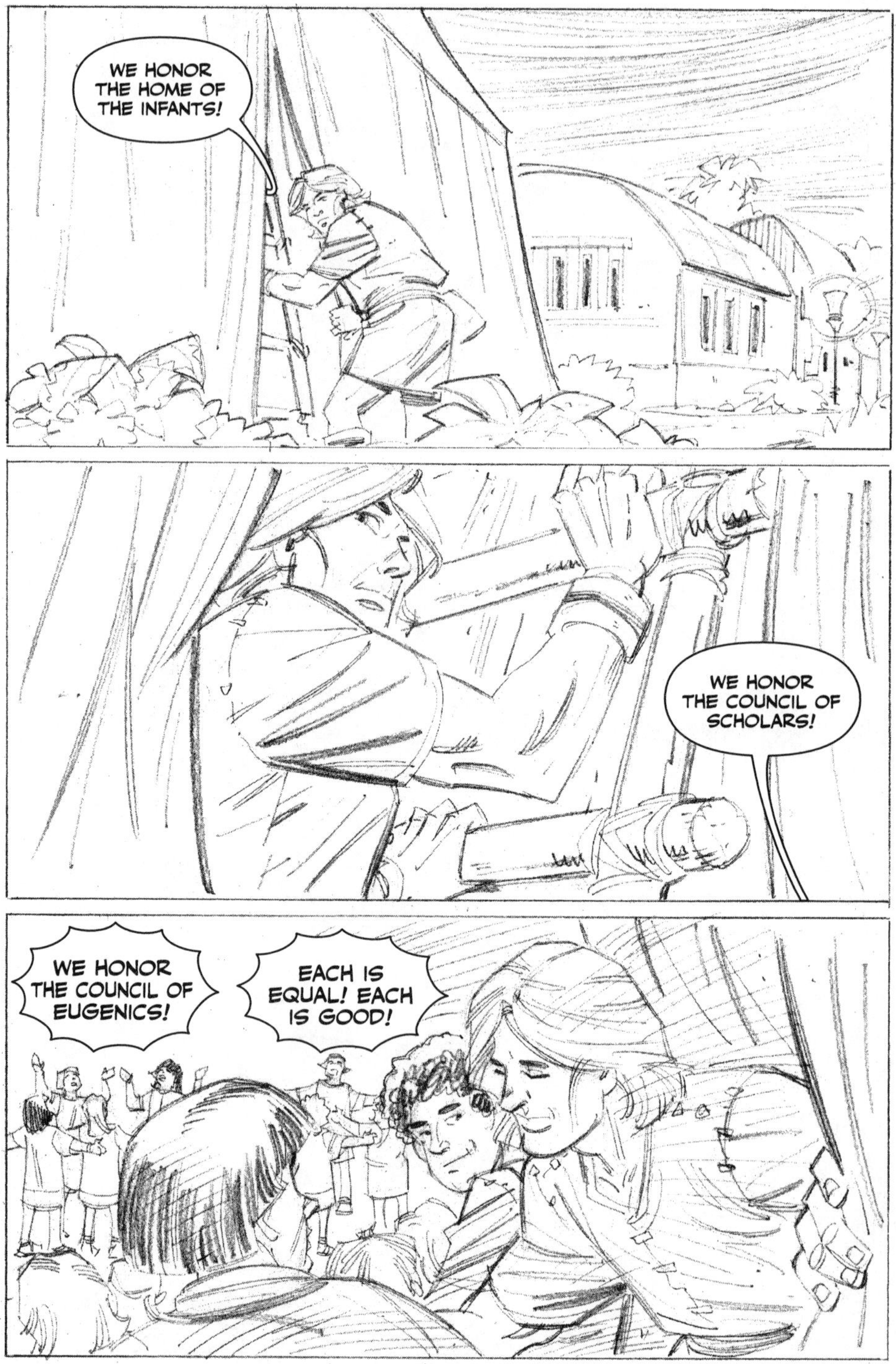
WE HONOR THE HOME OF THE INFANTS!
WE HONOR THE COUNCIL OF SCHOLARS!
WE HONOR THE COUNCIL OF EUGENICS!
EACH IS EQUAL! EACH IS GOOD!

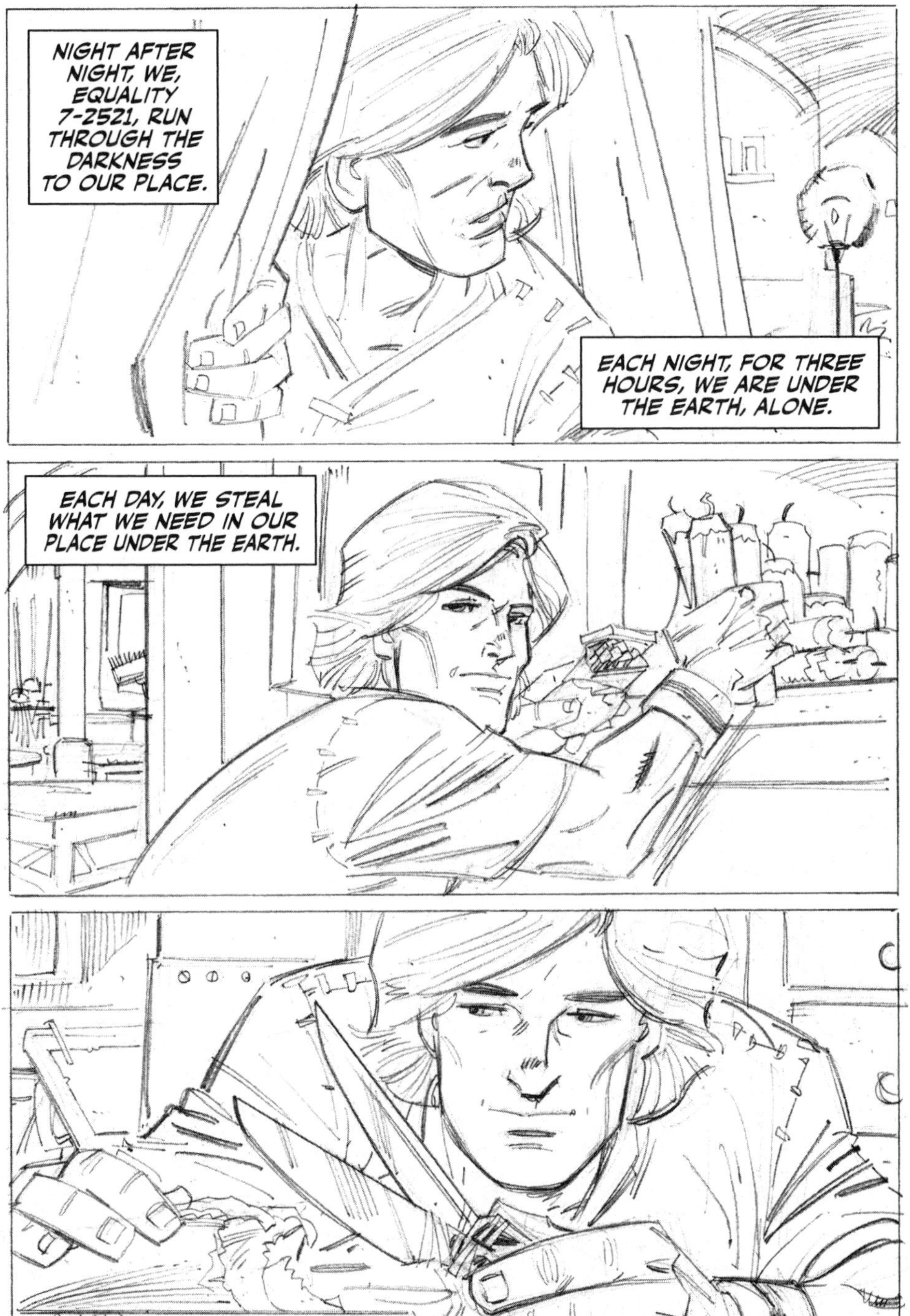
NIGHT AFTER NIGHT, WE, EQUALITY 7-2521, RUN THROUGH THE DARKNESS TO OUR PLACE.
EACH NIGHT, FOR THREE HOURS, WE ARE UNDER THE EARTH, ALONE.
EACH DAY, WE STEAL WHAT WE NEED IN OUR PLACE UNDER THE EARTH.

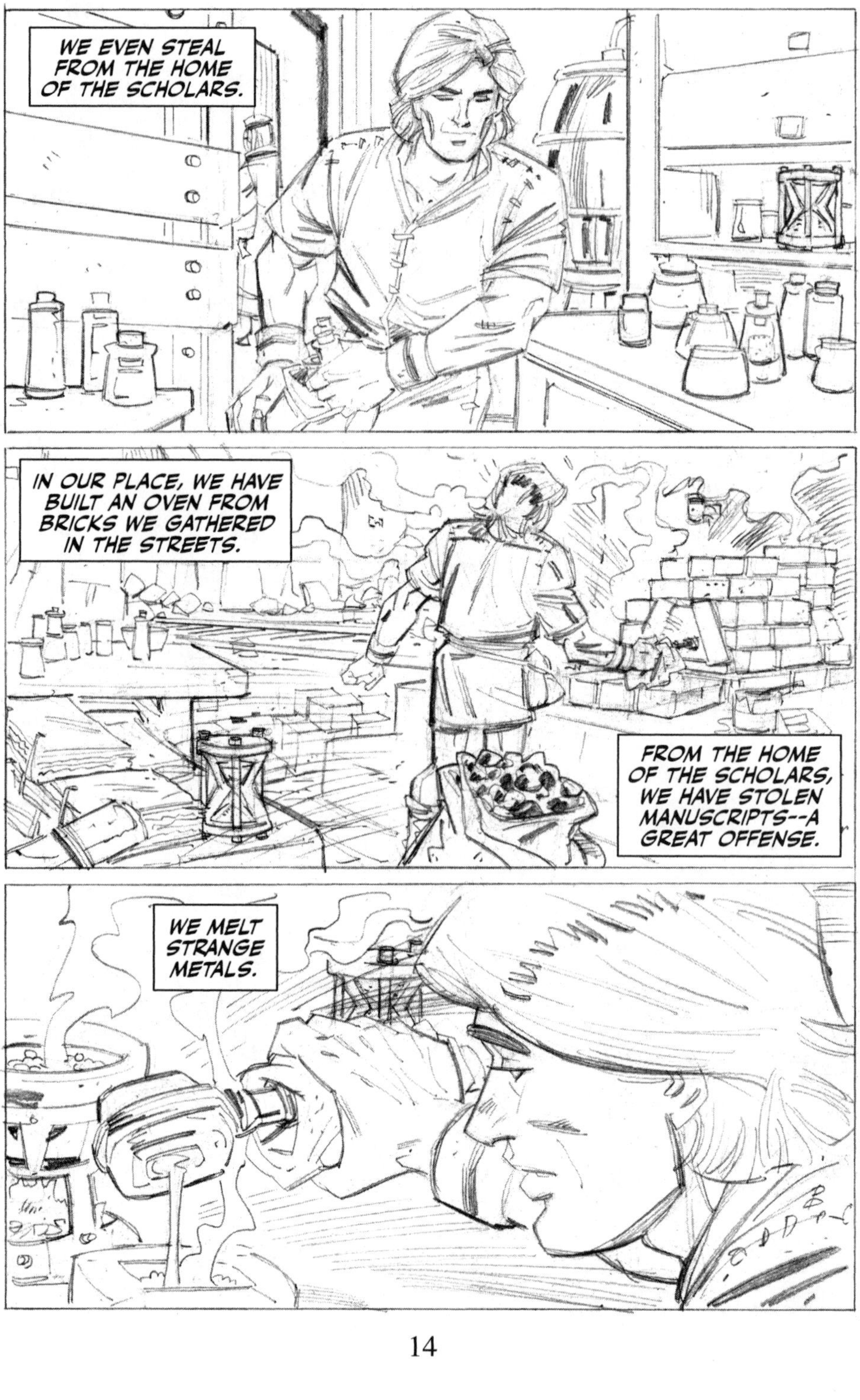
WE EVEN STEAL FROM THE HOME OF THE SCHOLARS.
IN OUR PLACE, WE HAVE BUILT AN OVEN FROM BRICKS WE GATHERED IN THE STREETS.
FROM THE HOME OF THE SCHOLARS, WE HAVE STOLEN MANUSCRIPTS--A GREAT OFFENSE.
WE MELT STRANGE METALS.

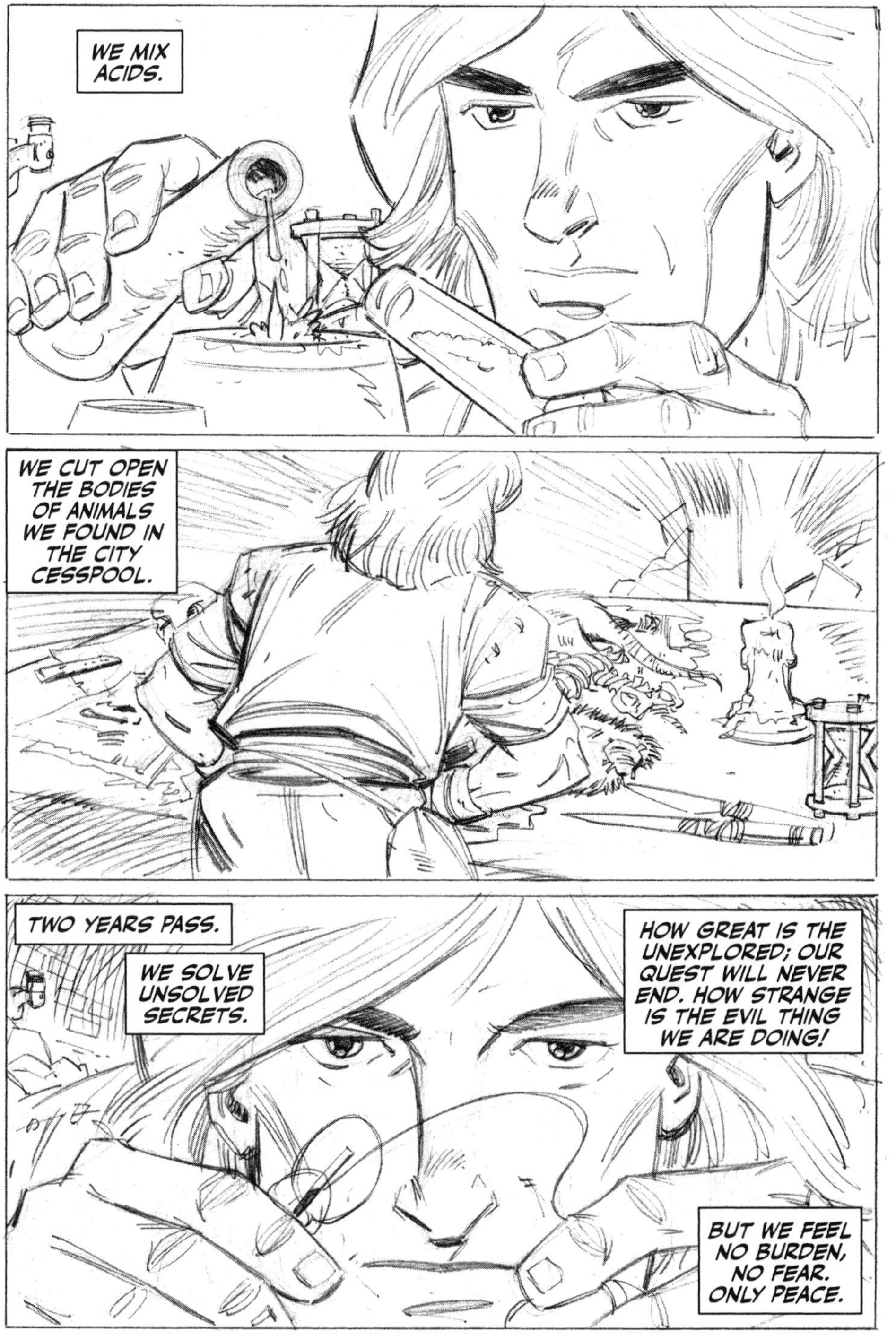
WE MIX ACIDS.
WE CUT OPEN THE BODIES OF ANIMALS WE FOUND IN THE CITY CESSPOOL.
TWO YEARS PASS.
WE SOLVE UNSOLVED SECRETS.
HOW GREAT IS THE UNEXPLORED; OUR QUEST WILL NEVER END. HOW STRANGE IS THE EVIL THING WE ARE DOING!
BUT WE FEEL NO BURDEN, NO FEAR. ONLY PEACE.

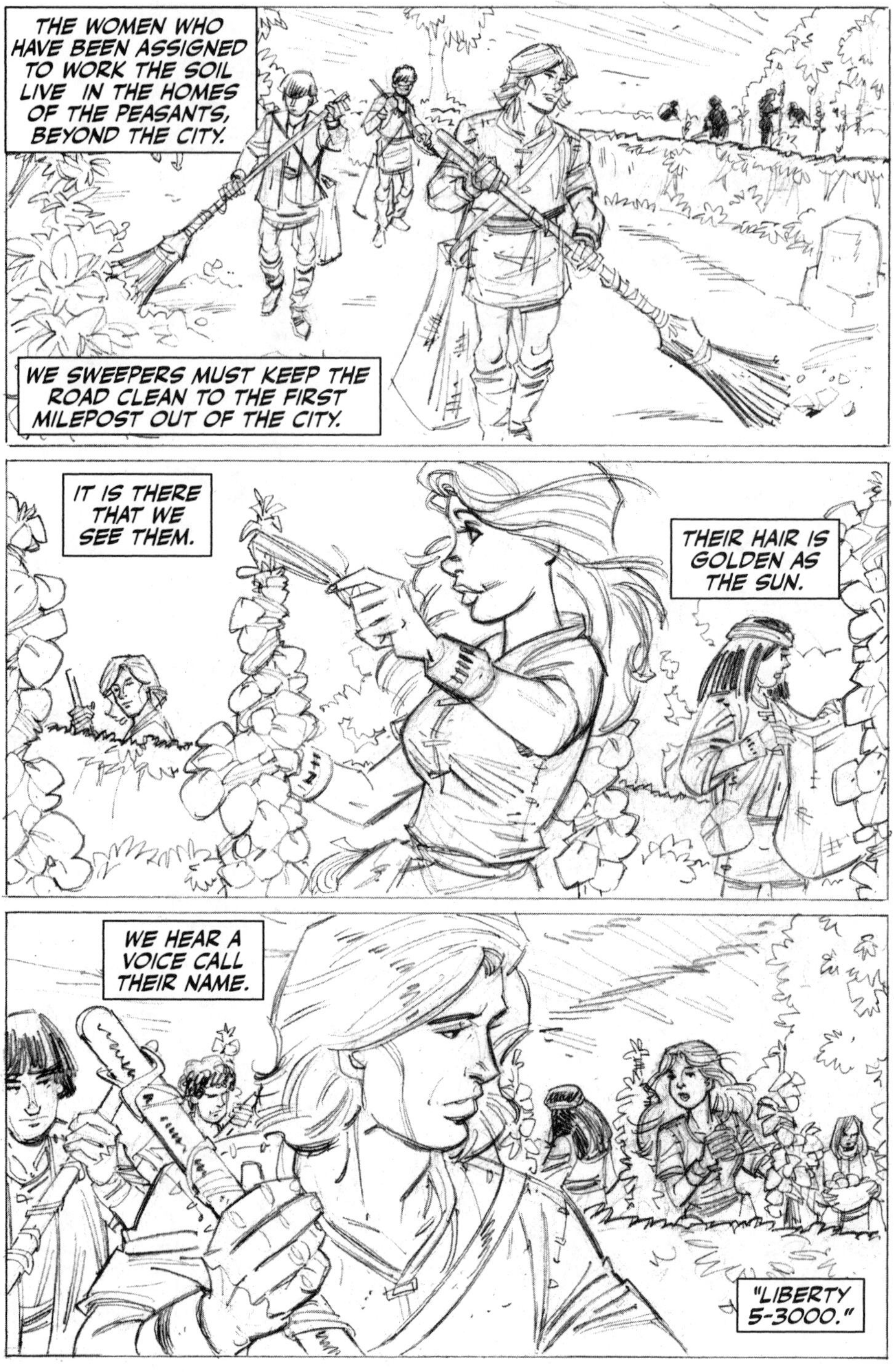
THE WOMEN WHO HAVE BEEN ASSIGNED TO WORK THE SOIL LIVE IN THE HOMES OF THE PEASANTS, BEYOND THE CITY.
WE SWEEPERS MUST KEEP THE ROAD CLEAN TO THE FIRST MILEPOST OUT OF THE CITY.
IT IS THERE THAT WE SEE THEM.
THEIR HAIR IS GOLDEN AS THE SUN.
WE HEAR A VOICE CALL THEIR NAME.
"LIBERTY 5-3000."

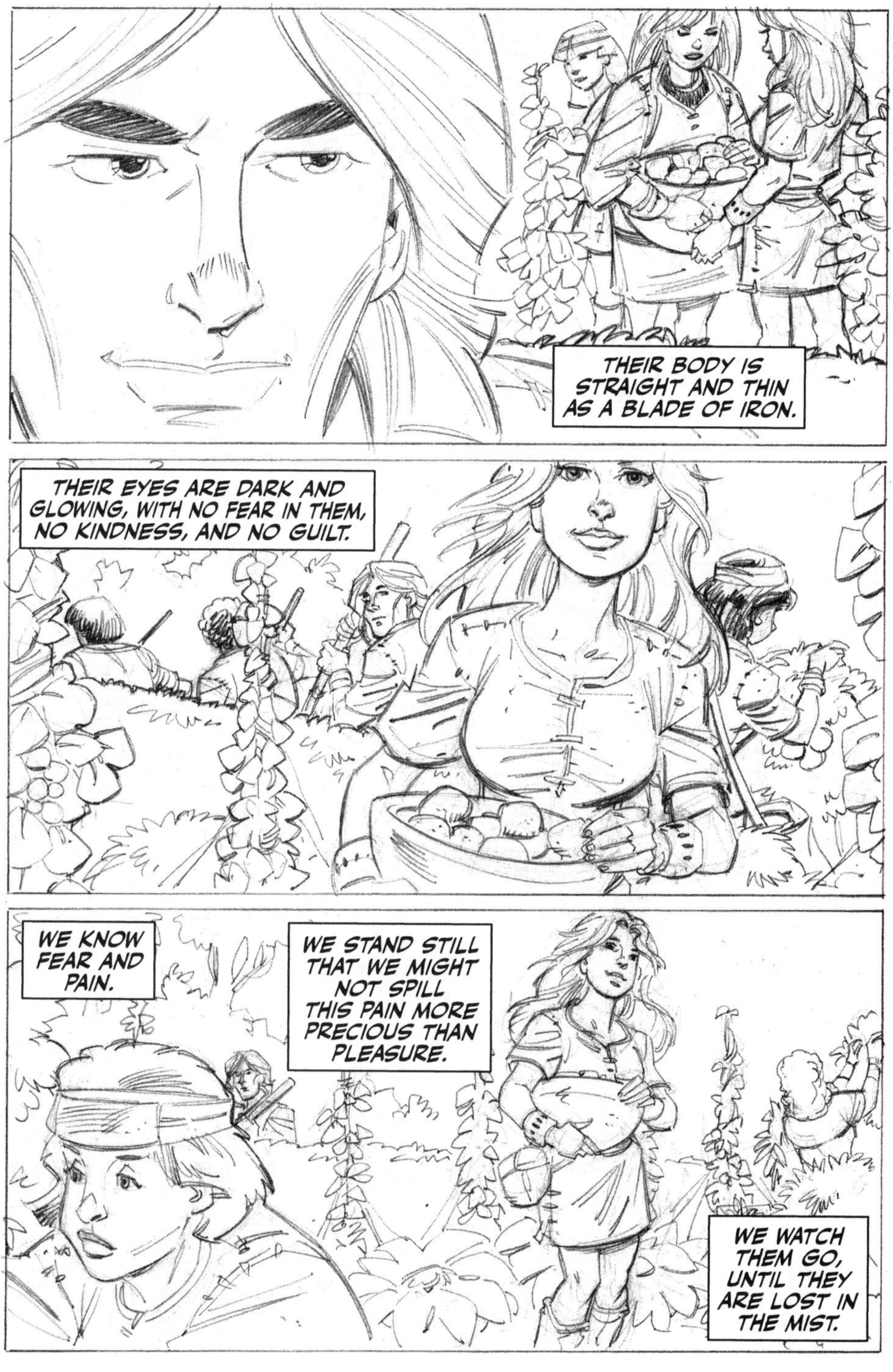
THEIR BODY IS STRAIGHT AND THIN AS A BLADE OF IRON.
THEIR EYES ARE DARK AND GLOWING, WITH NO FEAR IN THEM, NO KINDNESS, AND NO GUILT.
WE KNOW FEAR AND PAIN.
WE STAND STILL THAT WE MIGHT NOT SPILL THIS PAIN MORE PRECIOUS THAN PLEASURE.
WE WATCH THEM GO, UNTIL THEY ARE LOST IN THE MIST.

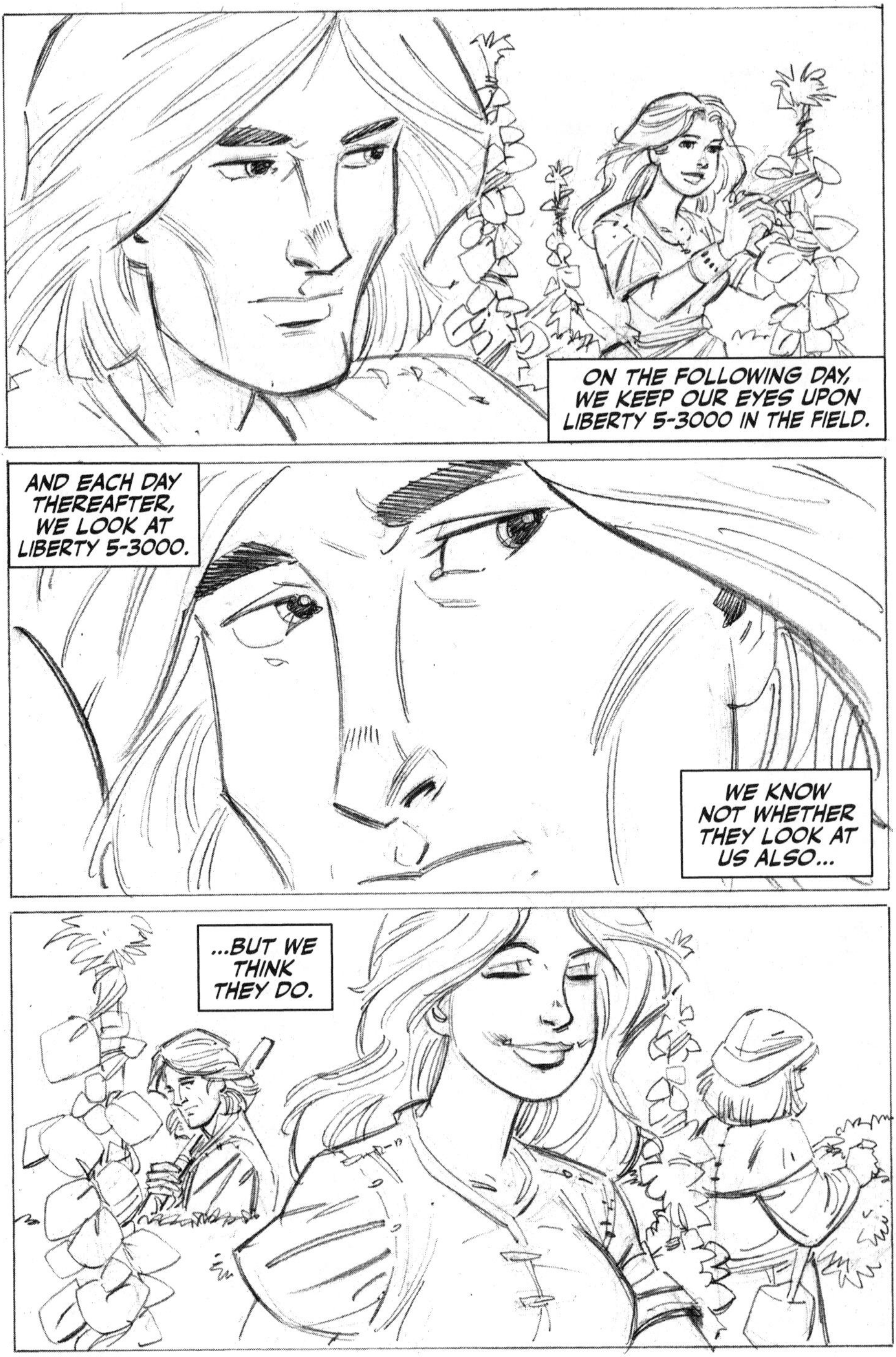
ON THE FOLLOWING DAY, WE KEEP OUR EYES UPON LIBERTY 5-3000 IN THE FIELD.
AND EACH DAY THEREAFTER, WE LOOK AT LIBERTY 5-3000.
WE KNOW NOT WHETHER THEY LOOK AT US ALSO...
...BUT WE THINK THEY DO.

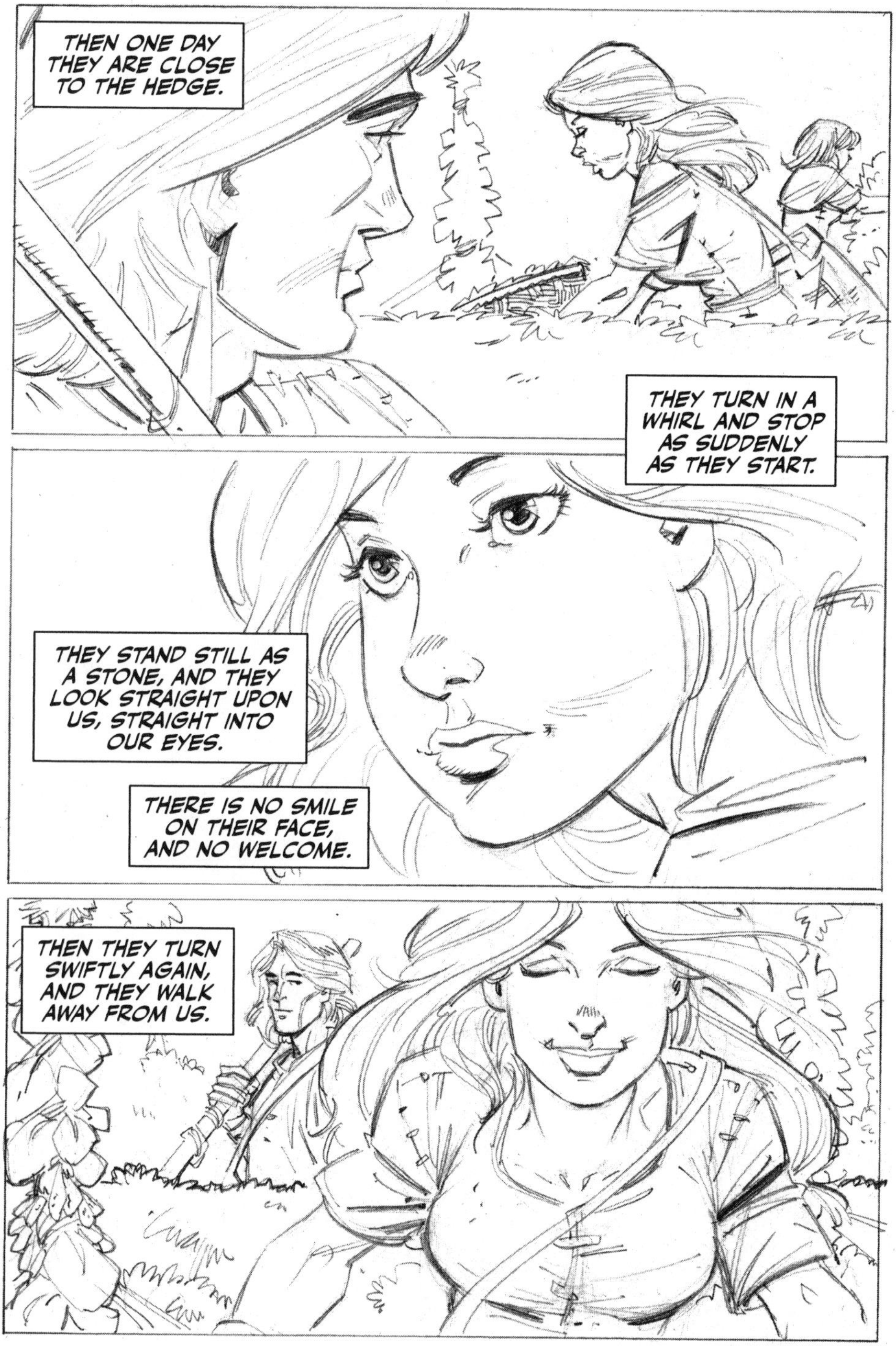
THEN ONE DAY THEY ARE CLOSE TO THE HEDGE.
THEY TURN IN A WHIRL AND STOP AS SUDDENLY AS THEY START.
THEY STAND STILL AS A STONE, AND THEY LOOK STRAIGHT UPON US, STRAIGHT INTO OUR EYES.
THERE IS NO SMILE ON THEIR FACE, AND NO WELCOME.
THEN THEY TURN SWIFTLY AGAIN, AND THEY WALK AWAY FROM US.

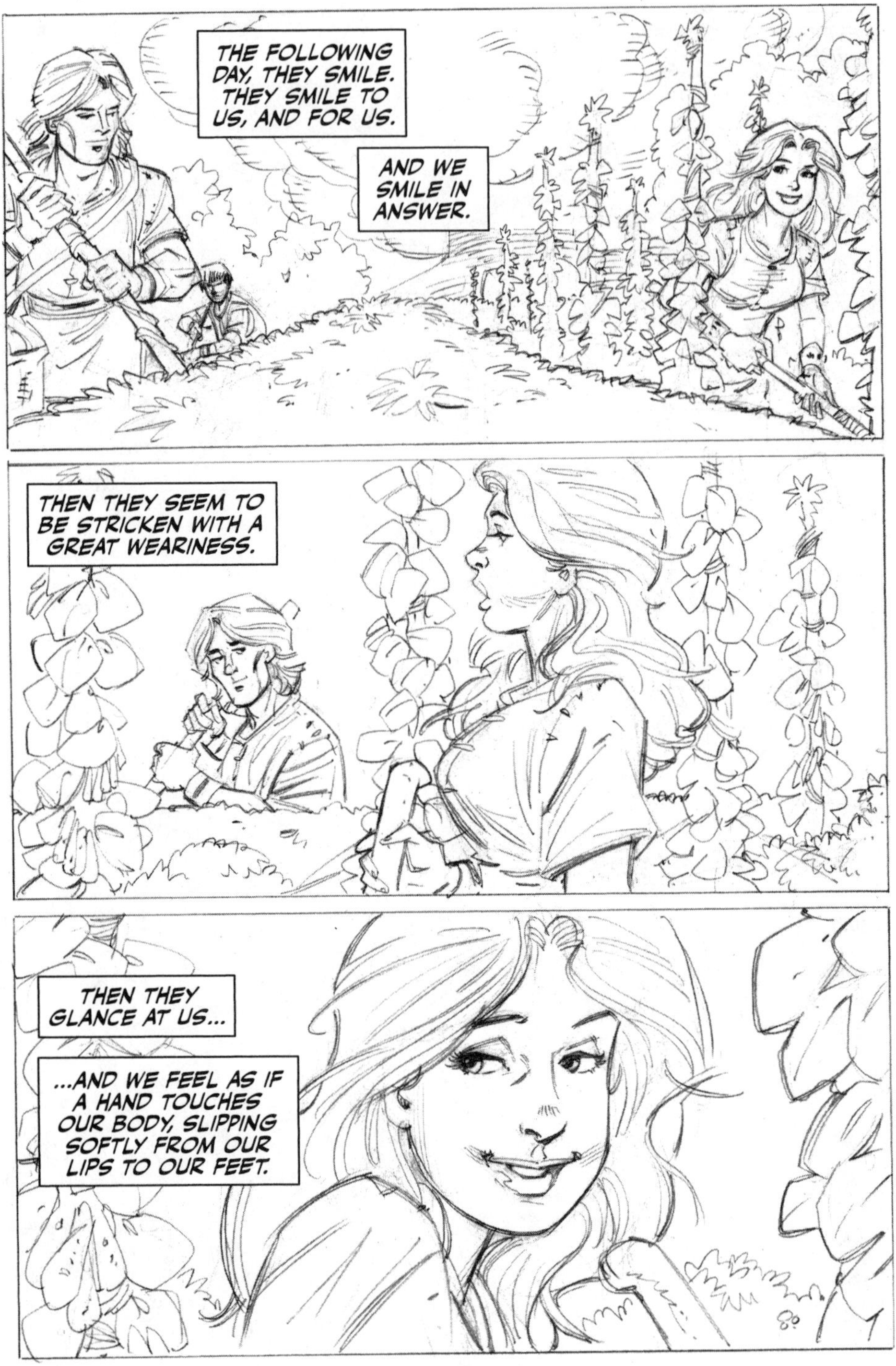
THE FOLLOWING DAY, THEY SMILE. THEY SMILE TO US, AND FOR US.
AND WE SMILE IN ANSWER.
THEN THEY SEEM TO BE STRICKEN WITH A GREAT WEARINESS.
THEN THEY GLANCE AT US...
...AND WE FEEL AS IF A HAND TOUCHES OUR BODY, SLIPPING SOFTLY FROM OUR LIPS TO OUR FEET.

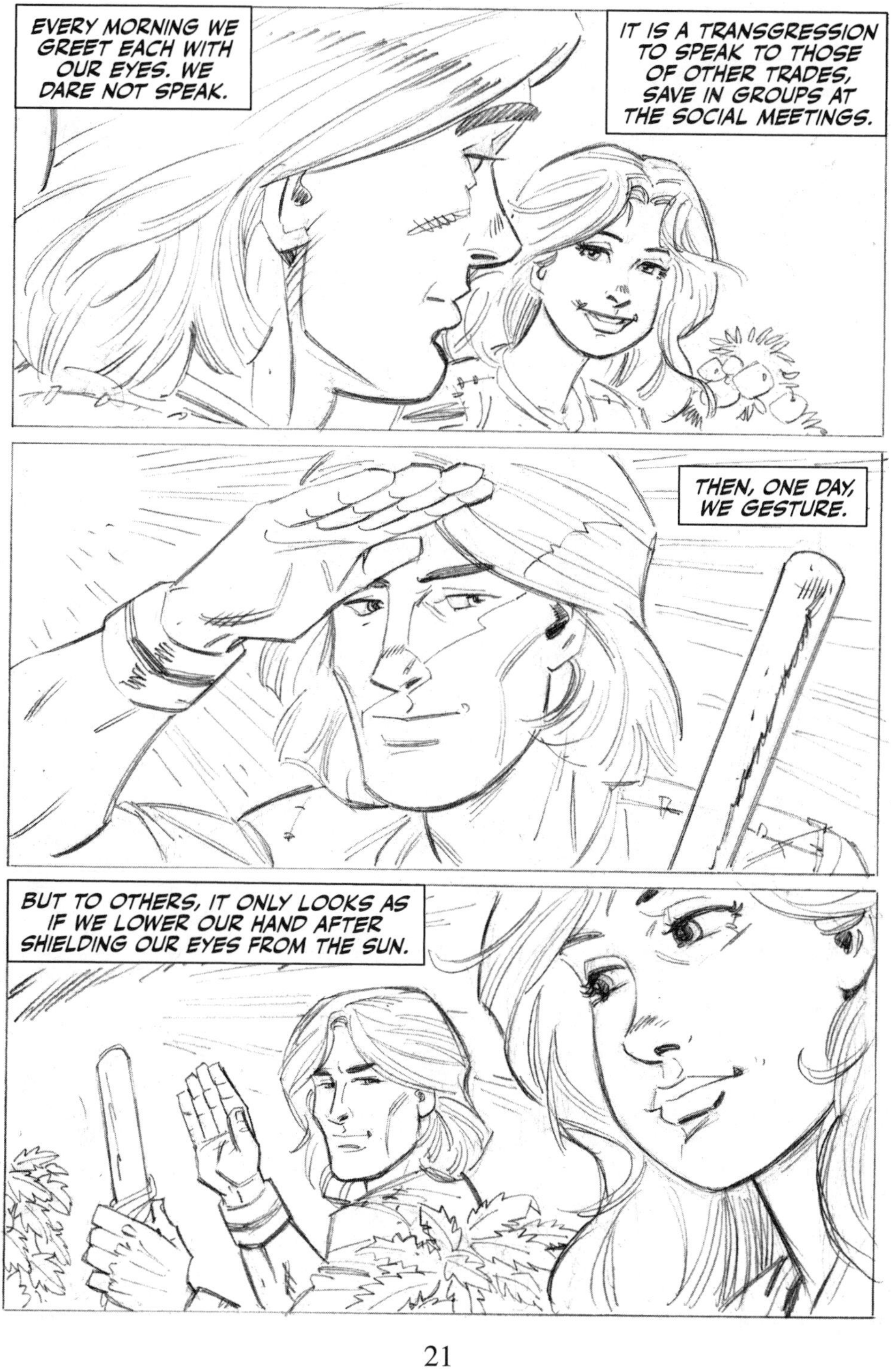
EVERY MORNING WE GREET EACH WITH OUR EYES. WE DARE NOT SPEAK.
IT IS A TRANSGRESSION TO SPEAK TO THOSE OF OTHER TRADES, SAVE IN GROUPS AT THE SOCIAL MEETINGS.
THEN, ONE DAY, WE GESTURE.
BUT TO OTHERS, IT ONLY LOOKS AS IF WE LOWER OUR HAND AFTER SHIELDING OUR EYES FROM THE SUN.

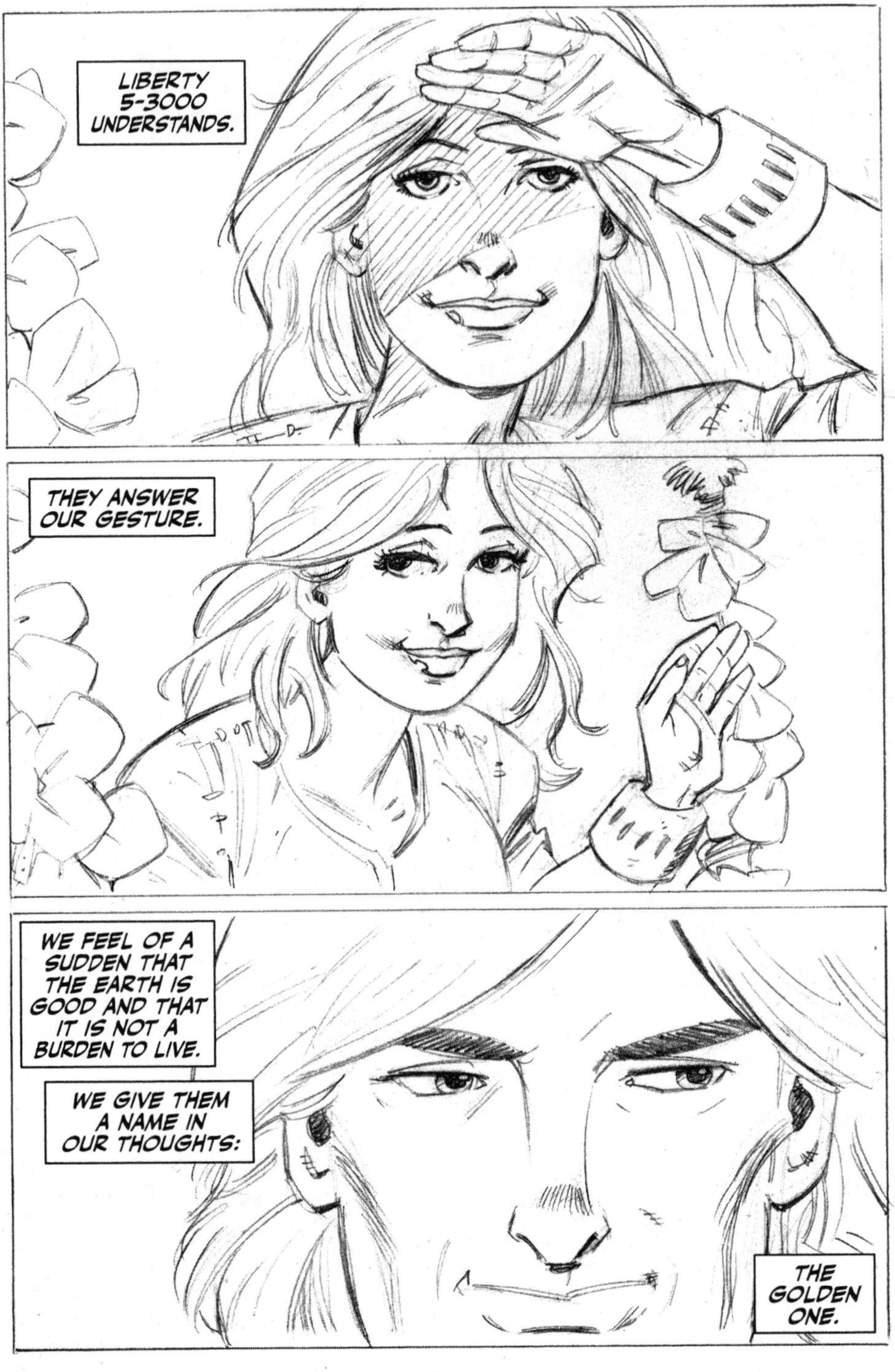
LIBERTY 5-3000 UNDERSTANDS.
THEY ANSWER OUR GESTURE.
WE FEEL OF A SUDDEN THAT THE EARTH IS GOOD AND THAT IT IS NOT A BURDEN TO LIVE.
WE GIVE THEM A NAME IN OUR THOUGHTS:
THE GOLDEN ONE.

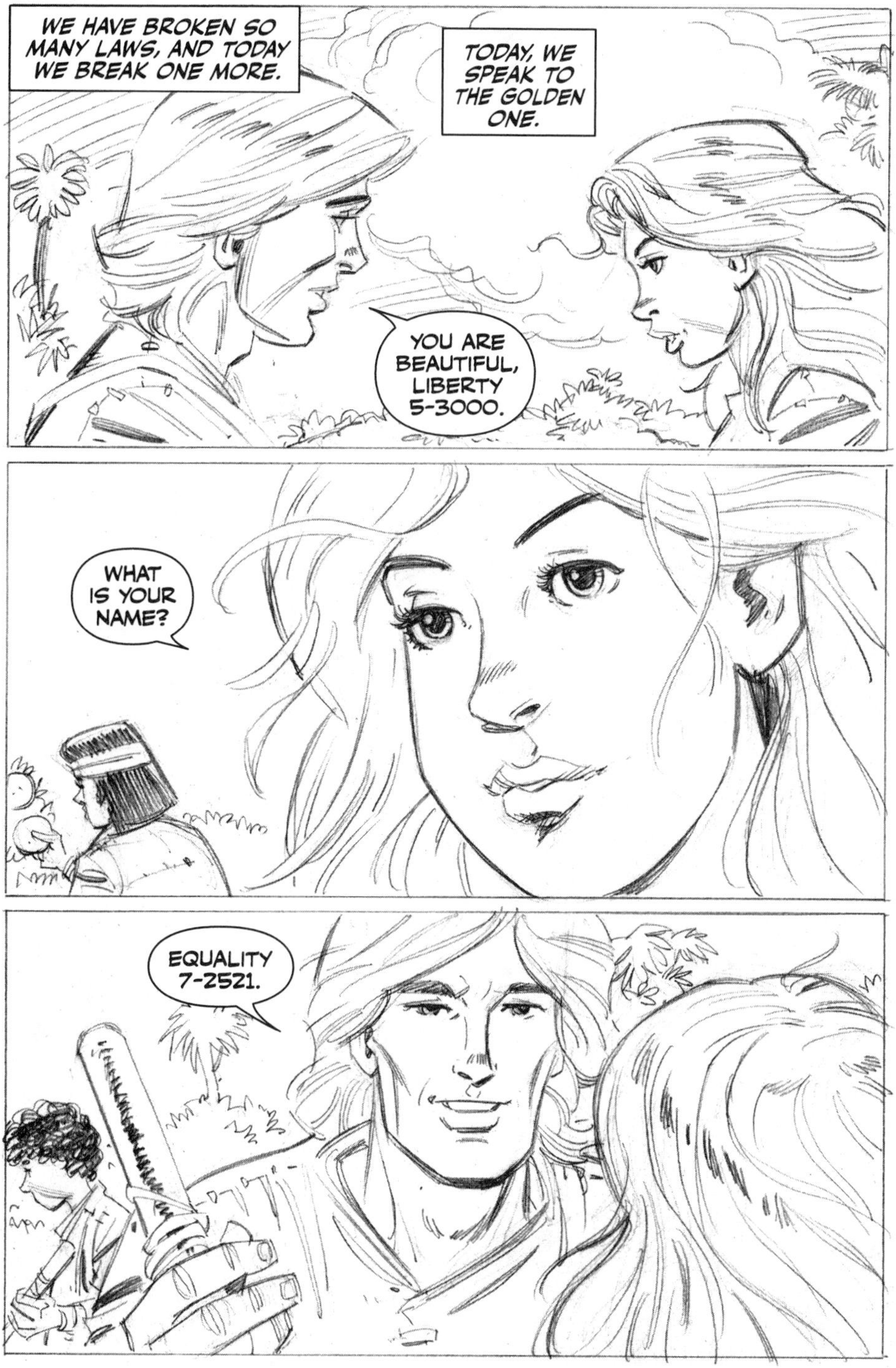
WE HAVE BROKEN SO MANY LAWS, AND TODAY WE BREAK ONE MORE.
TODAY, WE SPEAK TO THE GOLDEN ONE.
YOU ARE BEAUTIFUL, LIBERTY 5-3000.
WHAT IS YOUR NAME?
EQUALITY 7-2521.

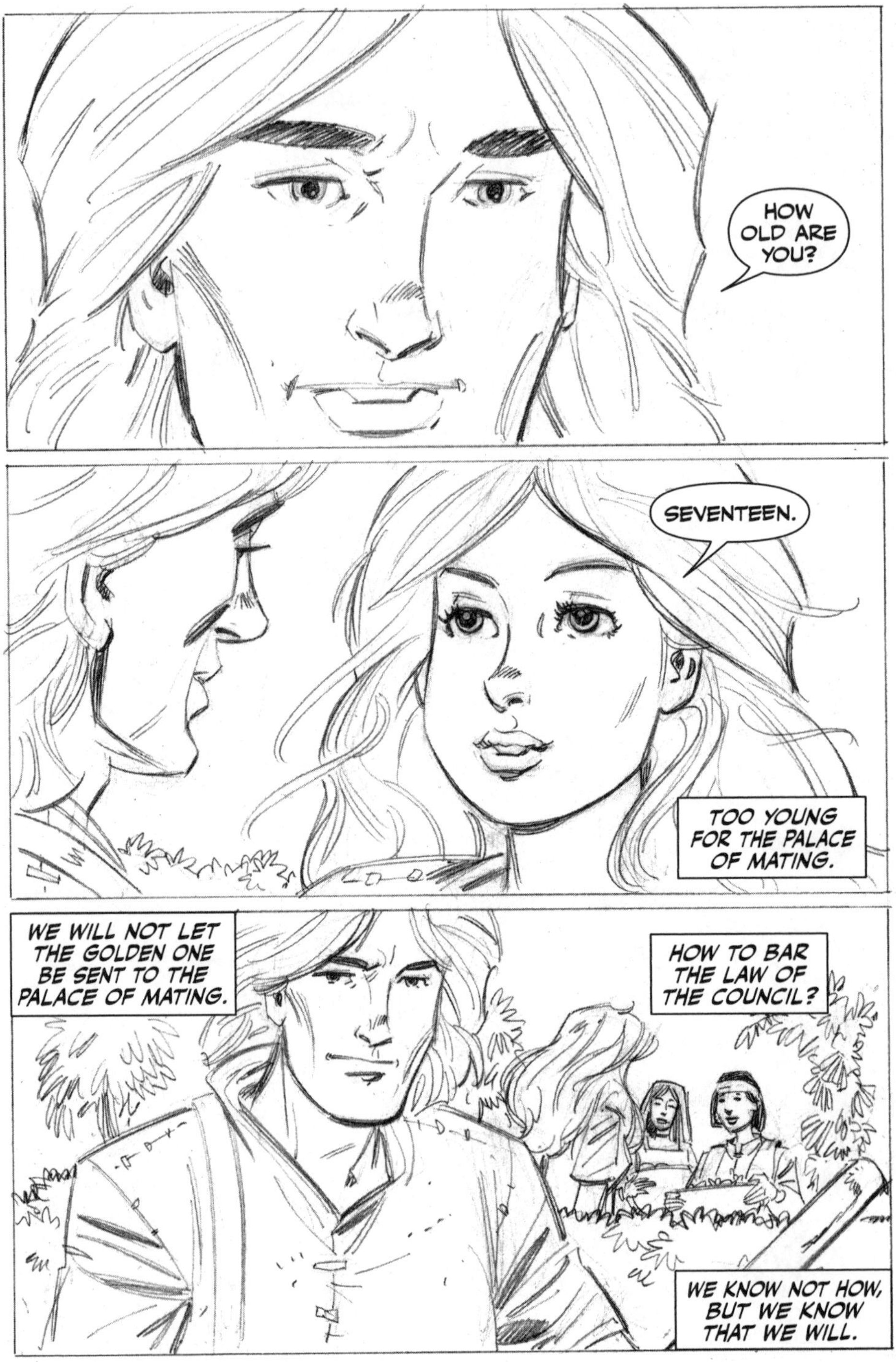
HOW OLD ARE YOU?
SEVENTEEN.
TOO YOUNG FOR THE PALACE OF MATING.
WE WILL NOT LET THE GOLDEN ONE BE SENT TO THE PALACE OF MATING.
HOW TO BAR THE LAW OF THE COUNCIL?
WE KNOW NOT HOW, BUT WE KNOW THAT WE WILL.

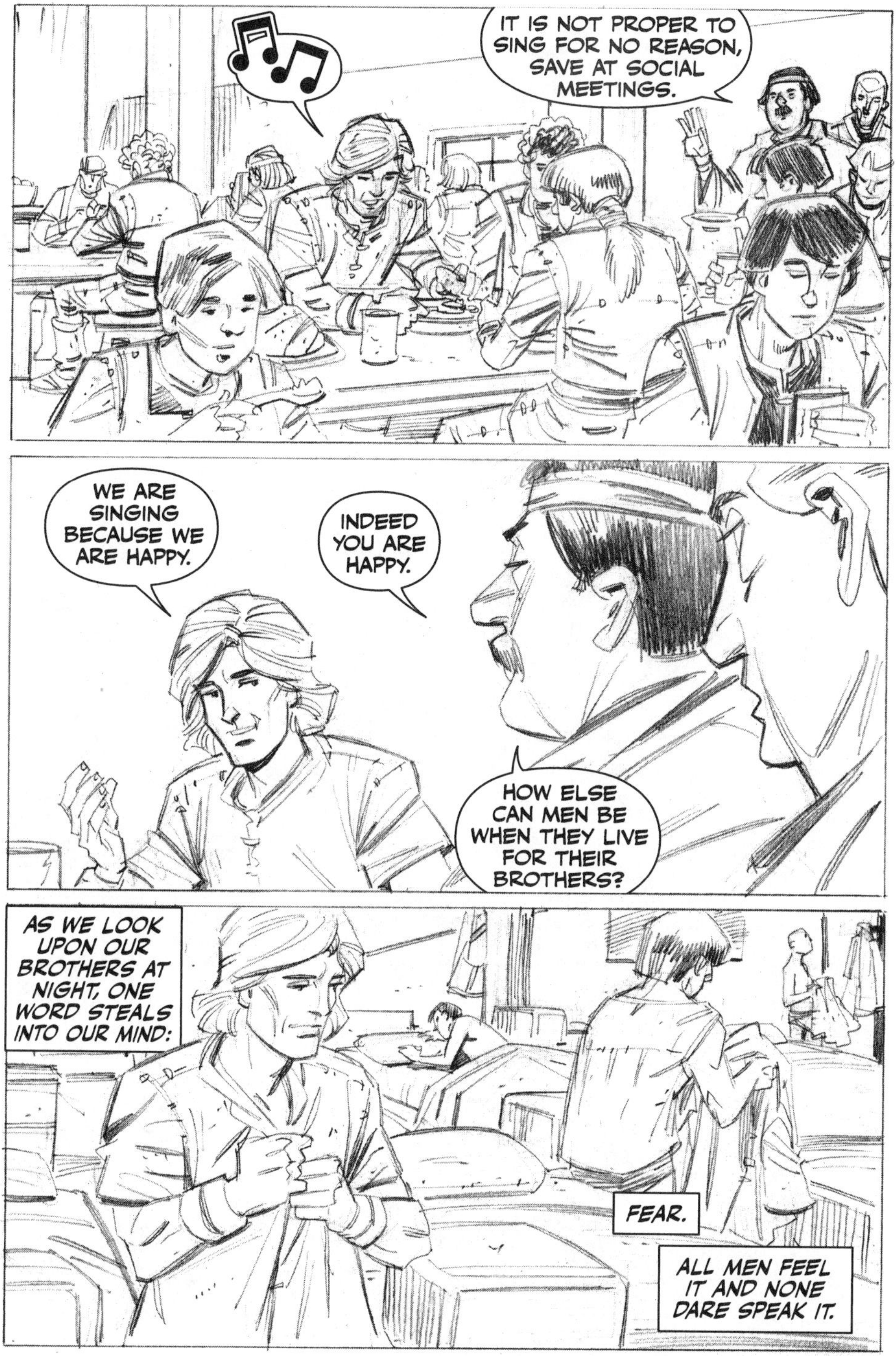
IT IS NOT PROPER TO SING FOR NO REASON, SAVE AT SOCIAL MEETINGS.
WE ARE SINGING BECAUSE WE ARE HAPPY.
INDEED YOU ARE HAPPY.
HOW ELSE CAN MEN BE WHEN THEY LIVE FOR THEIR BROTHERS?
AS WE LOOK UPON OUR BROTHERS AT NIGHT, ONE WORD STEALS INTO OUR MIND:
FEAR.
ALL MEN FEEL IT AND NONE DARE SPEAK IT.

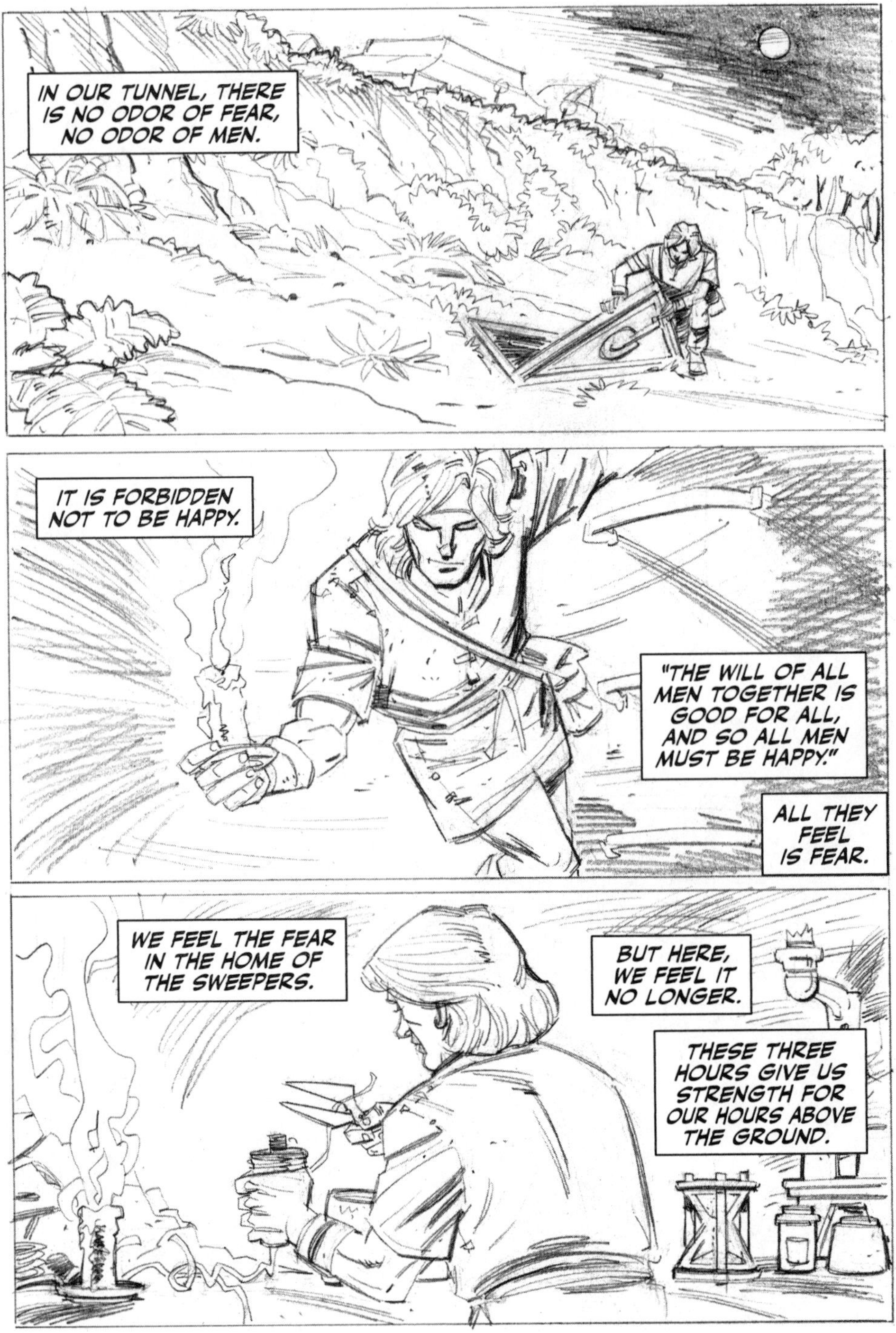
IN OUR TUNNEL, THERE IS NO ODOR OF FEAR, NO ODOR OF MEN.
IT IS FORBIDDEN NOT TO BE HAPPY.
"THE WILL OF ALL MEN TOGETHER IS GOOD FOR ALL, AND SO ALL MEN MUST BE HAPPY."
ALL THEY FEEL IS FEAR.
WE FEEL THE FEAR IN THE HOME OF THE SWEEPERS.
BUT HERE, WE FEEL IT NO LONGER.
THESE THREE HOURS GIVE US STRENGTH FOR OUR HOURS ABOVE THE GROUND.

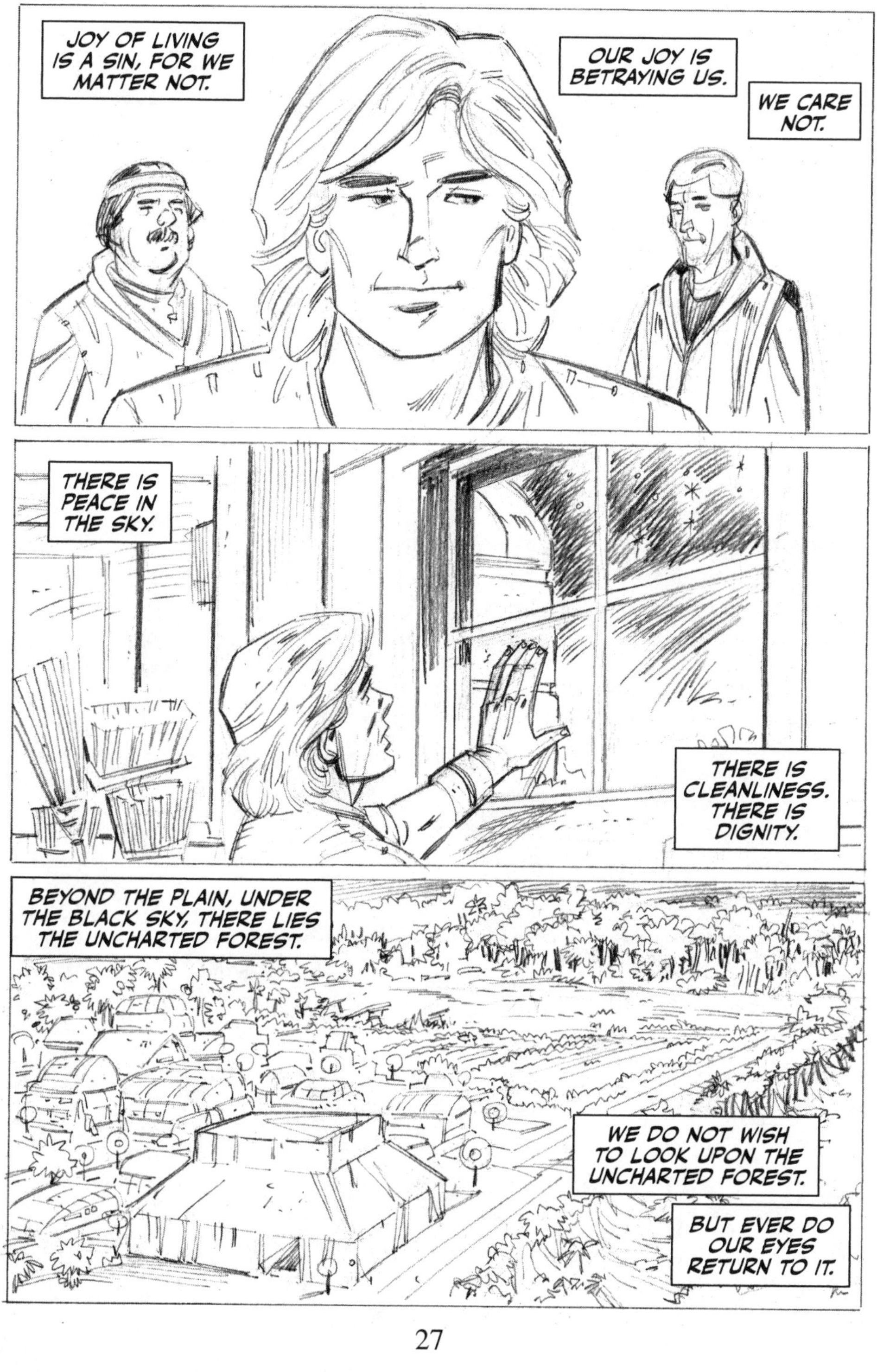
JOY OF LIVING IS A SIN, FOR WE MATTER NOT.
OUR JOY IS BETRAYING US.
WE CARE NOT.
THERE IS PEACE IN THE SKY.
THERE IS CLEANLINESS. THERE IS DIGNITY.
BEYOND THE PLAIN, UNDER THE BLACK SKY, THERE LIES THE UNCHARTED FOREST.
WE DO NOT WISH TO LOOK UPON THE UNCHARTED FOREST.
BUT EVER DO OUR EYES RETURN TO IT.

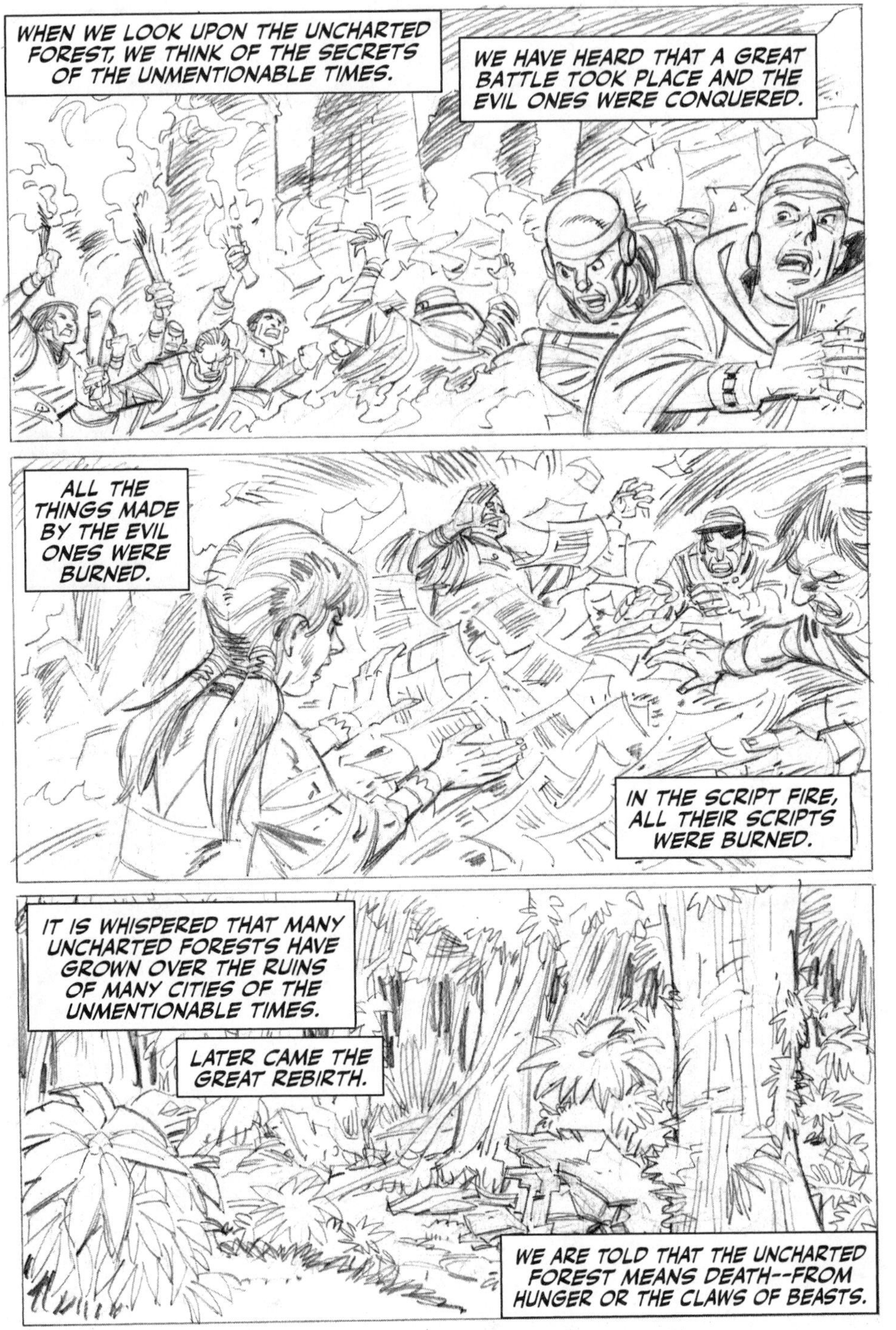
WHEN WE LOOK UPON THE UNCHARTED FOREST, WE THINK OF THE SECRETS OF THE UNMENTIONABLE TIMES.
WE HAVE HEARD THAT A GREAT BATTLE TOOK PLACE AND THE EVIL ONES WERE CONQUERED.
ALL THE THINGS MADE BY THE EVIL ONES WERE BURNED.
IN THE SCRIPT FIRE, ALL THEIR SCRIPTS WERE BURNED.
IT IS WHISPERED THAT MANY UNCHARTED FORESTS HAVE GROWN OVER THE RUINS OF MANY CITIES OF THE UNMENTIONABLE TIMES.
LATER CAME THE GREAT REBIRTH.
WE ARE TOLD THAT THE UNCHARTED FOREST MEANS DEATH--FROM HUNGER OR THE CLAWS OF BEASTS.

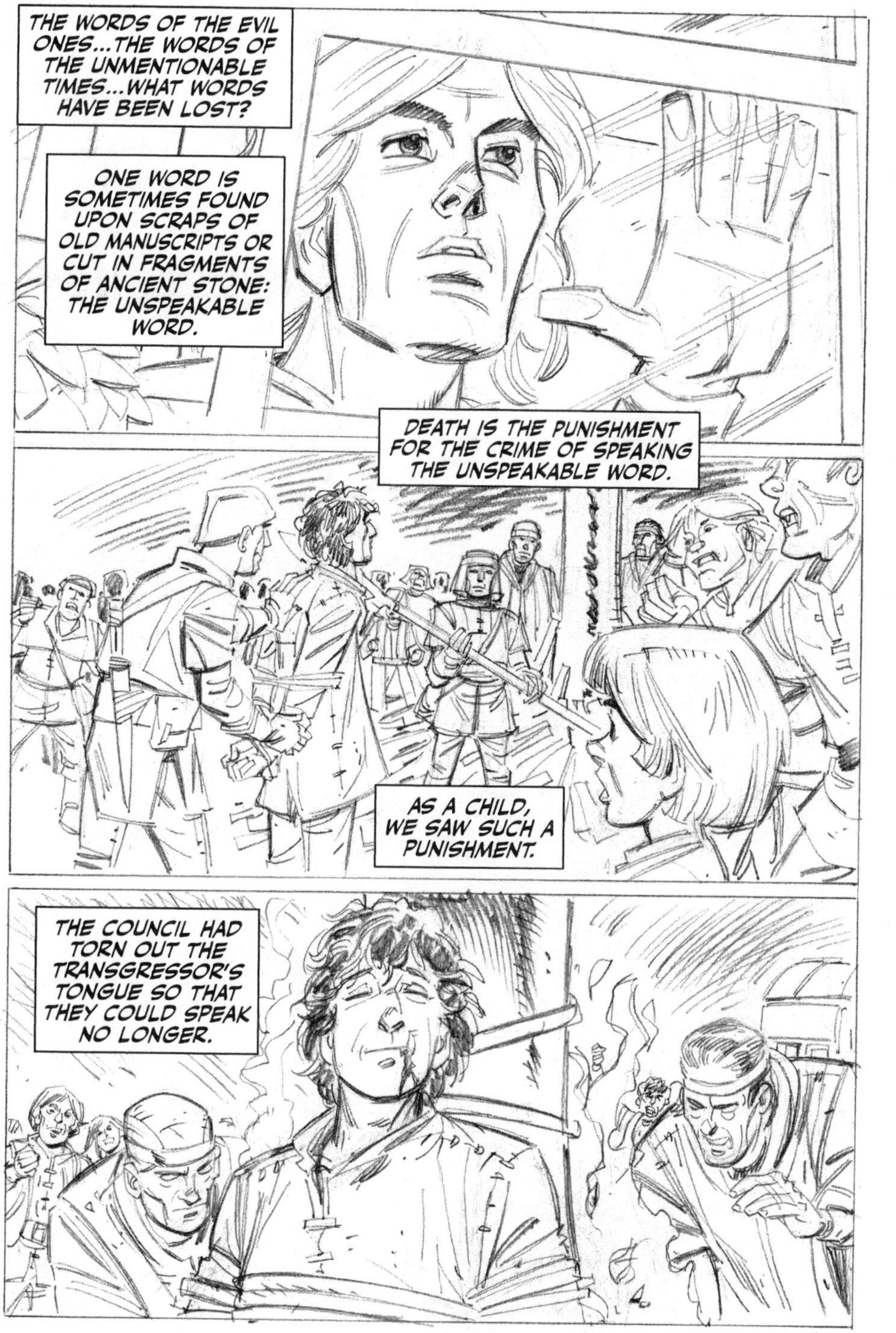
THE WORDS OF THE EVIL ONES...THE WORDS OF THE UNMENTIONABLE TIMES...WHAT WORDS HAVE BEEN LOST?
ONE WORD IS SOMETIMES FOUND UPON SCRAPS OF OLD MANUSCRIPTS OR CUT IN FRAGMENTS OF ANCIENT STONE: THE UNSPEAKABLE WORD.
DEATH IS THE PUNISHMENT FOR THE CRIME OF SPEAKING THE UNSPEAKABLE WORD.
AS A CHILD, WE SAW SUCH A PUNISHMENT.
THE COUNCIL HAD TORN OUT THE TRANSGRESSOR'S TONGUE SO THAT THEY COULD SPEAK NO LONGER.

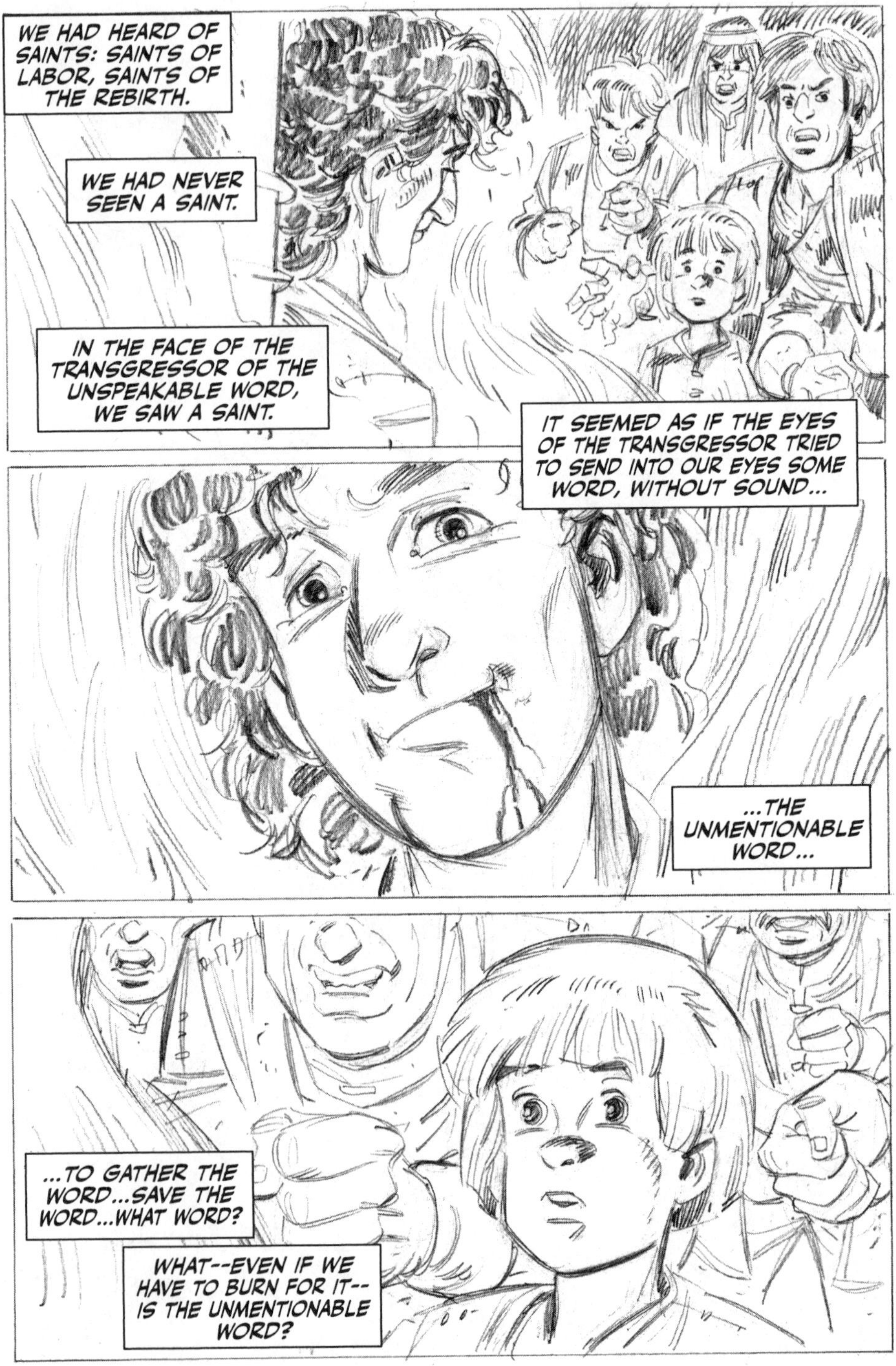
WE HAD HEARD OF SAINTS: SAINTS OF LABOR, SAINTS OF THE REBIRTH.
WE HAD NEVER SEEN A SAINT.
IN THE FACE OF THE TRANSGRESSOR OF THE UNSPEAKABLE WORD, WE SAW A SAINT.
IT SEEMED AS IF THE EYES OF THE TRANSGRESSOR TRIED TO SEND INTO OUR EYES SOME WORD, WITHOUT SOUND...
...THE UNMENTIONABLE WORD...
...TO GATHER THE WORD...SAVE THE WORD...WHAT WORD?
WHAT--EVEN IF WE HAVE TO BURN FOR IT--IS THE UNMENTIONABLE WORD?

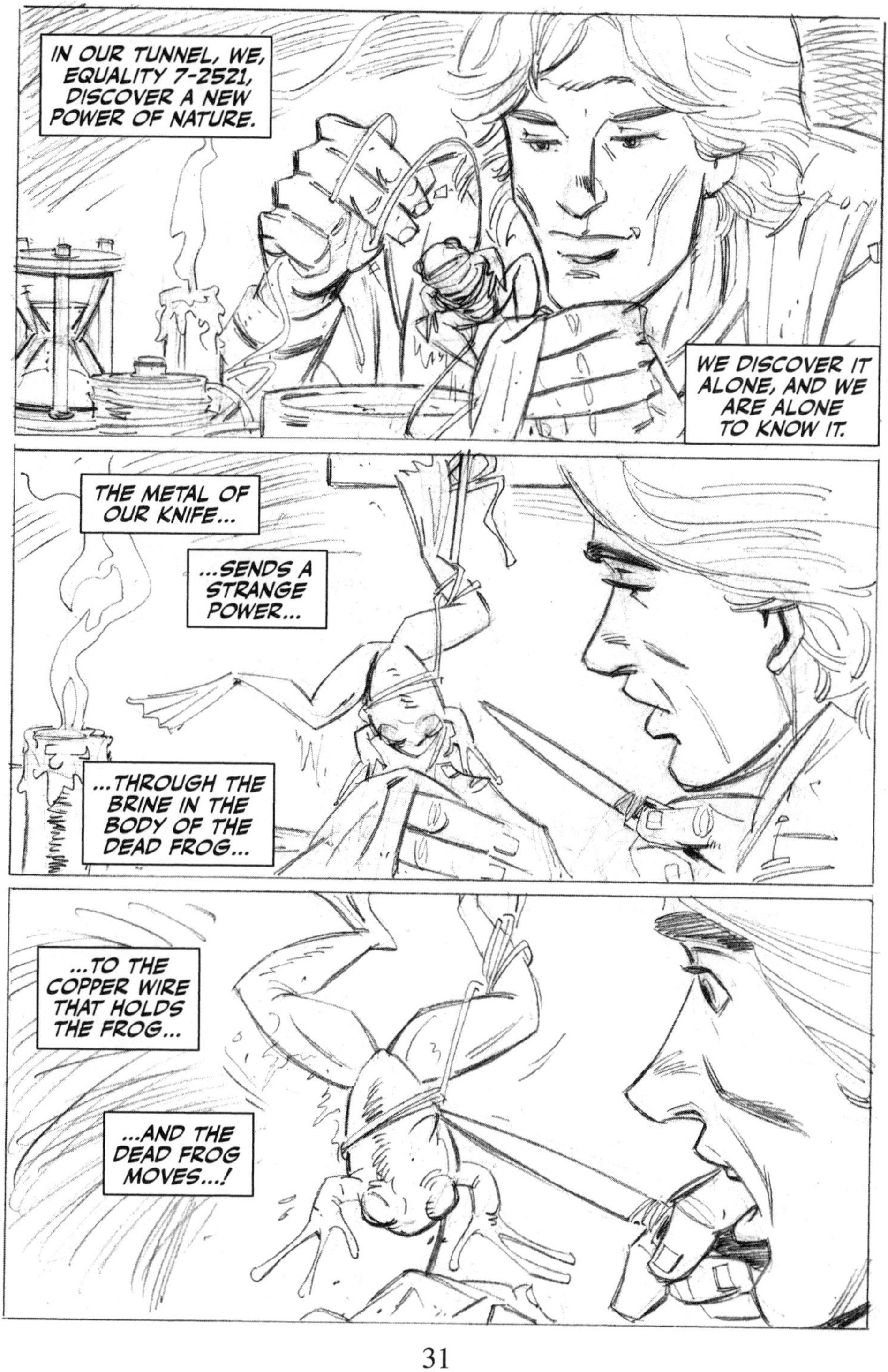
IN OUR TUNNEL, WE, EQUALITY 7-2521, DISCOVER A NEW POWER OF NATURE.
WE DISCOVER IT ALONE, AND WE ARE ALONE TO KNOW IT.
THE METAL OF OUR KNIFE...
...SENDS A STRANGE POWER...
...THROUGH THE BRINE IN THE BODY OF THE DEAD FROG...
...TO THE COPPER WIRE THAT HOLDS THE FROG...
...AND THE DEAD FROG MOVES...!

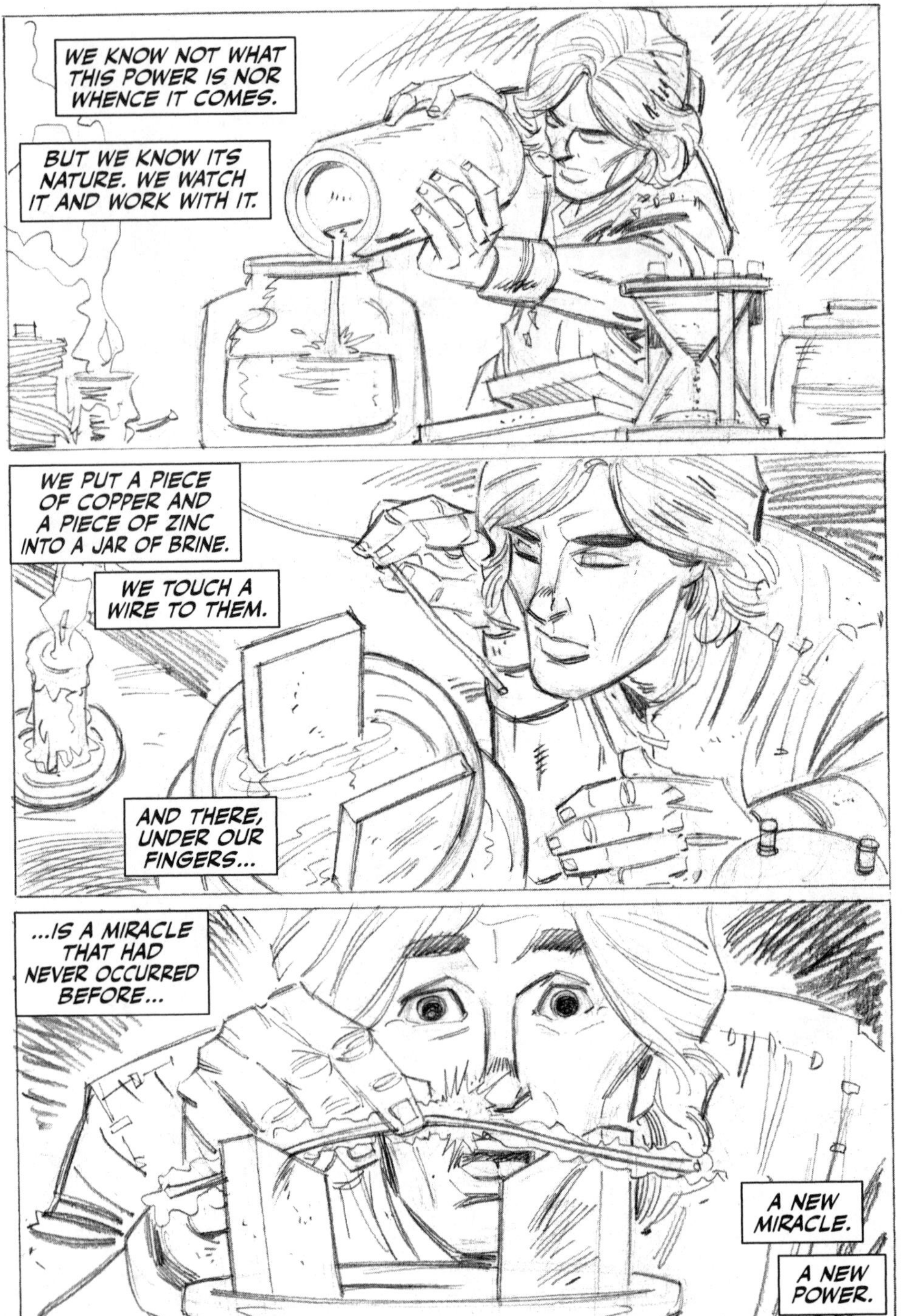
WE KNOW NOT WHAT THIS POWER IS NOR WHENCE IT COMES.
BUT WE KNOW ITS NATURE. WE WATCH IT AND WORK WITH IT.
WE PUT A PIECE OF COPPER AND A PIECE OF ZINC INTO A JAR OF BRINE.
WE TOUCH A WIRE TO THEM.
AND THERE, UNDER OUR FINGERS...
...IS A MIRACLE THAT HAD NEVER OCCURRED BEFORE...
A NEW MIRACLE.
A NEW POWER.

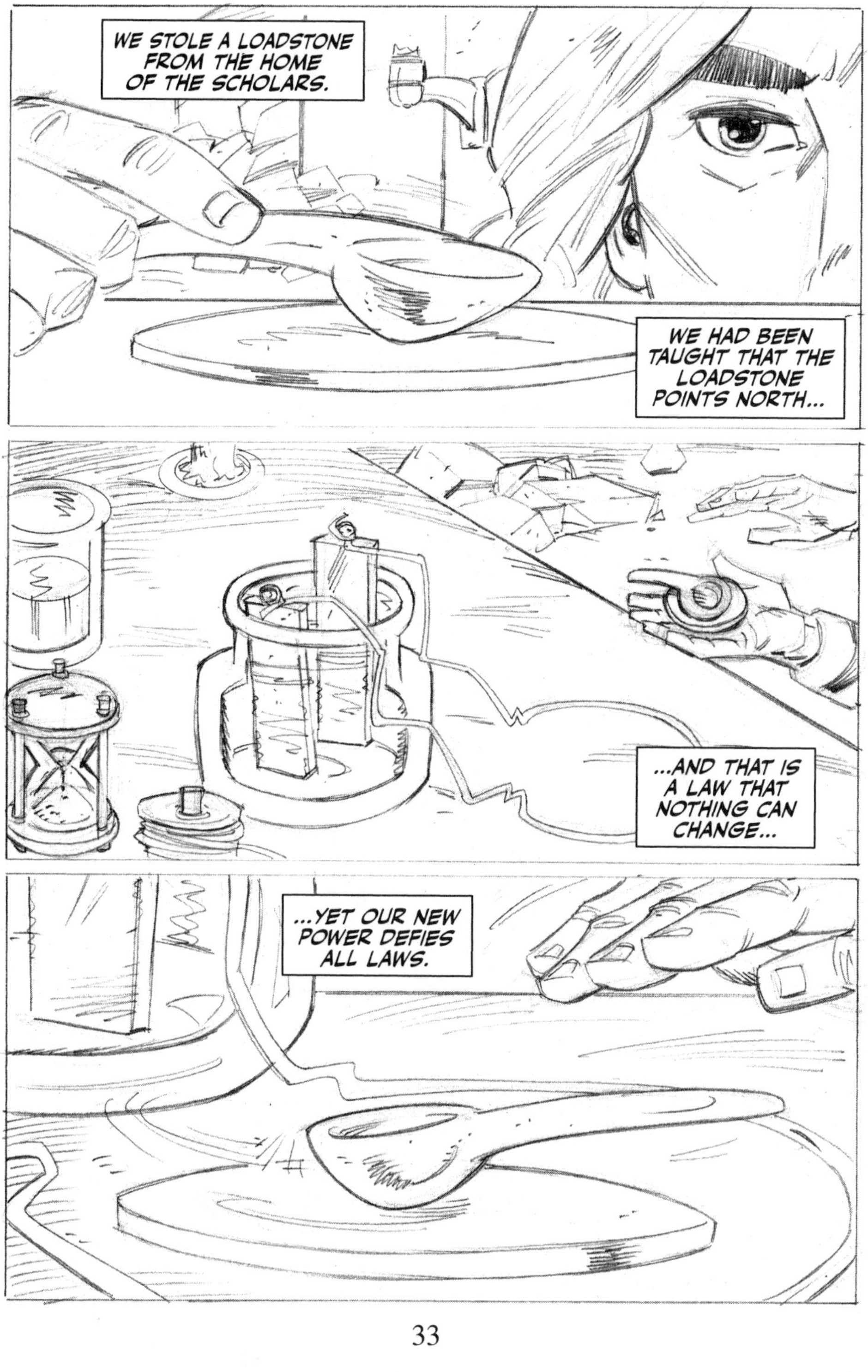
WE STOLE A LOADSTONE FROM THE HOME OF THE SCHOLARS.
WE HAD BEEN TAUGHT THAT THE LOADSTONE POINTS NORTH...
...AND THAT IS A LAW THAT NOTHING CAN CHANGE...
...YET OUR NEW POWER DEFIES ALL LAWS.

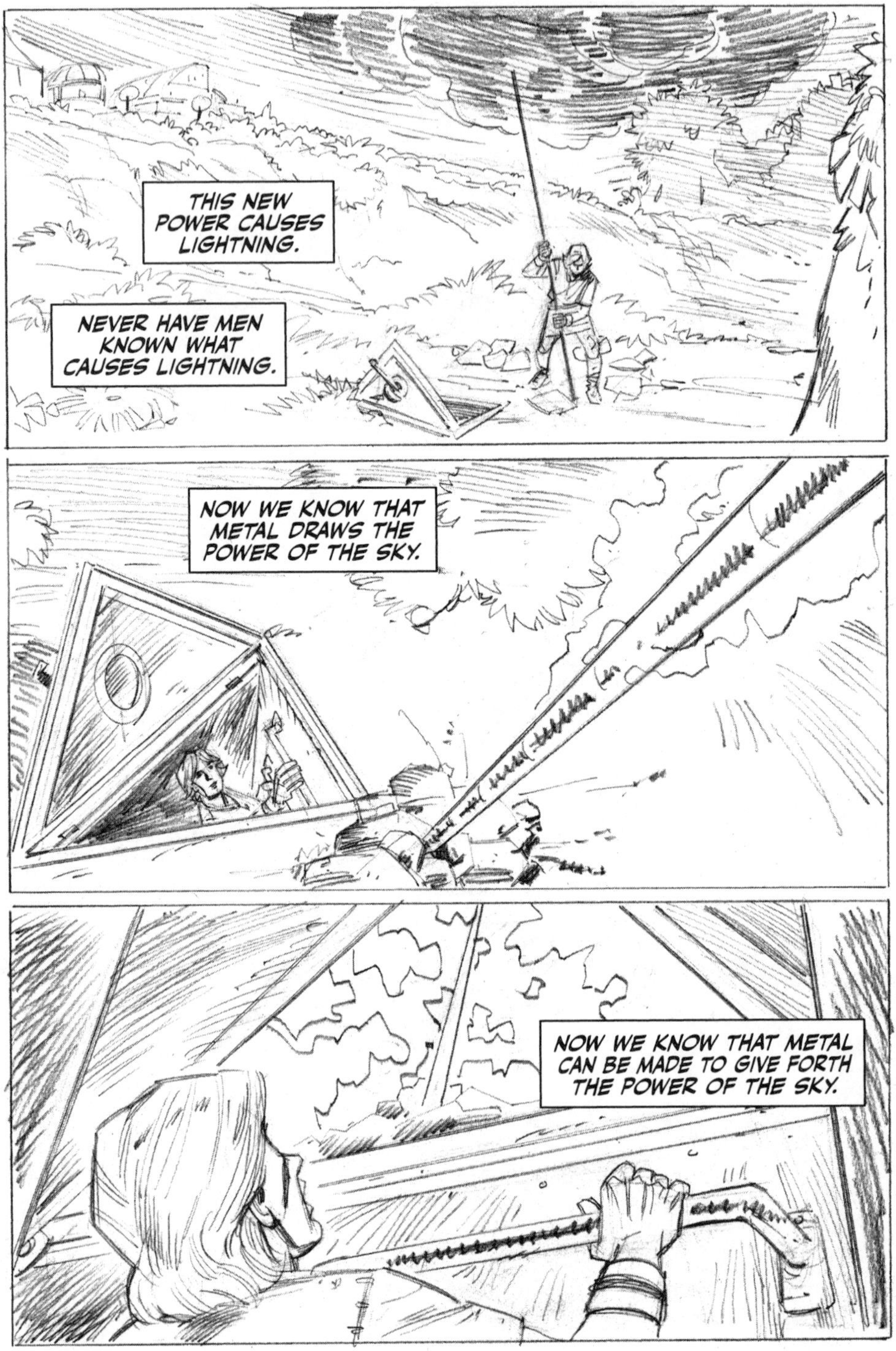
THIS NEW POWER CAUSES LIGHTNING.
NEVER HAVE MEN KNOWN WHAT CAUSES LIGHTNING.
NOW WE KNOW THAT METAL DRAWS THE POWER OF THE SKY.
NOW WE KNOW THAT METAL CAN BE MADE TO GIVE FORTH THE POWER OF THE SKY.

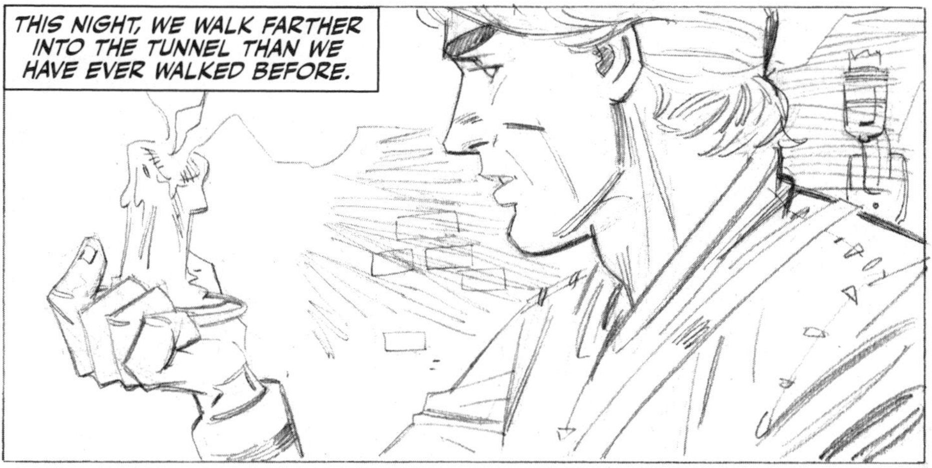
THIS NIGHT, WE WALK FARTHER INTO THE TUNNEL THAN WE HAVE EVER WALKED BEFORE.

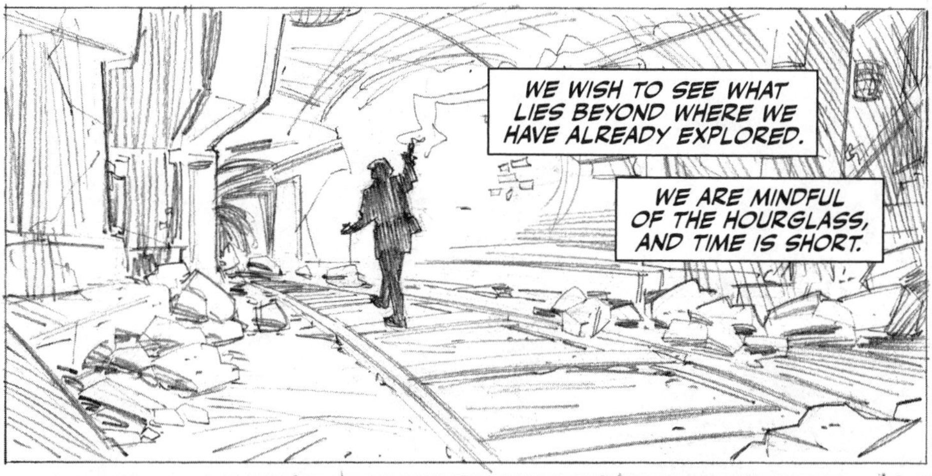
WE WISH TO SEE WHAT LIES BEYOND WHERE WE HAVE ALREADY EXPLORED.
WE ARE MINDFUL OF THE HOURGLASS, AND TIME IS SHORT.

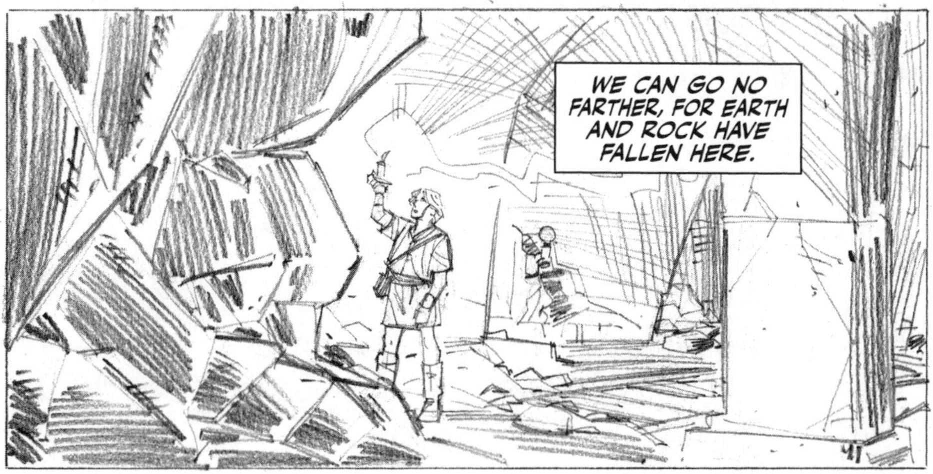
WE CAN GO NO FARTHER, FOR EARTH AND ROCK HAVE FALLEN HERE.

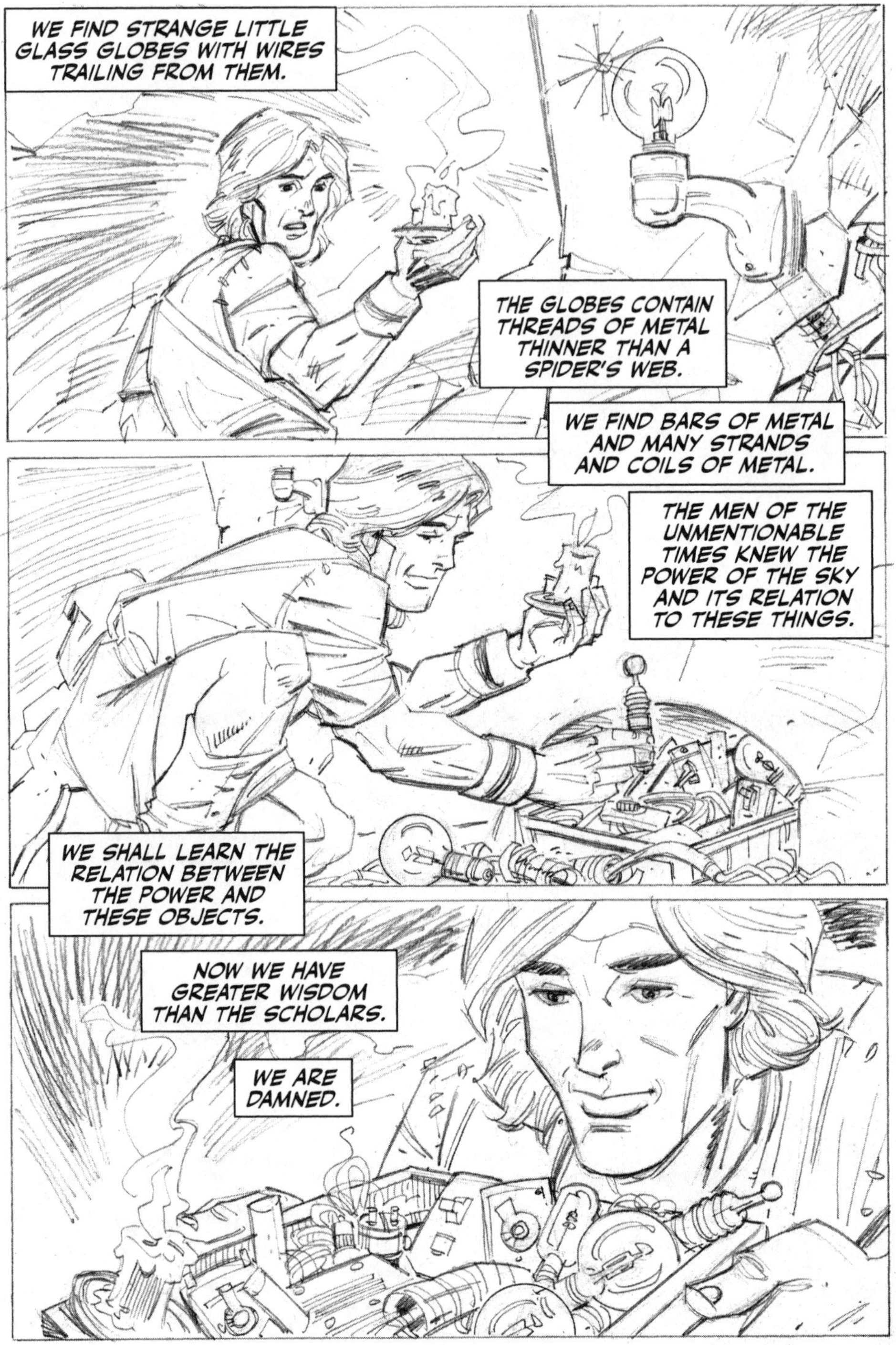
WE FIND STRANGE LITTLE GLASS GLOBES WITH WIRES TRAILING FROM THEM.
THE GLOBES CONTAIN THREADS OF METAL THINNER THAN A SPIDER'S WEB.
WE FIND BARS OF METAL AND MANY STRANDS AND COILS OF METAL.
THE MEN OF THE UNMENTIONABLE TIMES KNEW THE POWER OF THE SKY AND ITS RELATION TO THESE THINGS.
WE SHALL LEARN THE RELATION BETWEEN THE POWER AND THESE OBJECTS.
NOW WE HAVE GREATER WISDOM THAN THE SCHOLARS.
WE ARE DAMNED.

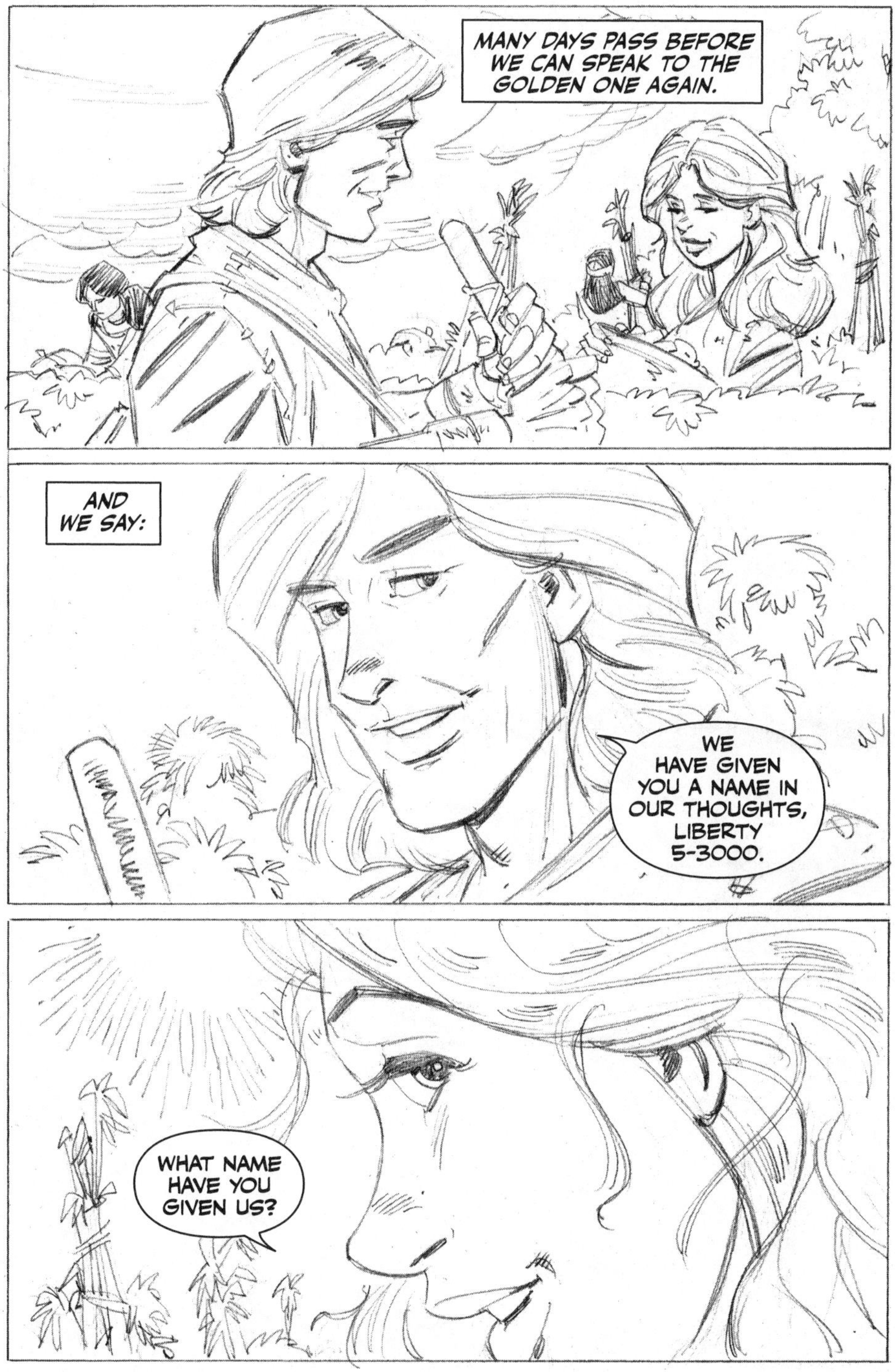
MANY DAYS PASS BEFORE WE CAN SPEAK TO THE GOLDEN ONE AGAIN.
AND WE SAY:
WE HAVE GIVEN YOU A NAME IN OUR THOUGHTS, LIBERTY 5-3000.
WHAT NAME HAVE YOU GIVEN US?

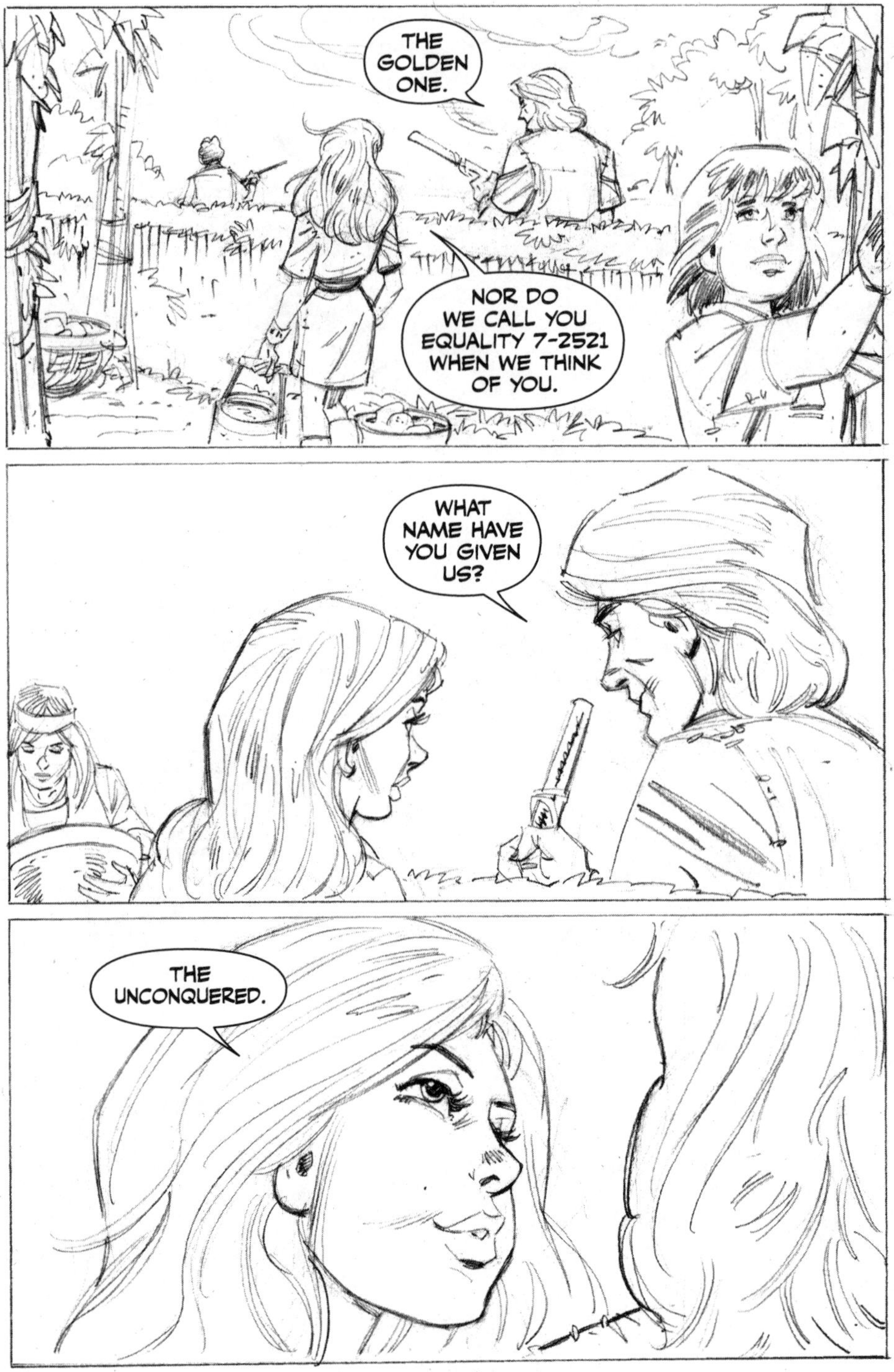
THE GOLDEN ONE.
NOR DO WE CALL YOU EQUALITY 7-2521 WHEN WE THINK OF YOU.
WHAT NAME HAVE YOU GIVEN US?
THE UNCONQUERED.

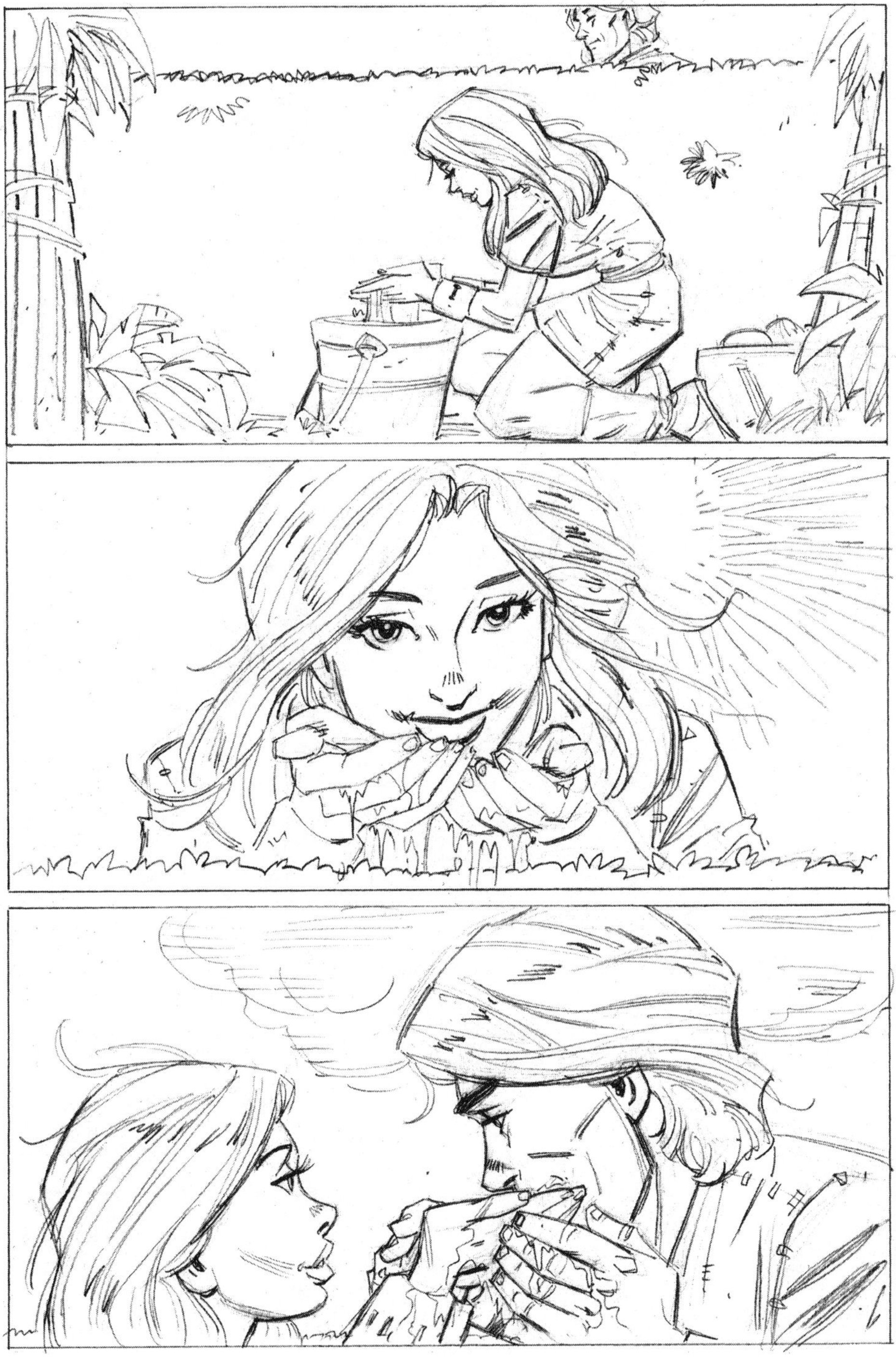

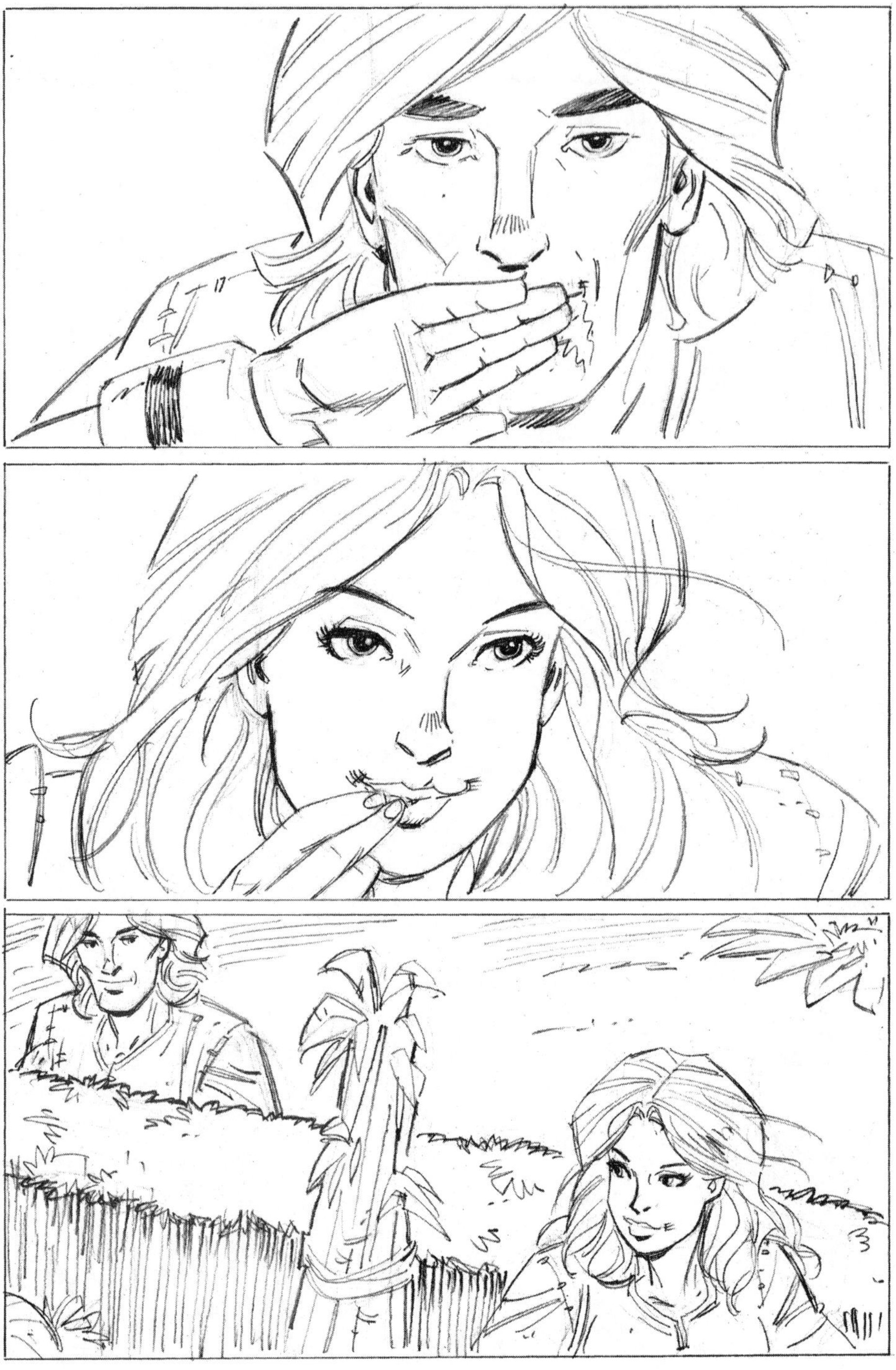

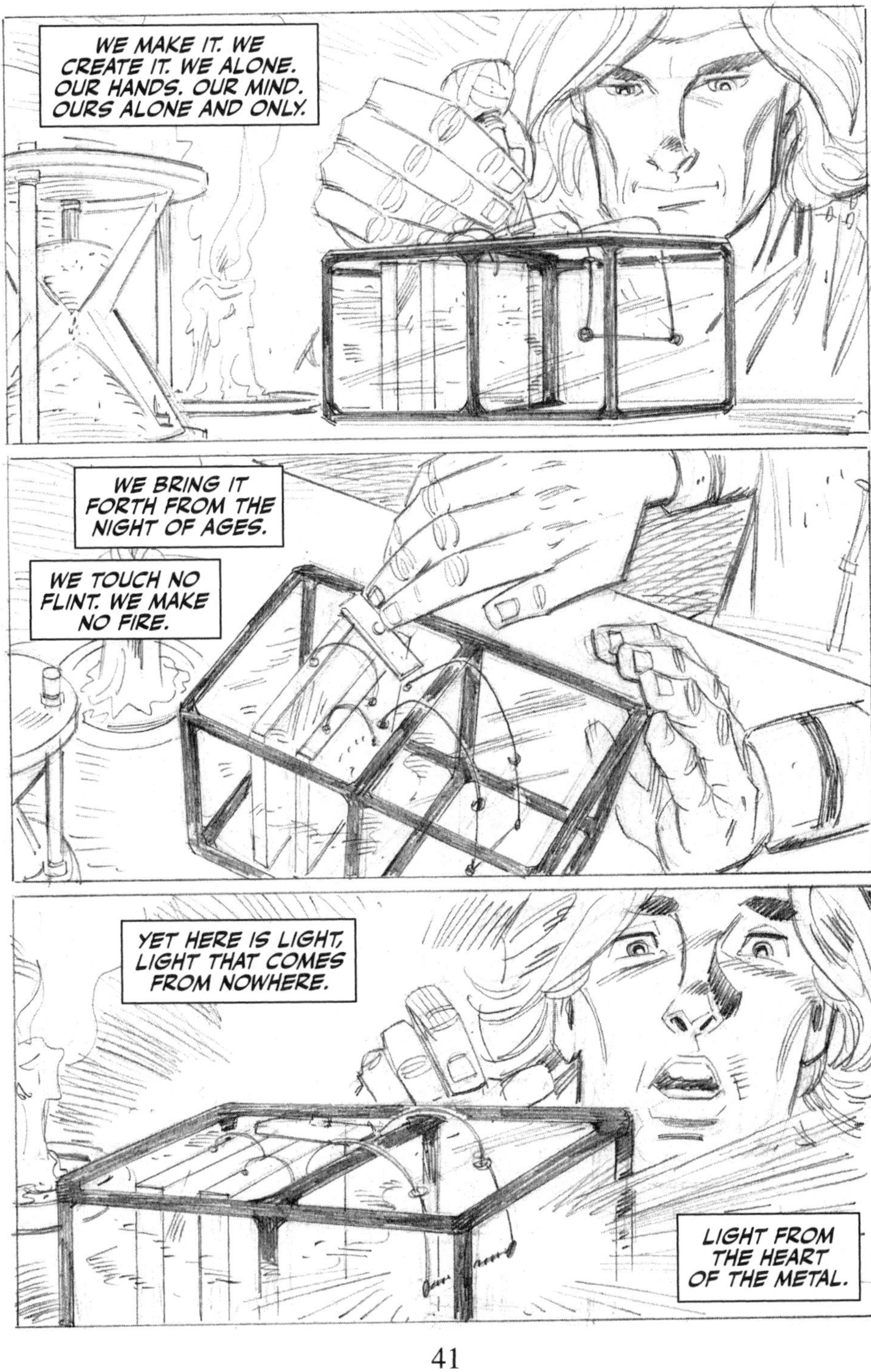
WE MAKE IT. WE CREATE IT. WE ALONE. OUR HANDS. OUR MIND. OURS ALONE AND ONLY.
WE BRING IT FORTH FROM THE NIGHT OF AGES.
WE TOUCH NO FLINT. WE MAKE NO FIRE.
YET HERE IS LIGHT, LIGHT THAT COMES FROM NOWHERE.
LIGHT FROM THE HEART OF THE METAL.

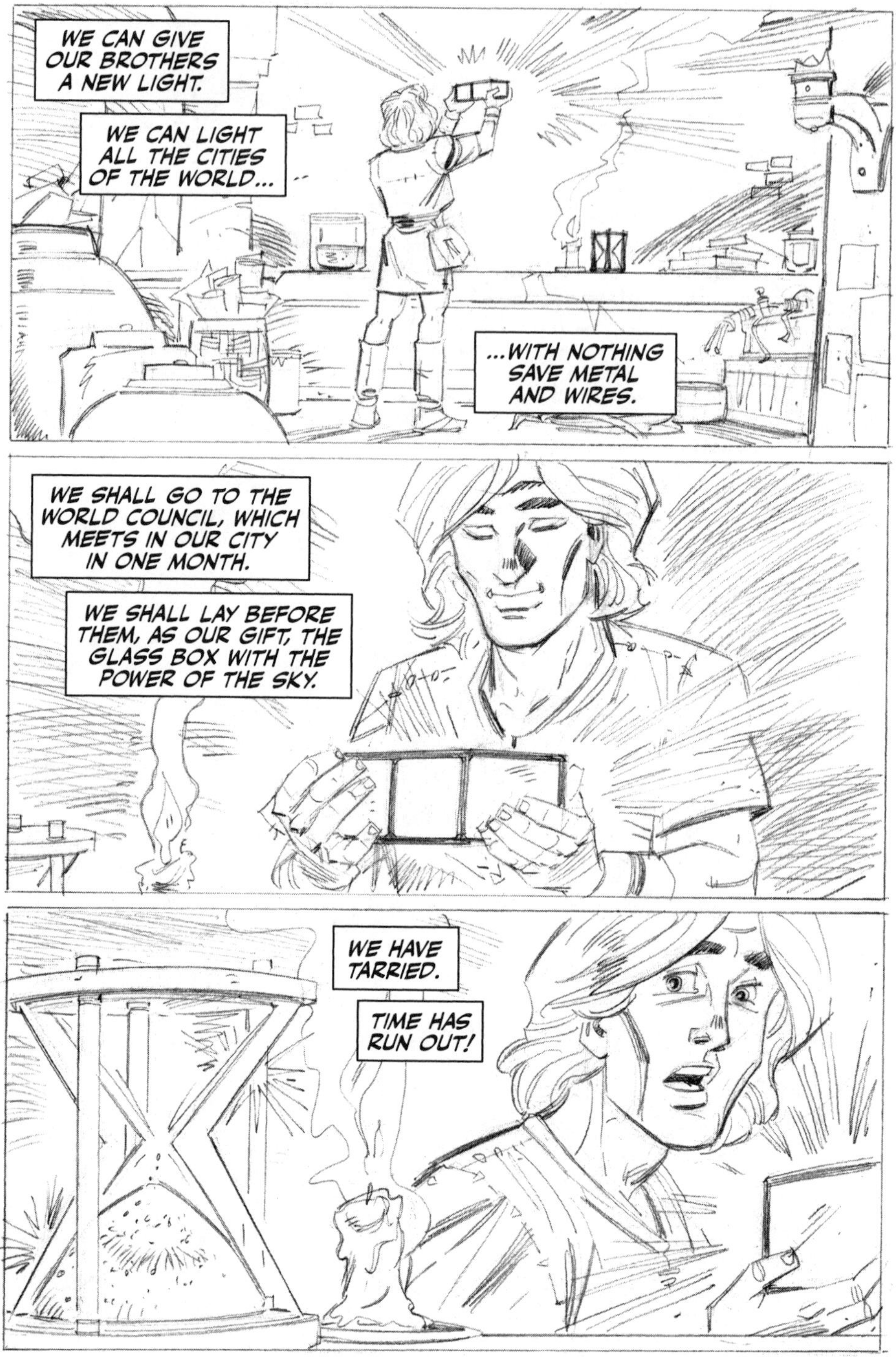
WE CAN GIVE OUR BROTHERS A NEW LIGHT.
WE CAN LIGHT ALL THE CITIES OF THE WORLD...
...WITH NOTHING SAVE METAL AND WIRES.
WE SHALL GO TO THE WORLD COUNCIL, WHICH MEETS IN OUR CITY IN ONE MONTH.
WE SHALL LAY BEFORE THEM, AS OUR GIFT, THE GLASS BOX WITH THE POWER OF THE SKY.
WE HAVE TARRIED.
TIME HAS RUN OUT!

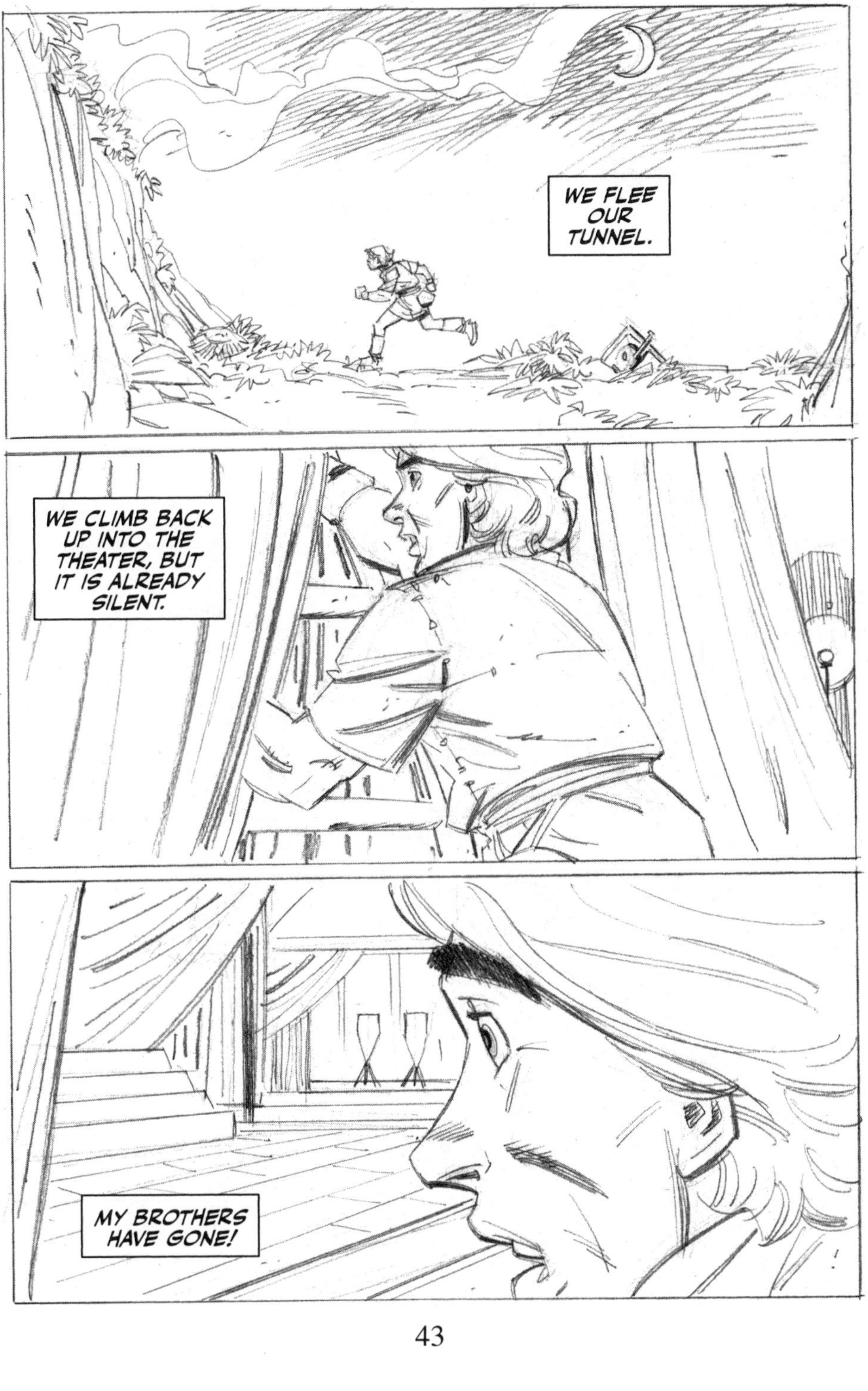
WE FLEE OUR TUNNEL.
WE CLIMB BACK UP INTO THE THEATER, BUT IT IS ALREADY SILENT.
MY BROTHERS HAVE GONE!

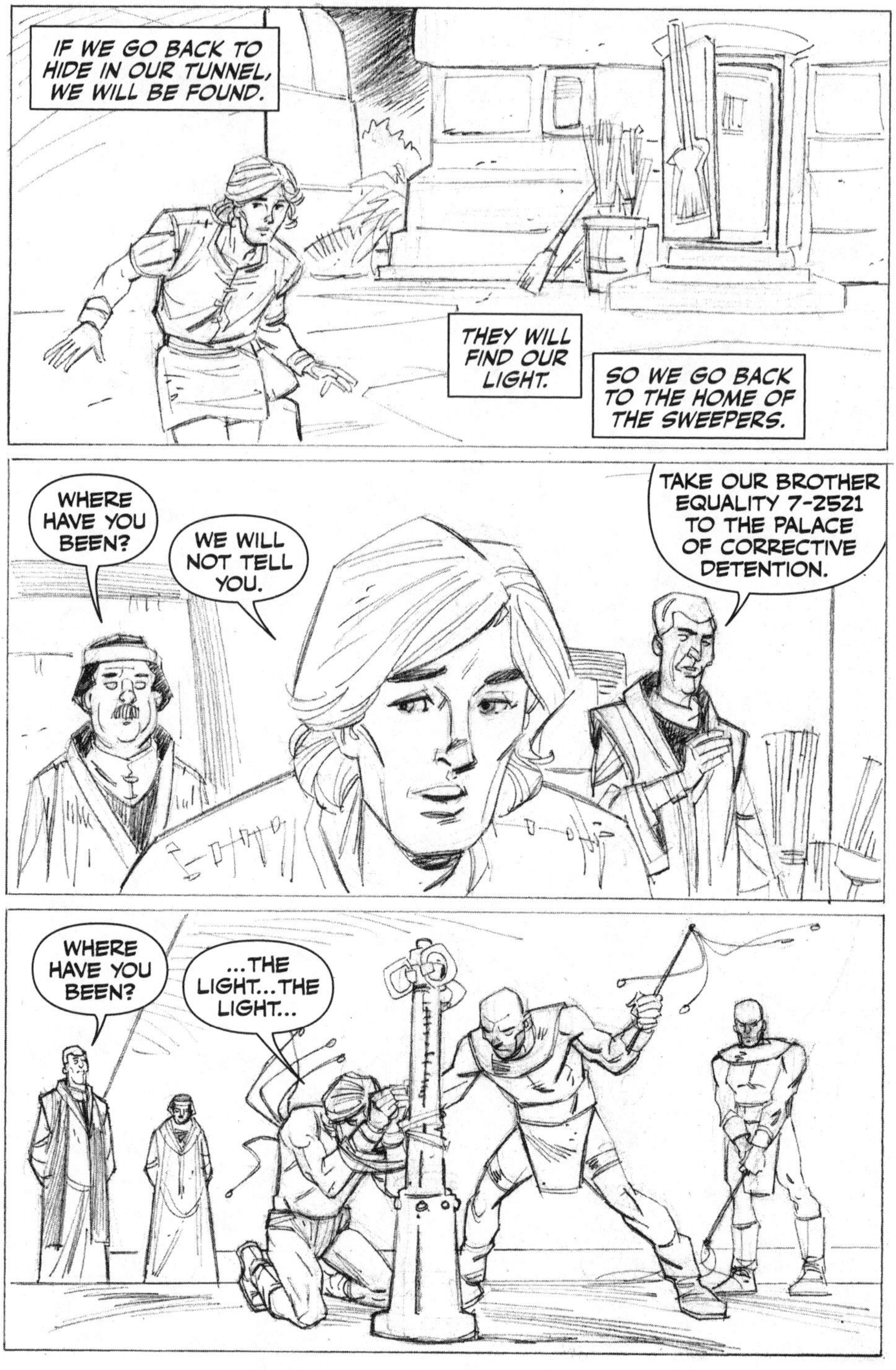
IF WE GO BACK TO HIDE IN OUR TUNNEL, WE WILL BE FOUND.
THEY WILL FIND OUR LIGHT.
SO WE GO BACK TO THE HOME OF THE SWEEPERS.
WHERE HAVE YOU BEEN?
WE WILL NOT TELL YOU.
TAKE OUR BROTHER EQUALITY 7-2521 TO THE PALACE OF CORRECTIVE DETENTION.
WHERE HAVE YOU BEEN?
...THE LIGHT...THE LIGHT...

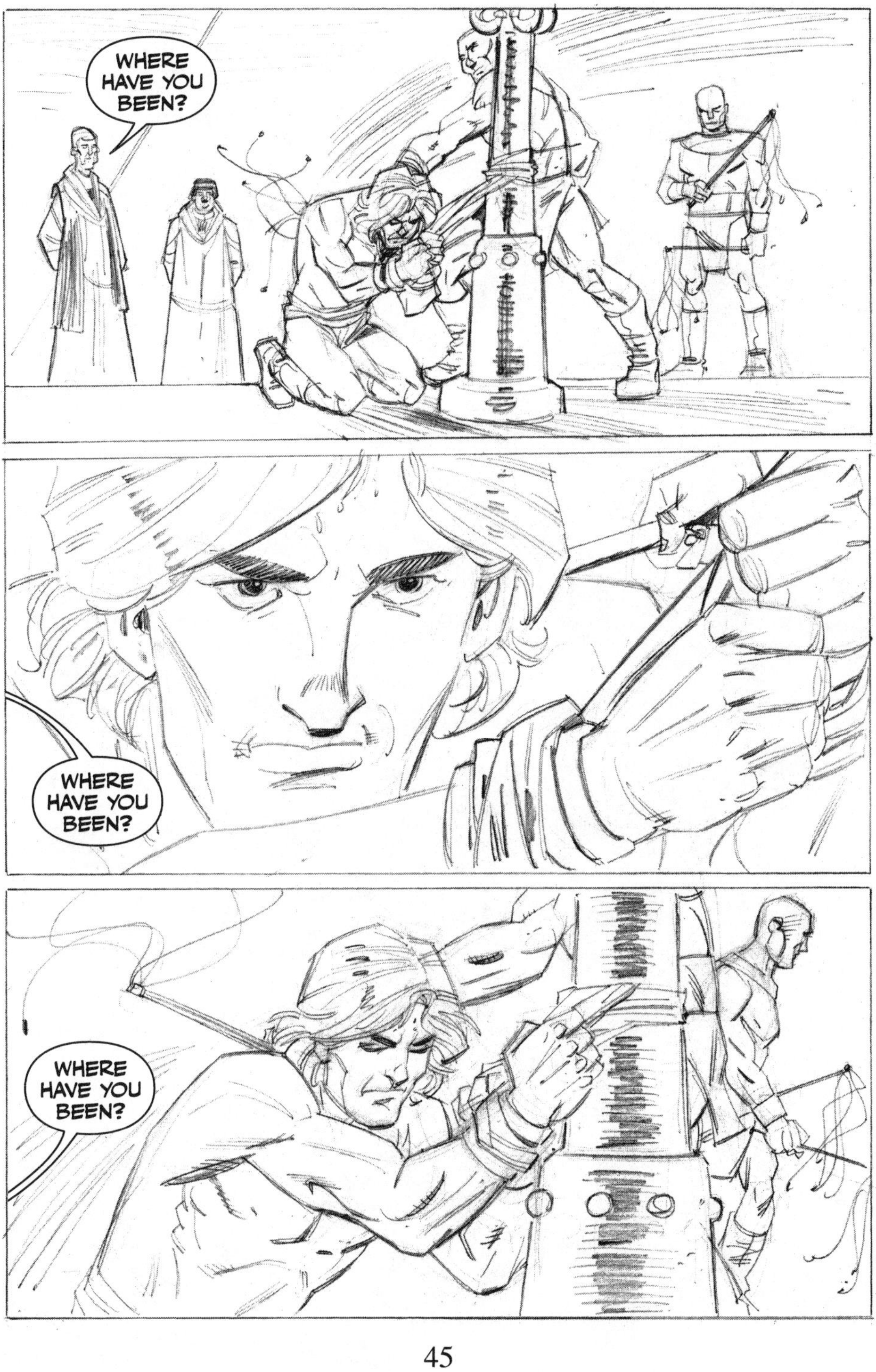
WHERE HAVE YOU BEEN?
WHERE HAVE YOU BEEN?
WHERE HAVE YOU BEEN?

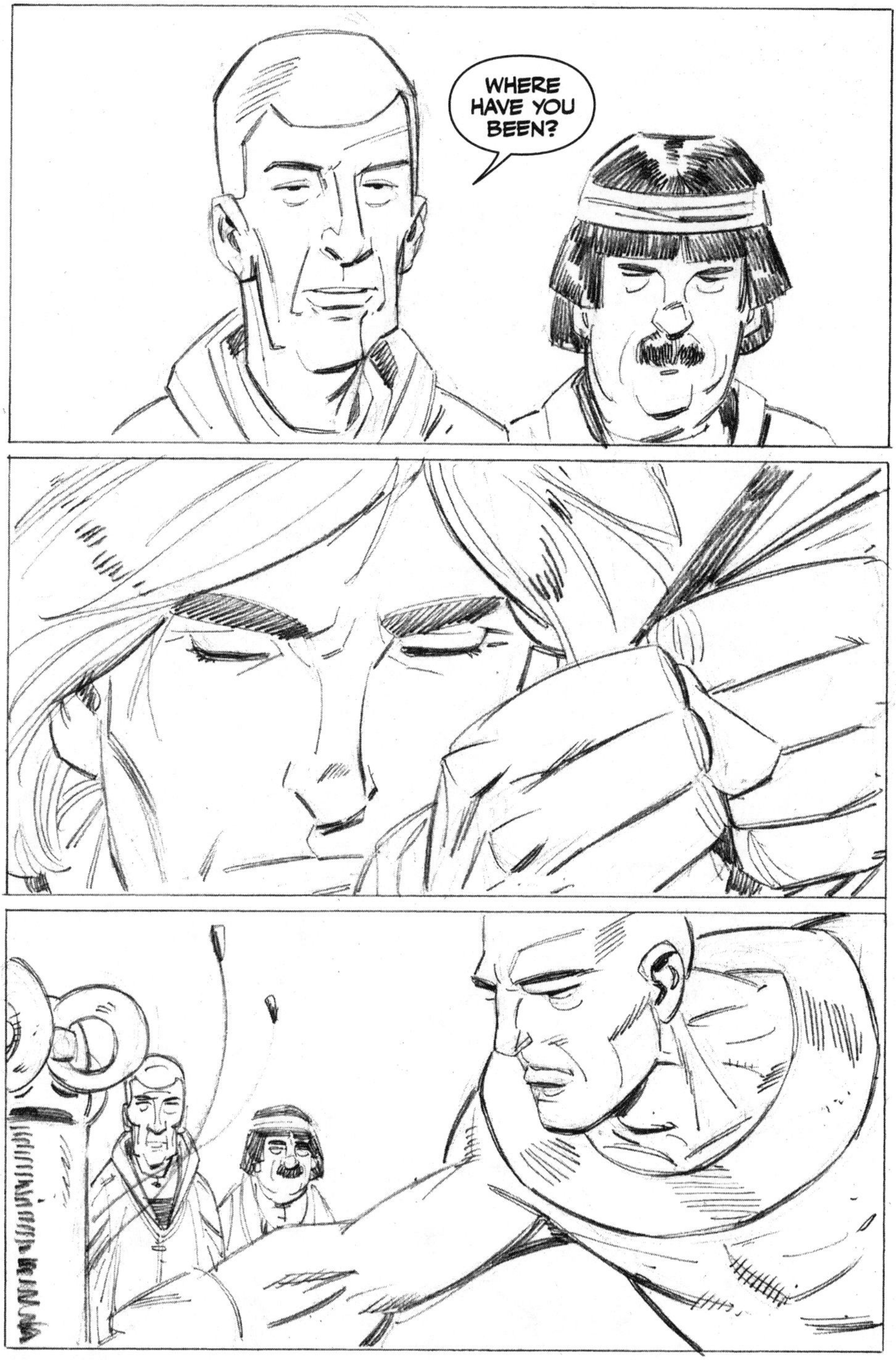
WHERE HAVE YOU BEEN?

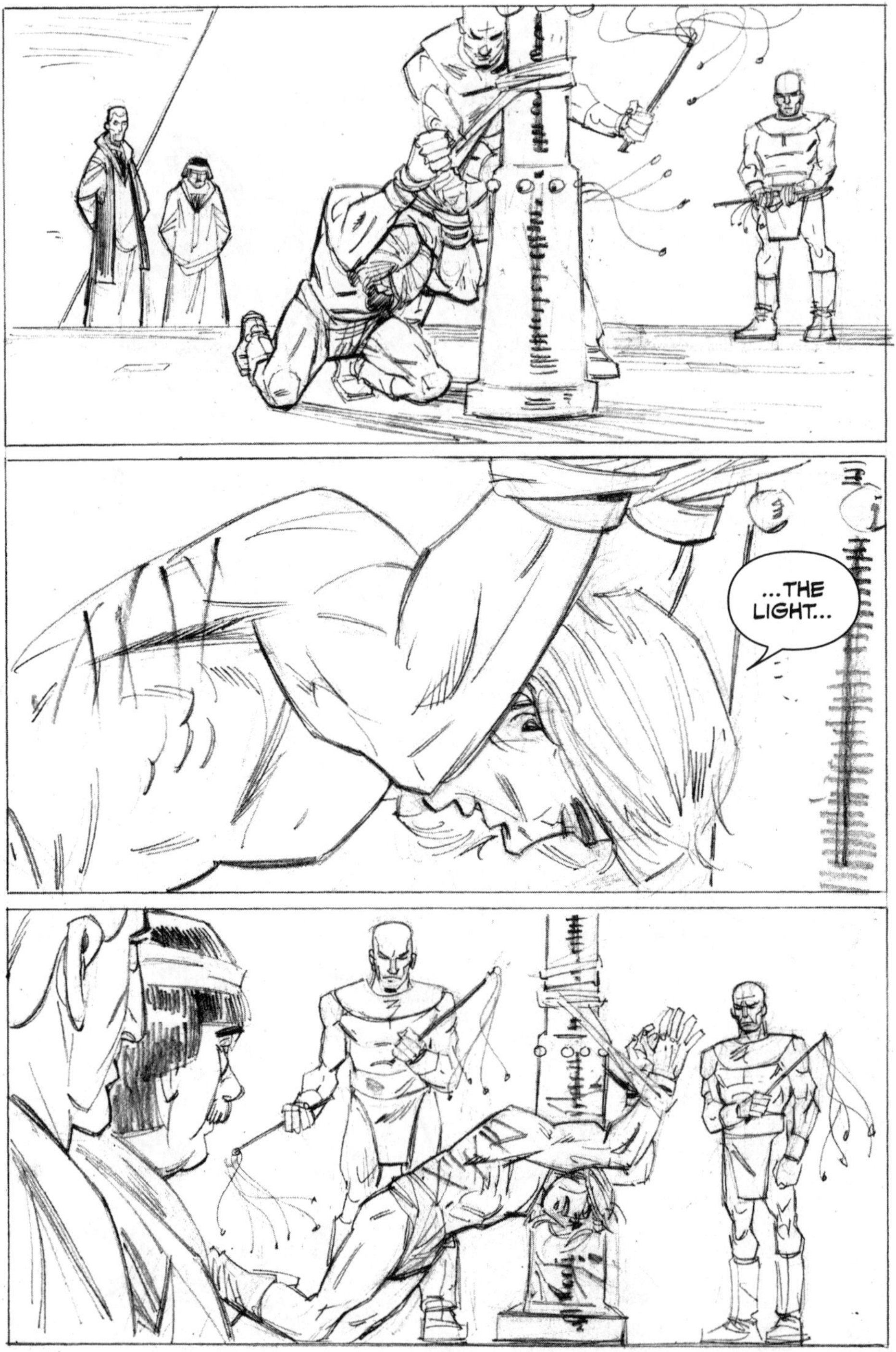
...THE LIGHT...

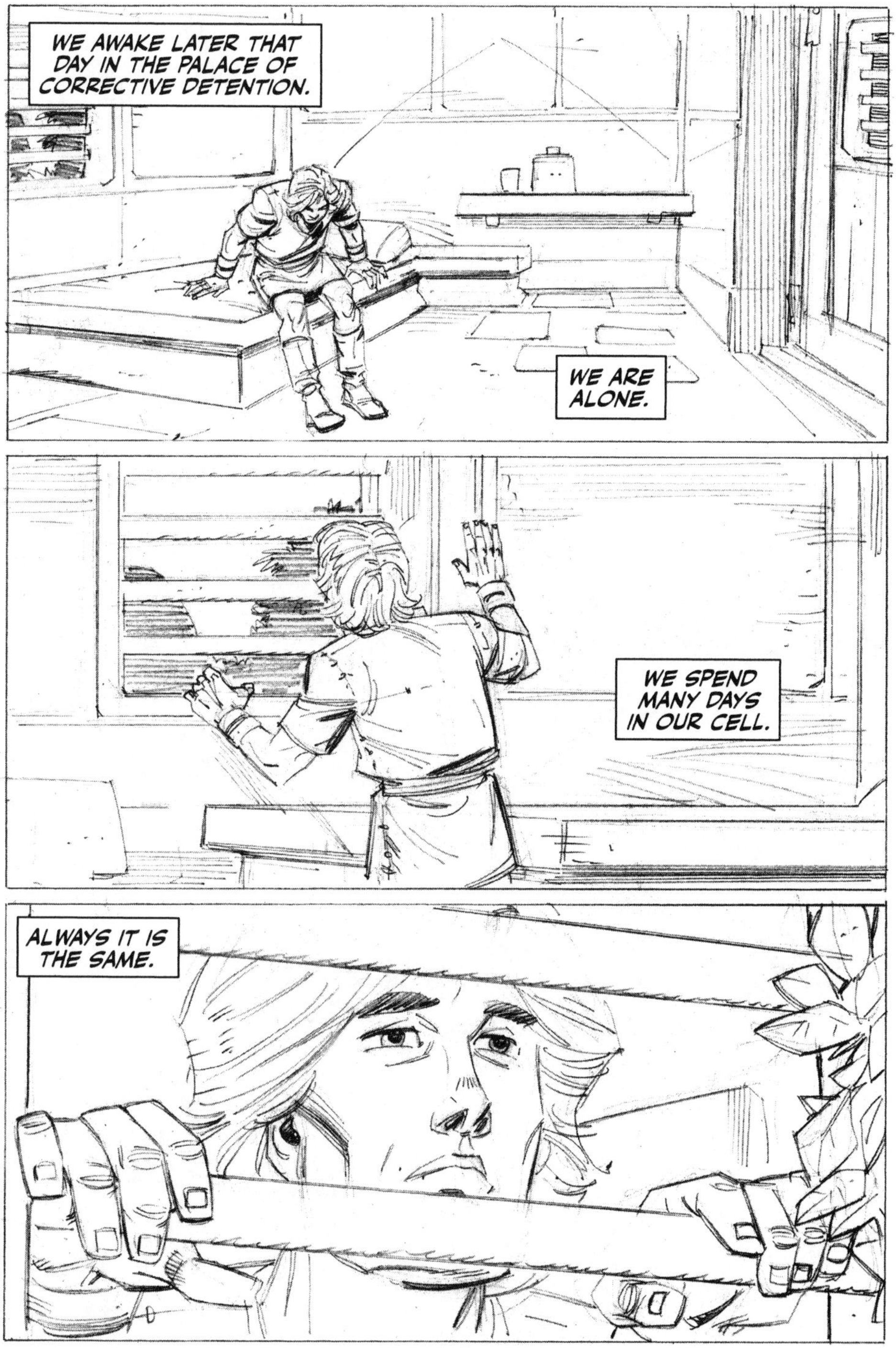
WE AWAKE LATER THAT DAY IN THE PALACE OF CORRECTIVE DETENTION.
WE ARE ALONE.
WE SPEND MANY DAYS IN OUR CELL.
ALWAYS IT IS THE SAME.

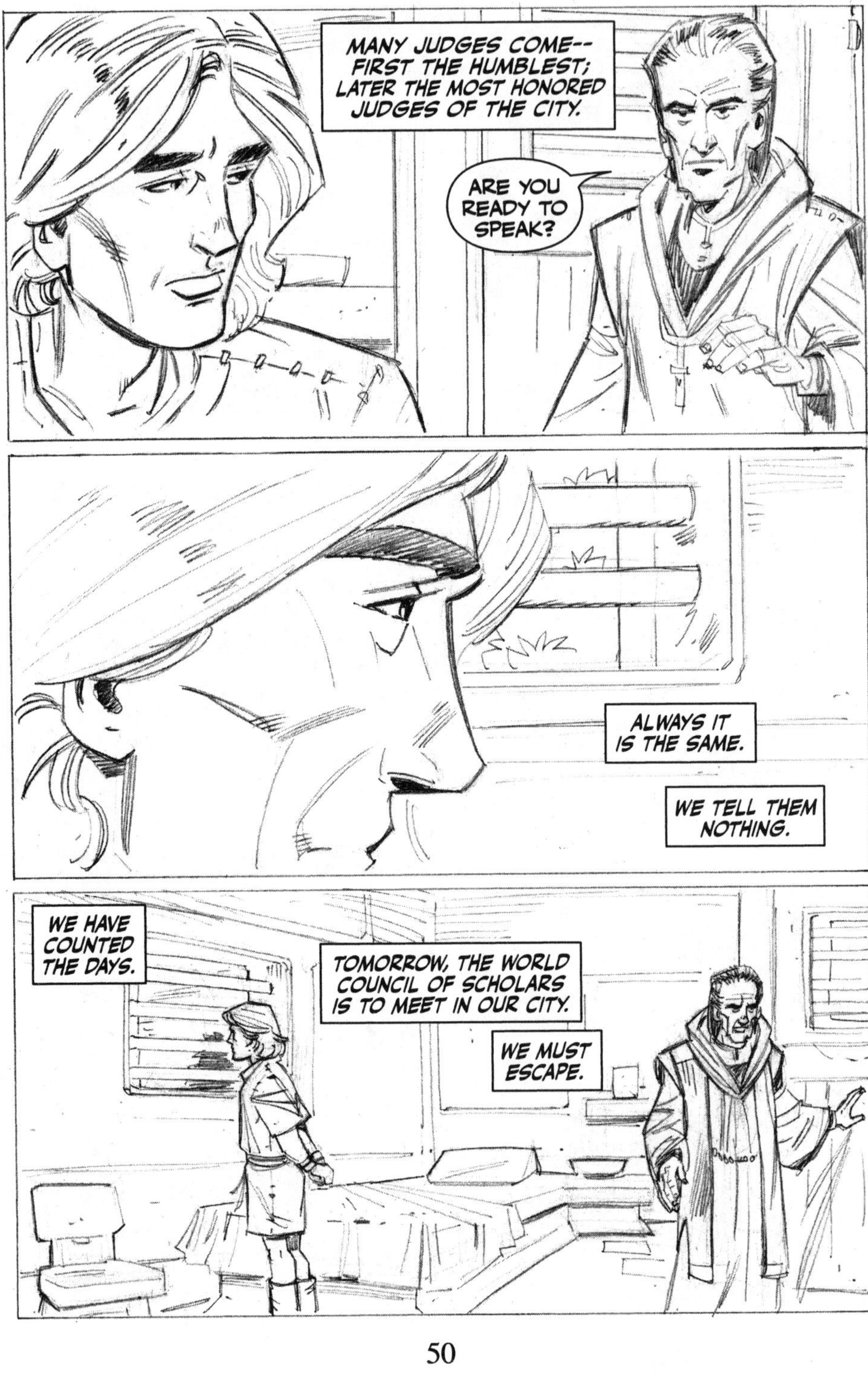
MANY JUDGES COME--
FIRST THE HUMBLEST;
LATER THE MOST HONORED
JUDGES OF THE CITY.
ARE YOU READY TO SPEAK?
ALWAYS IT IS THE SAME.
WE TELL THEM NOTHING.
WE HAVE COUNTED THE DAYS.
TOMORROW, THE WORLD COUNCIL OF SCHOLARS IS TO MEET IN OUR CITY.
WE MUST ESCAPE.

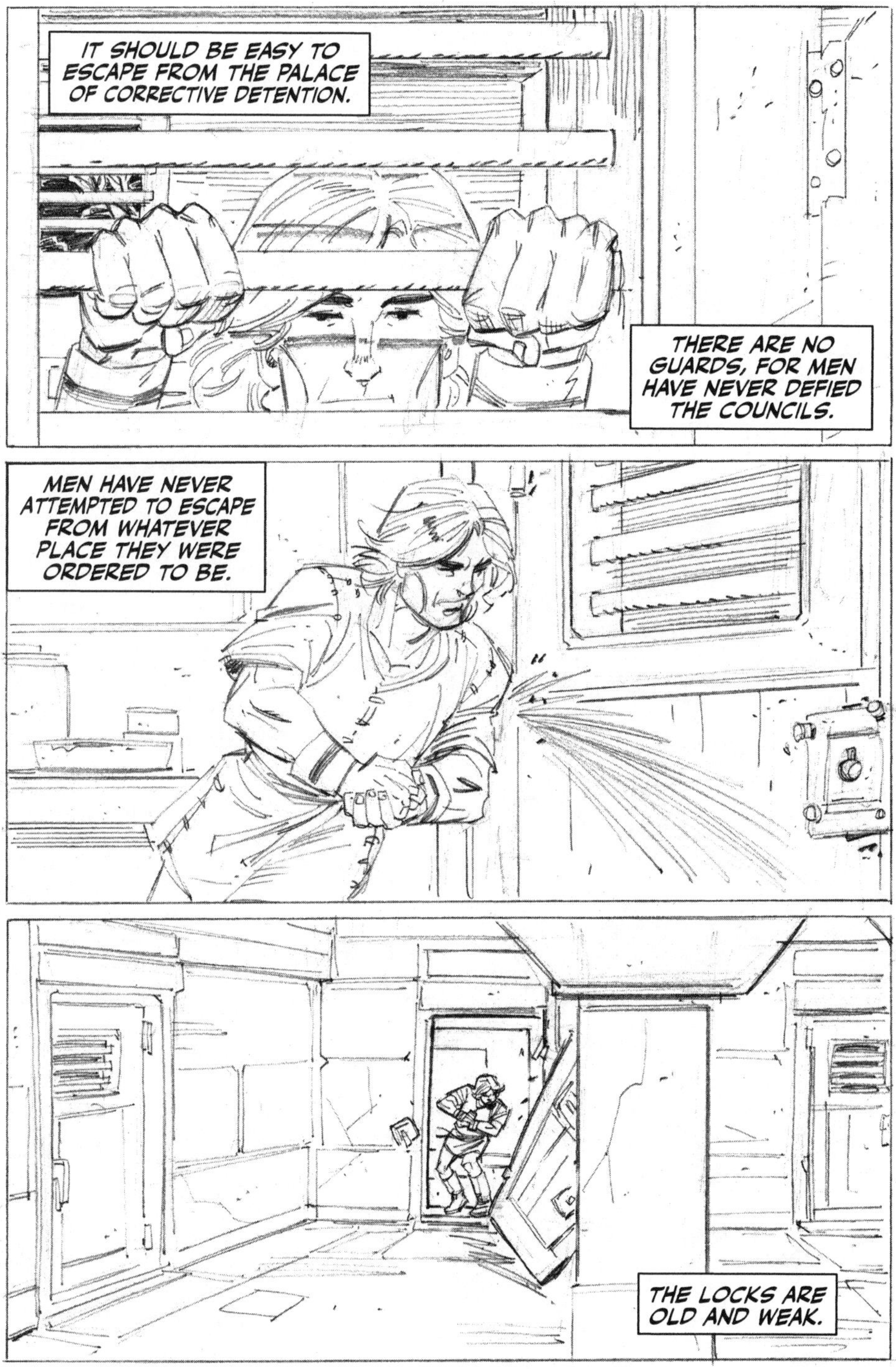
IT SHOULD BE EASY TO ESCAPE FROM THE PALACE OF CORRECTIVE DETENTION.
THERE ARE NO GUARDS, FOR MEN HAVE NEVER DEFIED THE COUNCILS.
MEN HAVE NEVER ATTEMPTED TO ESCAPE FROM WHATEVER PLACE THEY WERE ORDERED TO BE.
THE LOCKS ARE OLD AND WEAK.

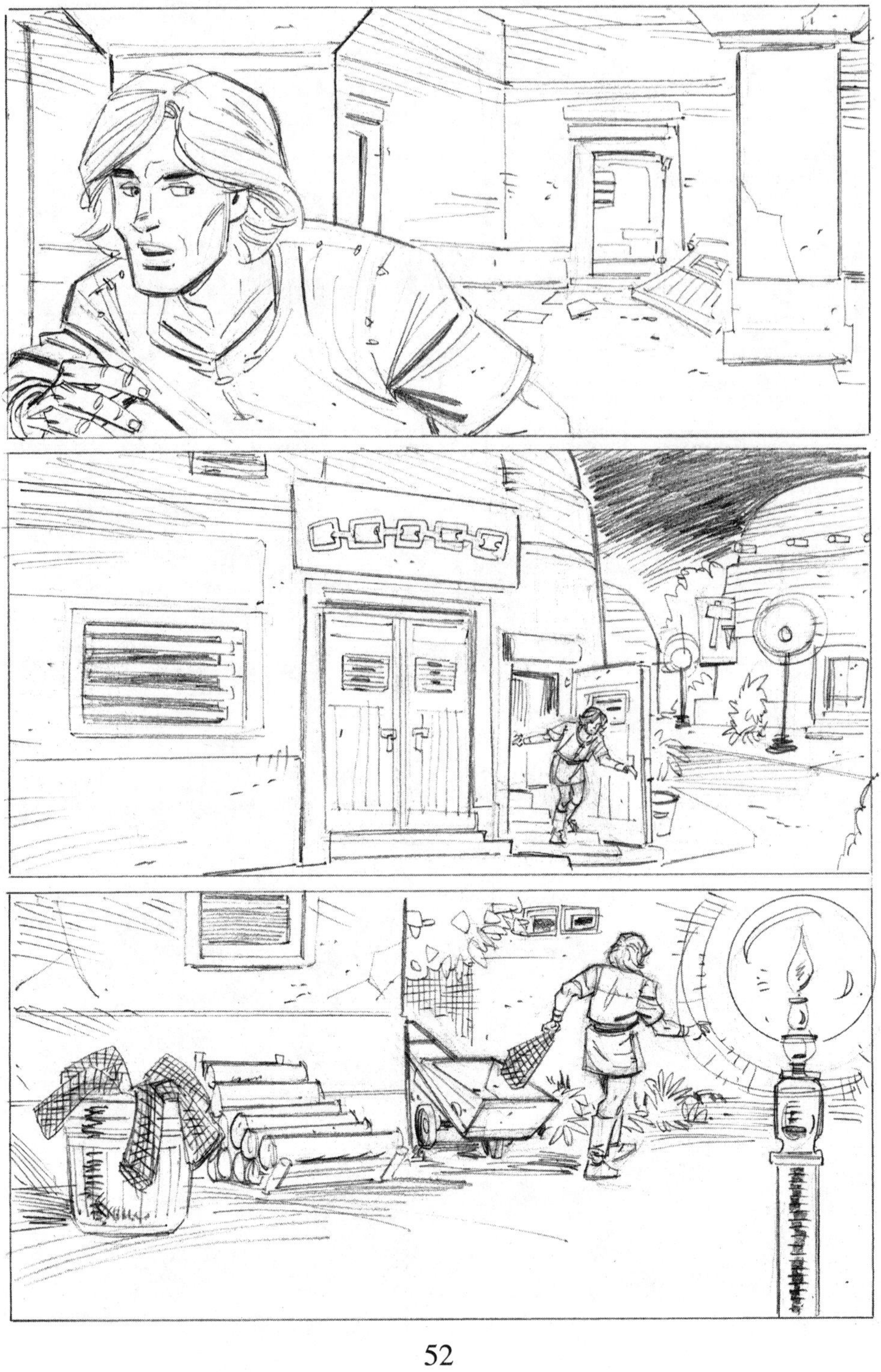

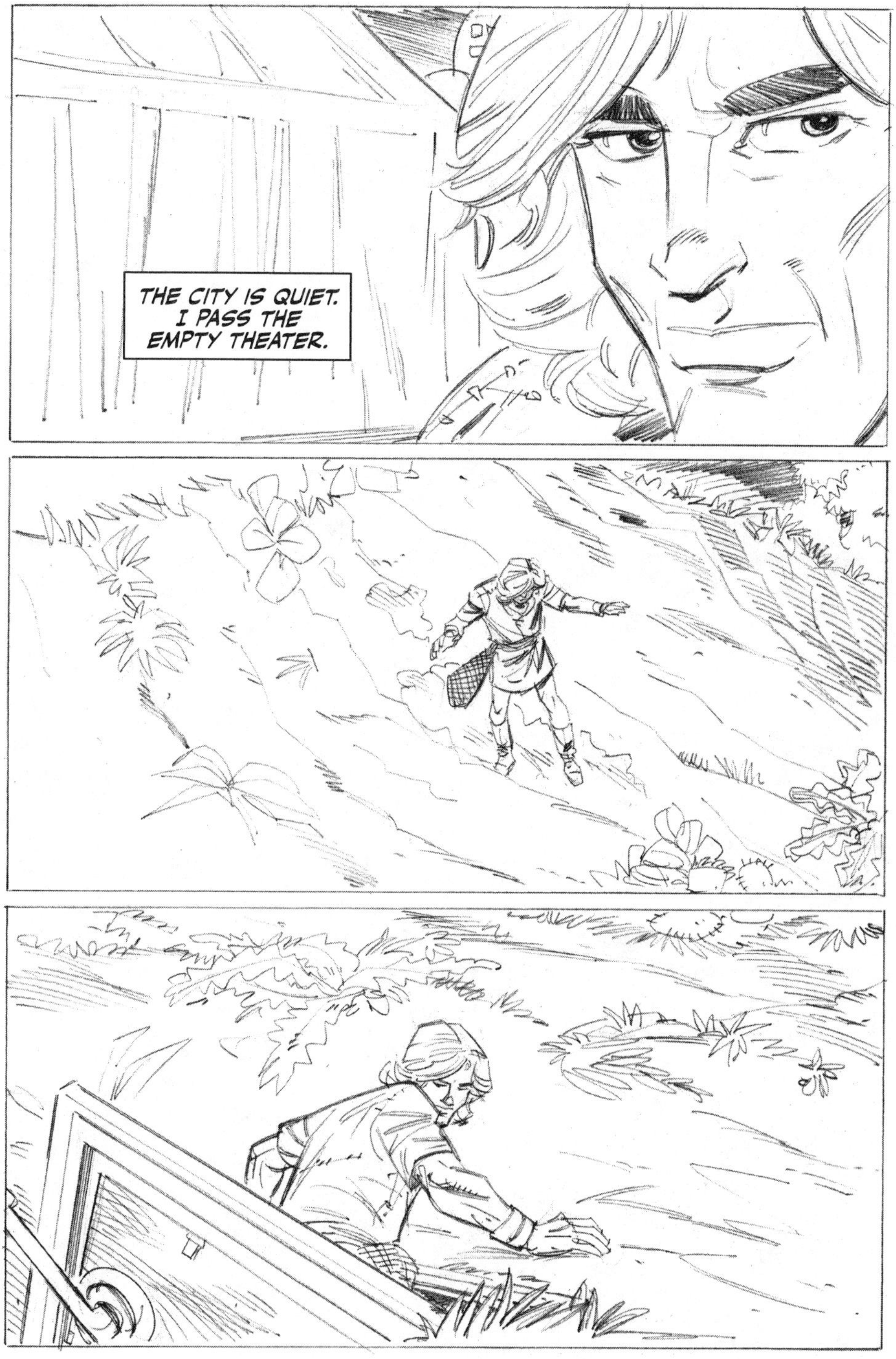
THE CITY IS QUIET. I PASS THE EMPTY THEATER.

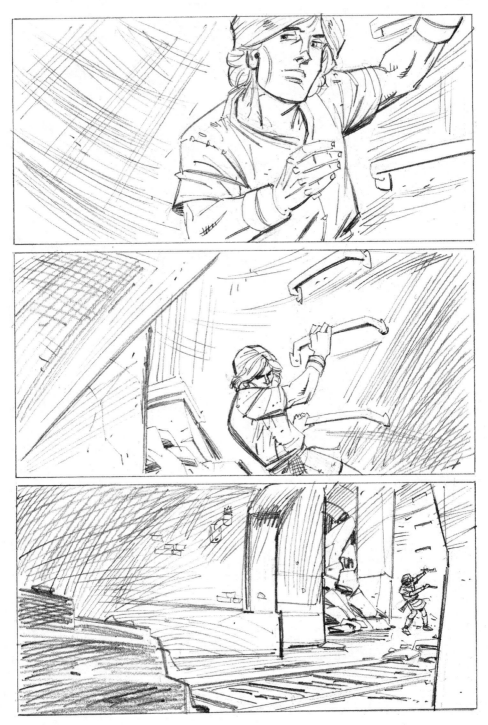

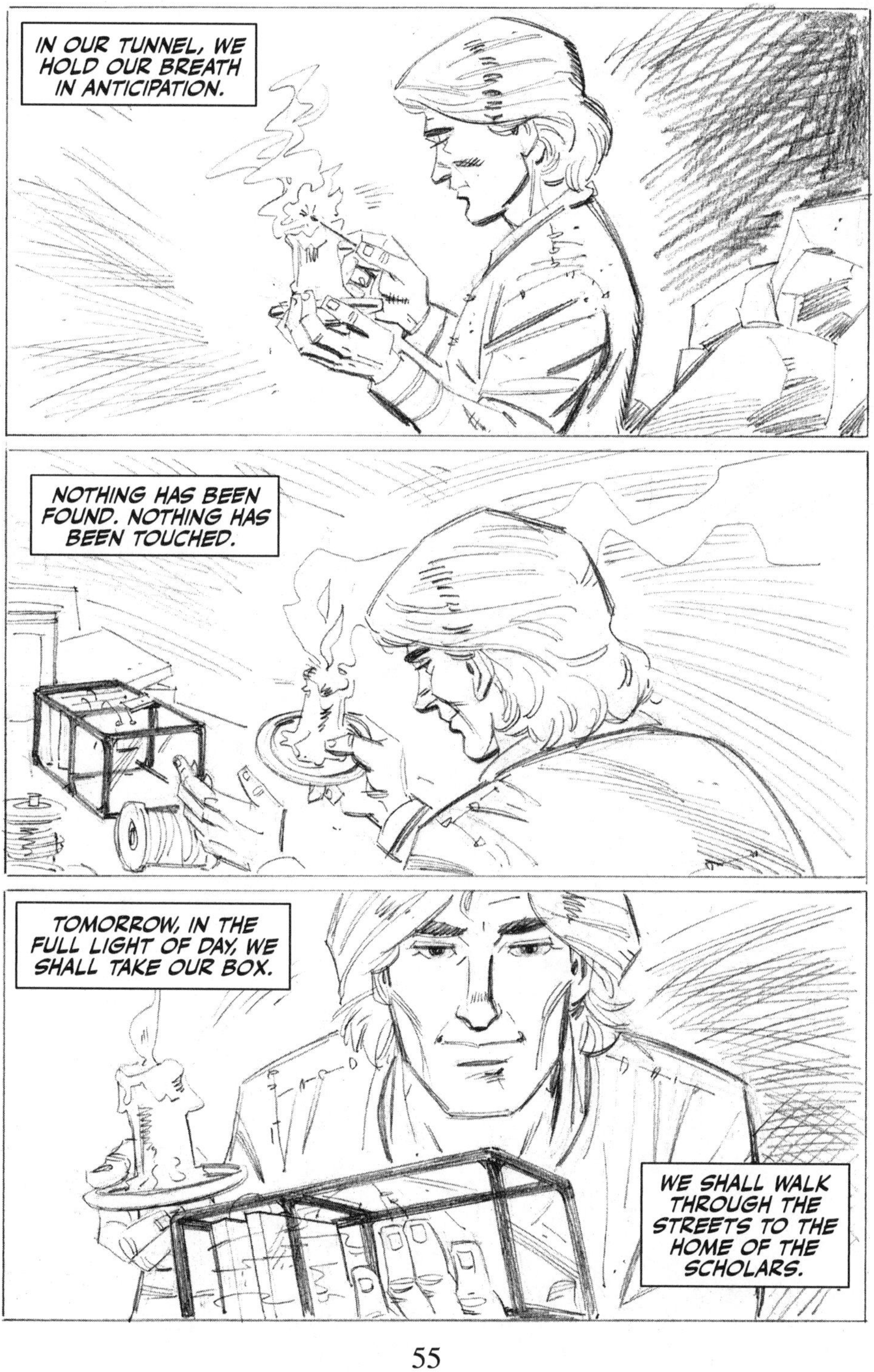
IN OUR TUNNEL, WE HOLD OUR BREATH IN ANTICIPATION.
NOTHING HAS BEEN FOUND. NOTHING HAS BEEN TOUCHED.
TOMORROW, IN THE FULL LIGHT OF DAY, WE SHALL TAKE OUR BOX.
WE SHALL WALK THROUGH THE STREETS TO THE HOME OF THE SCHOLARS.

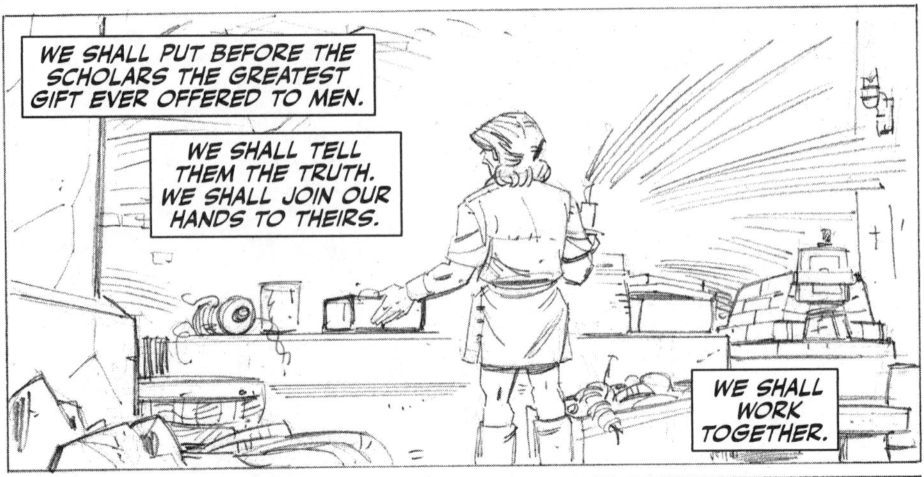
WE SHALL PUT BEFORE THE SCHOLARS THE GREATEST GIFT EVER OFFERED TO MEN.
WE SHALL TELL THEM THE TRUTH. WE SHALL JOIN OUR HANDS TO THEIRS.
WE SHALL WORK TOGETHER.

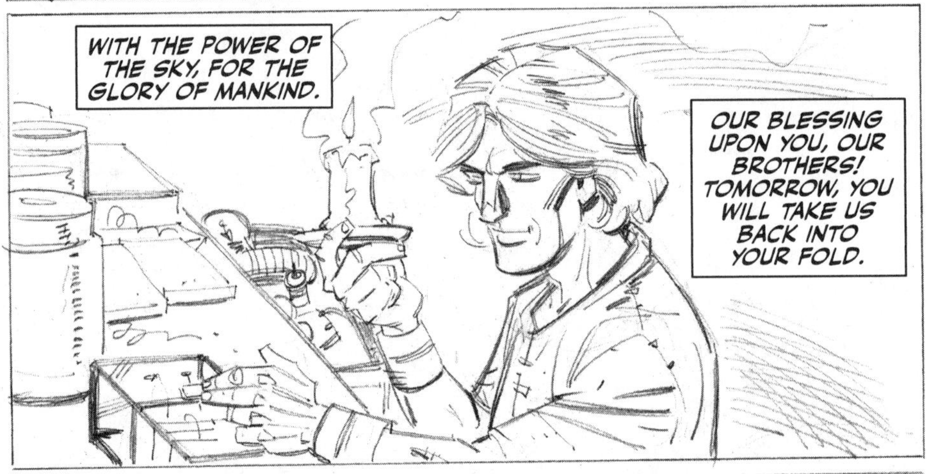
WITH THE POWER OF THE SKY, FOR THE GLORY OF MANKIND.
OUR BLESSING UPON YOU, OUR BROTHERS! TOMORROW, YOU WILL TAKE US BACK INTO YOUR FOLD.

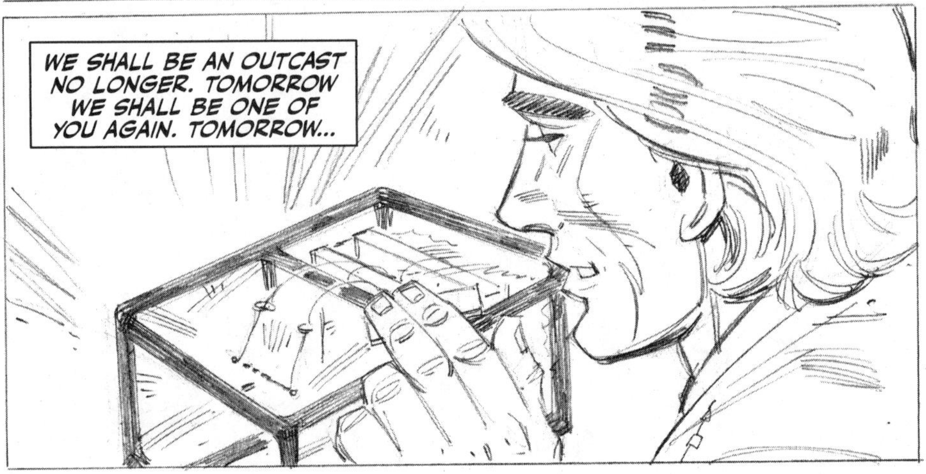
WE SHALL BE AN OUTCAST NO LONGER. TOMORROW WE SHALL BE ONE OF YOU AGAIN. TOMORROW...

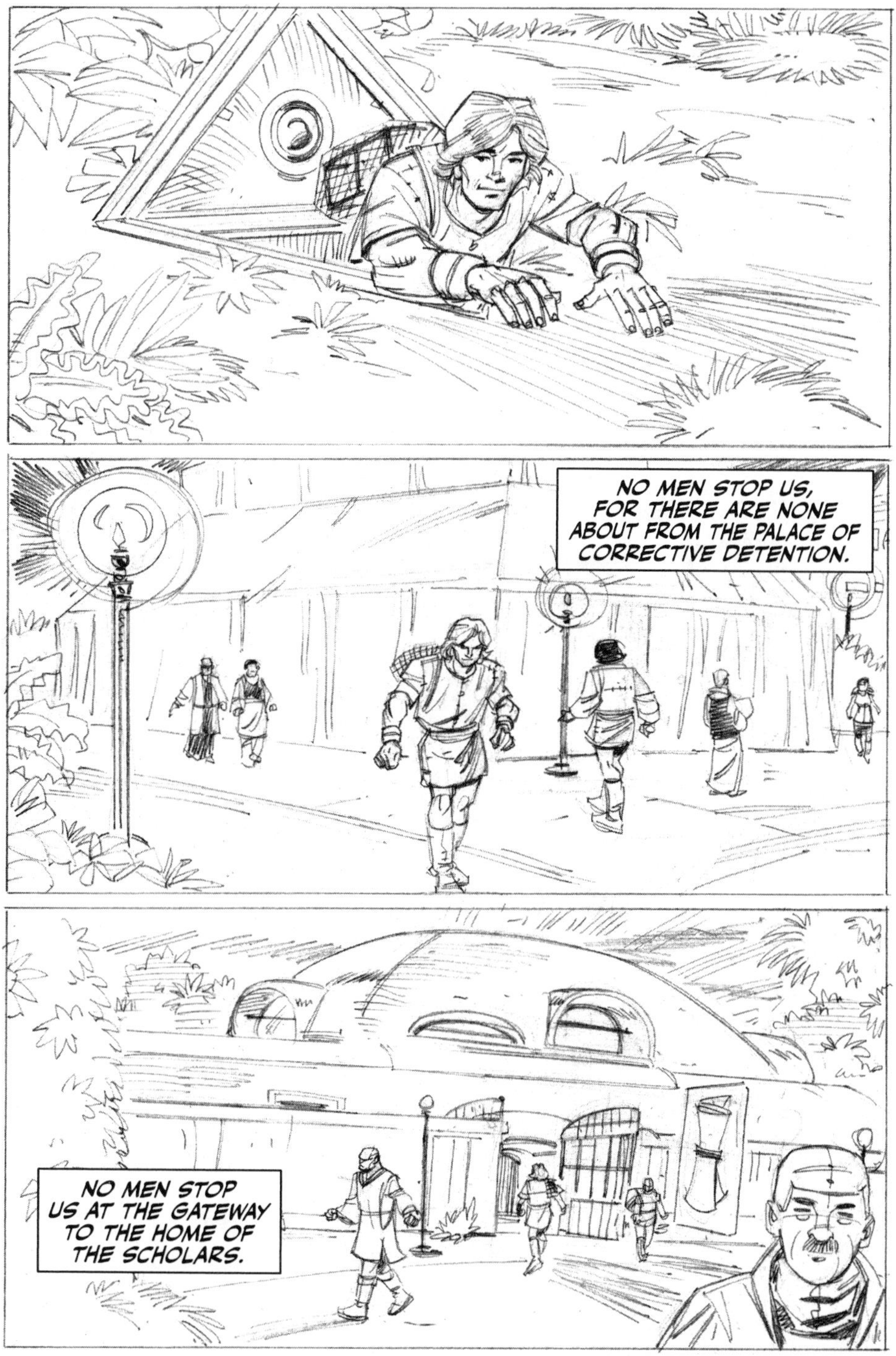
NO MEN STOP US, FOR THERE ARE NONE ABOUT FROM THE PALACE OF CORRECTIVE DETENTION.
NO MEN STOP US AT THE GATEWAY TO THE HOME OF THE SCHOLARS.

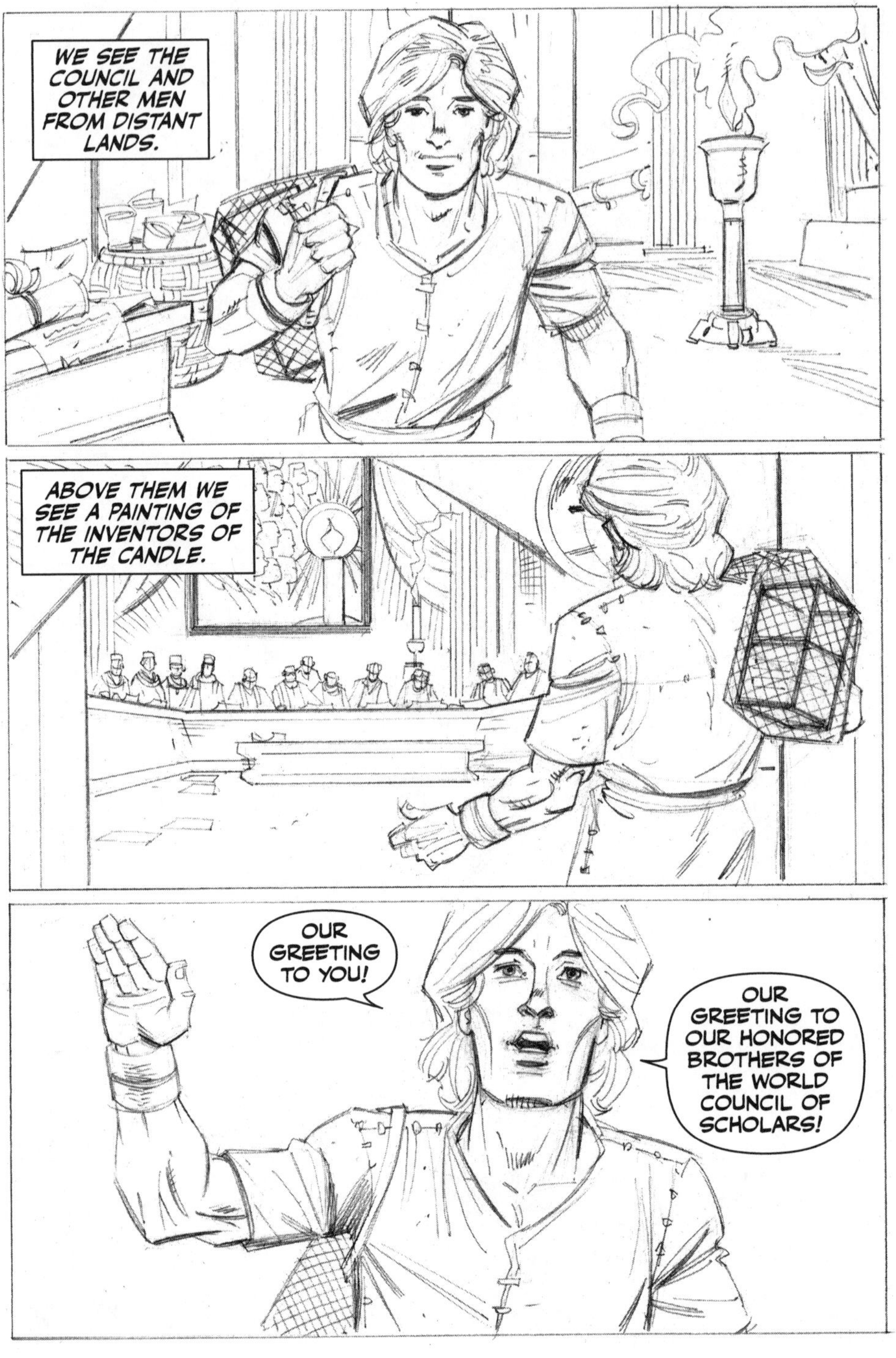
WE SEE THE COUNCIL AND OTHER MEN FROM DISTANT LANDS.
ABOVE THEM WE SEE A PAINTING OF THE INVENTORS OF THE CANDLE.
OUR GREETING TO YOU!
OUR GREETING TO OUR HONORED BROTHERS OF THE WORLD COUNCIL OF SCHOLARS!

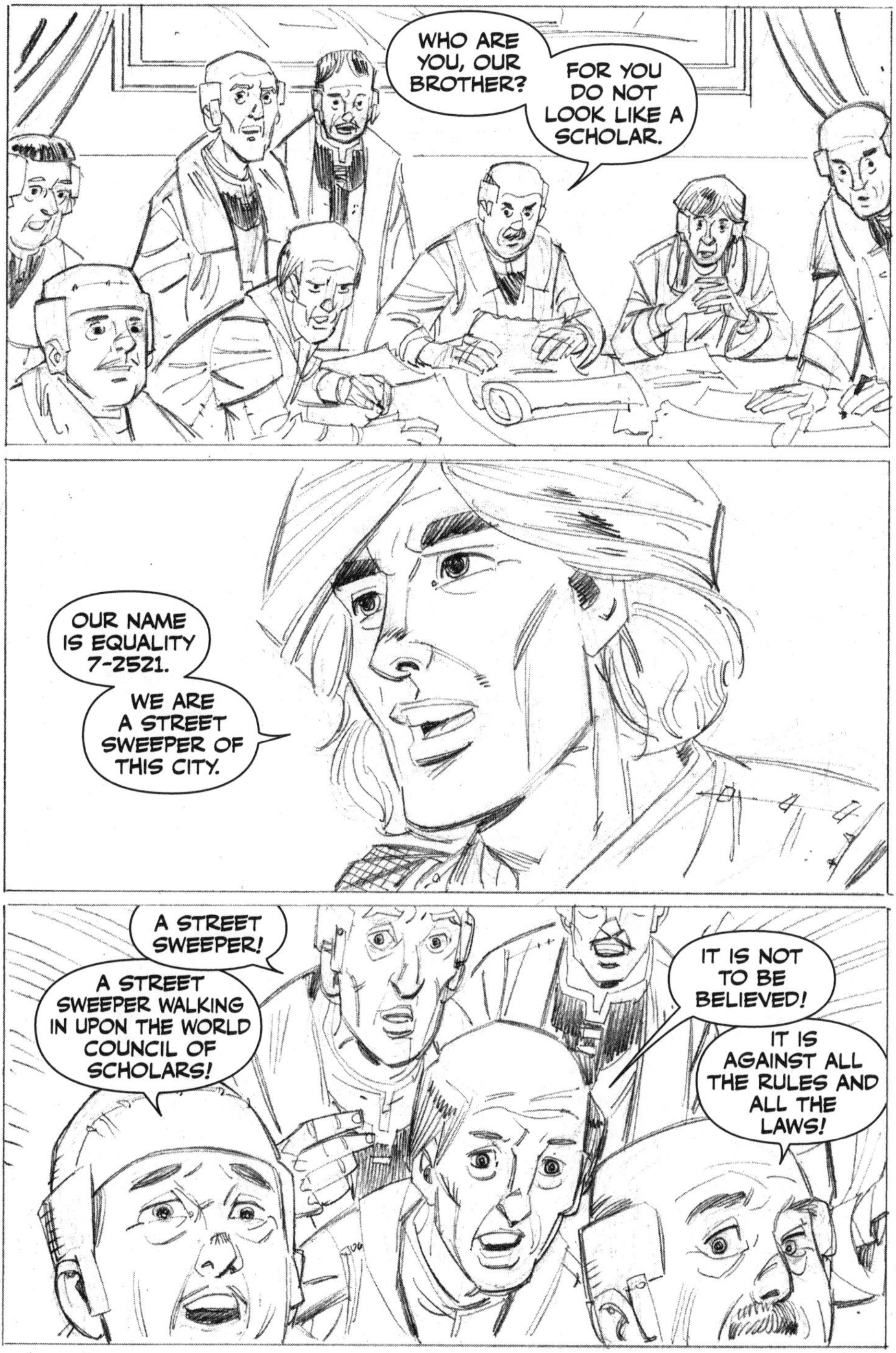
WHO ARE YOU, OUR BROTHER?
FOR YOU DO NOT LOOK LIKE A SCHOLAR.
OUR NAME IS EQUALITY 7-2521.
WE ARE A STREET SWEEPER OF THIS CITY.
A STREET SWEEPER!
A STREET SWEEPER WALKING IN UPON THE WORLD COUNCIL OF SCHOLARS!
IT IS NOT TO BE BELIEVED!
IT IS AGAINST ALL THE RULES AND ALL THE LAWS!

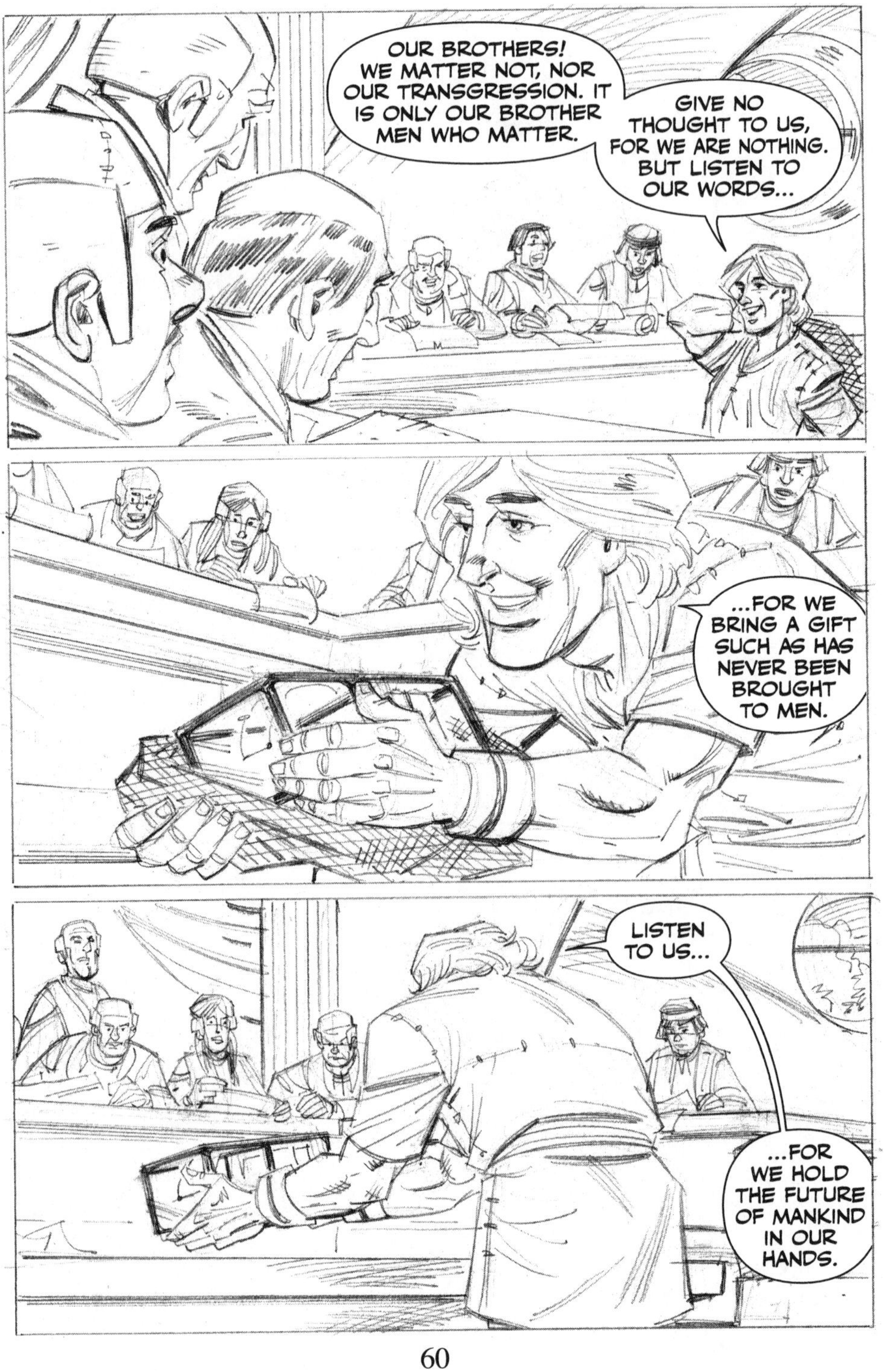
OUR BROTHERS! WE MATTER NOT, NOR OUR TRANSGRESSION. IT IS ONLY OUR BROTHER MEN WHO MATTER.
GIVE NO THOUGHT TO US, FOR WE ARE NOTHING. BUT LISTEN TO OUR WORDS...
...FOR WE BRING A GIFT SUCH AS HAS NEVER BEEN BROUGHT TO MEN.
LISTEN TO US...
...FOR WE HOLD THE FUTURE OF MANKIND IN OUR HANDS.

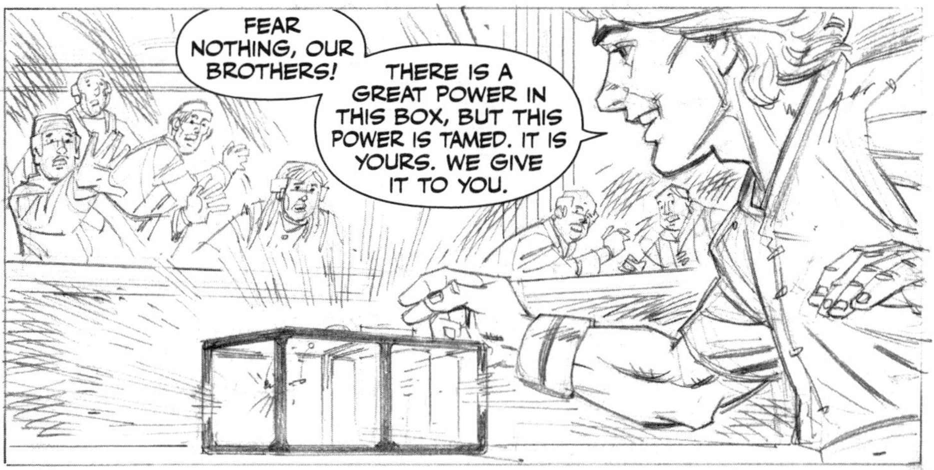
FEAR NOTHING, OUR BROTHERS!
THERE IS A GREAT POWER IN THIS BOX, BUT THIS POWER IS TAMED. IT IS YOURS. WE GIVE IT TO YOU.

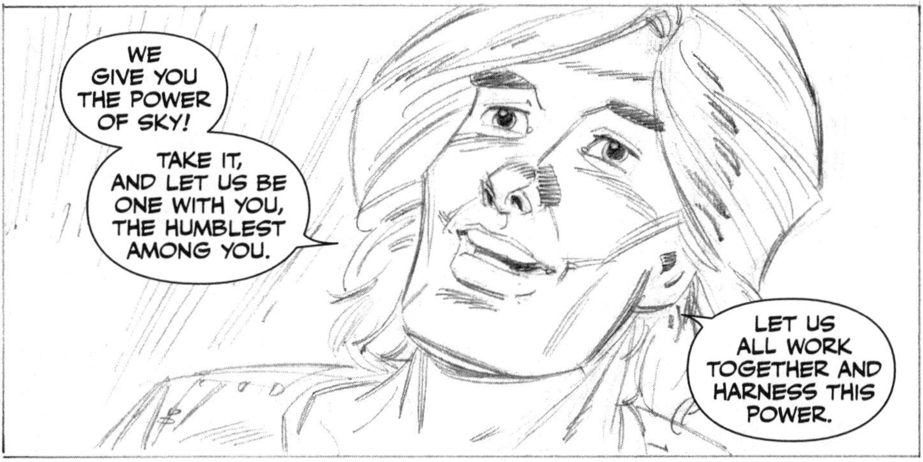
WE GIVE YOU THE POWER OF SKY!
TAKE IT, AND LET US BE ONE WITH YOU, THE HUMBLEST AMONG YOU.
LET US ALL WORK TOGETHER AND HARNESS THIS POWER.

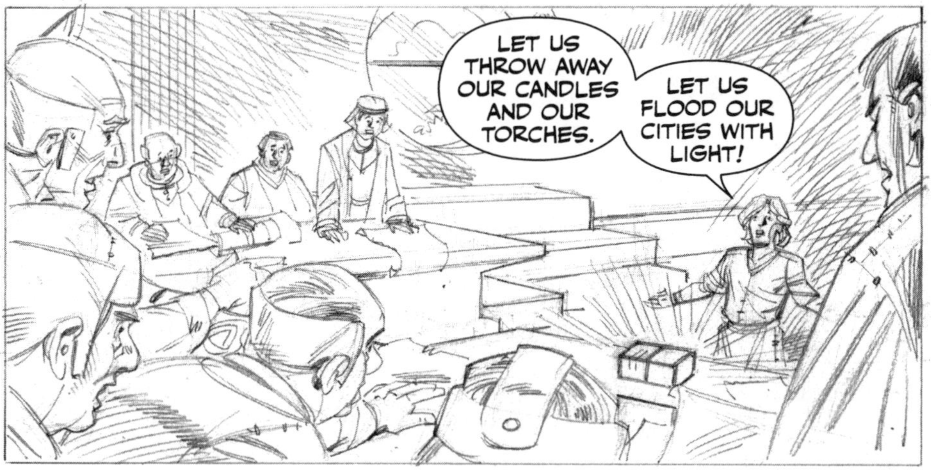
LET US THROW AWAY OUR CANDLES AND OUR TORCHES.
LET US FLOOD OUR CITIES WITH LIGHT!

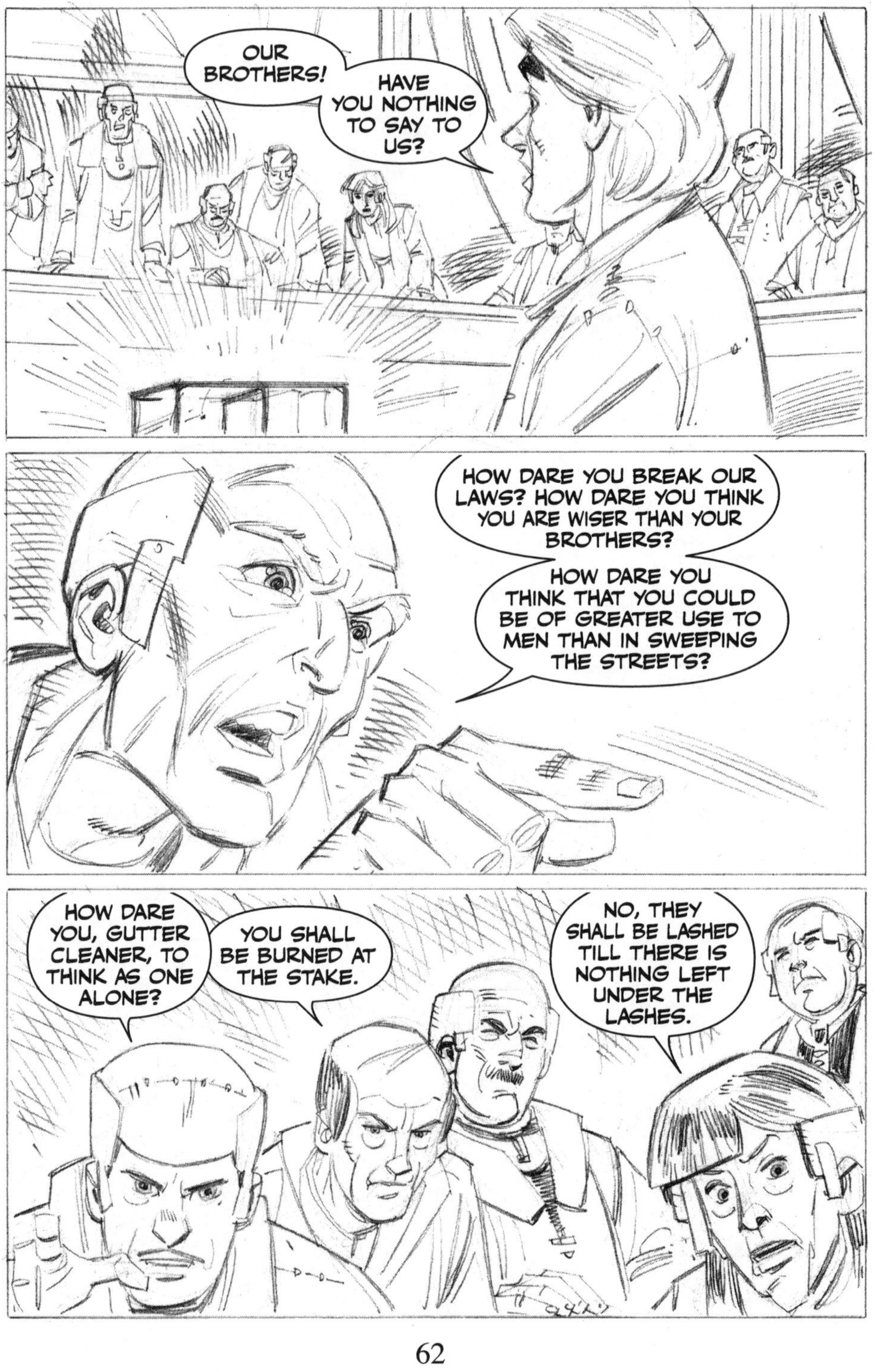
OUR BROTHERS!
HAVE YOU NOTHING TO SAY TO US?
HOW DARE YOU BREAK OUR LAWS? HOW DARE YOU THINK YOU ARE WISER THAN YOUR BROTHERS?
HOW DARE YOU THINK THAT YOU COULD BE OF GREATER USE TO MEN THAN IN SWEEPING THE STREETS?
HOW DARE YOU, GUTTER CLEANER, TO THINK AS ONE ALONE?
YOU SHALL BE BURNED AT THE STAKE.
NO, THEY SHALL BE LASHED TILL THERE IS NOTHING LEFT UNDER THE LASHES.

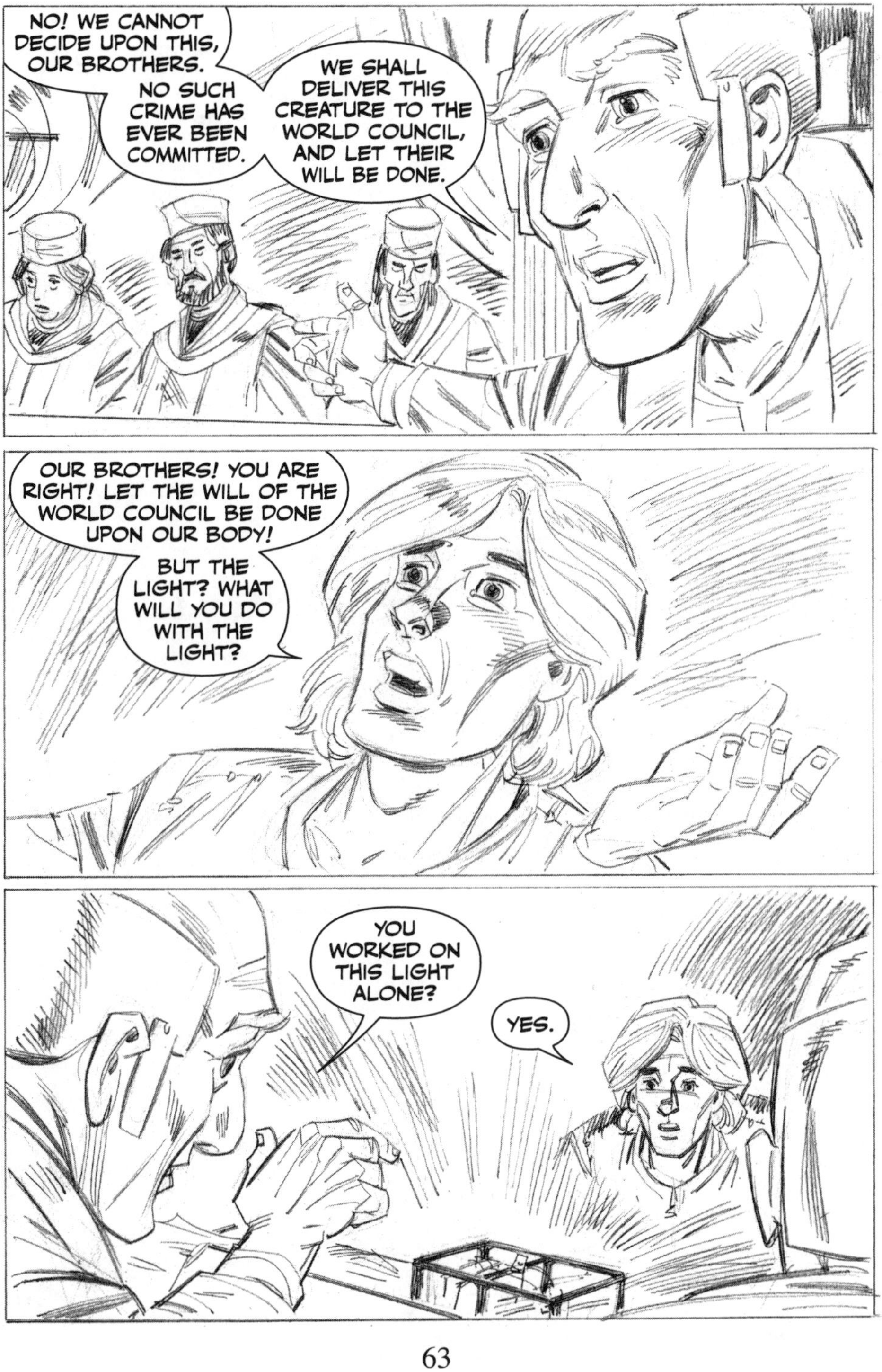
NO! WE CANNOT DECIDE UPON THIS, OUR BROTHERS.
NO SUCH CRIME HAS EVER BEEN COMMITTED.
WE SHALL DELIVER THIS CREATURE TO THE WORLD COUNCIL, AND LET THEIR WILL BE DONE.
OUR BROTHERS! YOU ARE RIGHT! LET THE WILL OF THE WORLD COUNCIL BE DONE UPON OUR BODY!
BUT THE LIGHT? WHAT WILL YOU DO WITH THE LIGHT?
YOU WORKED ON THIS LIGHT ALONE?
YES.

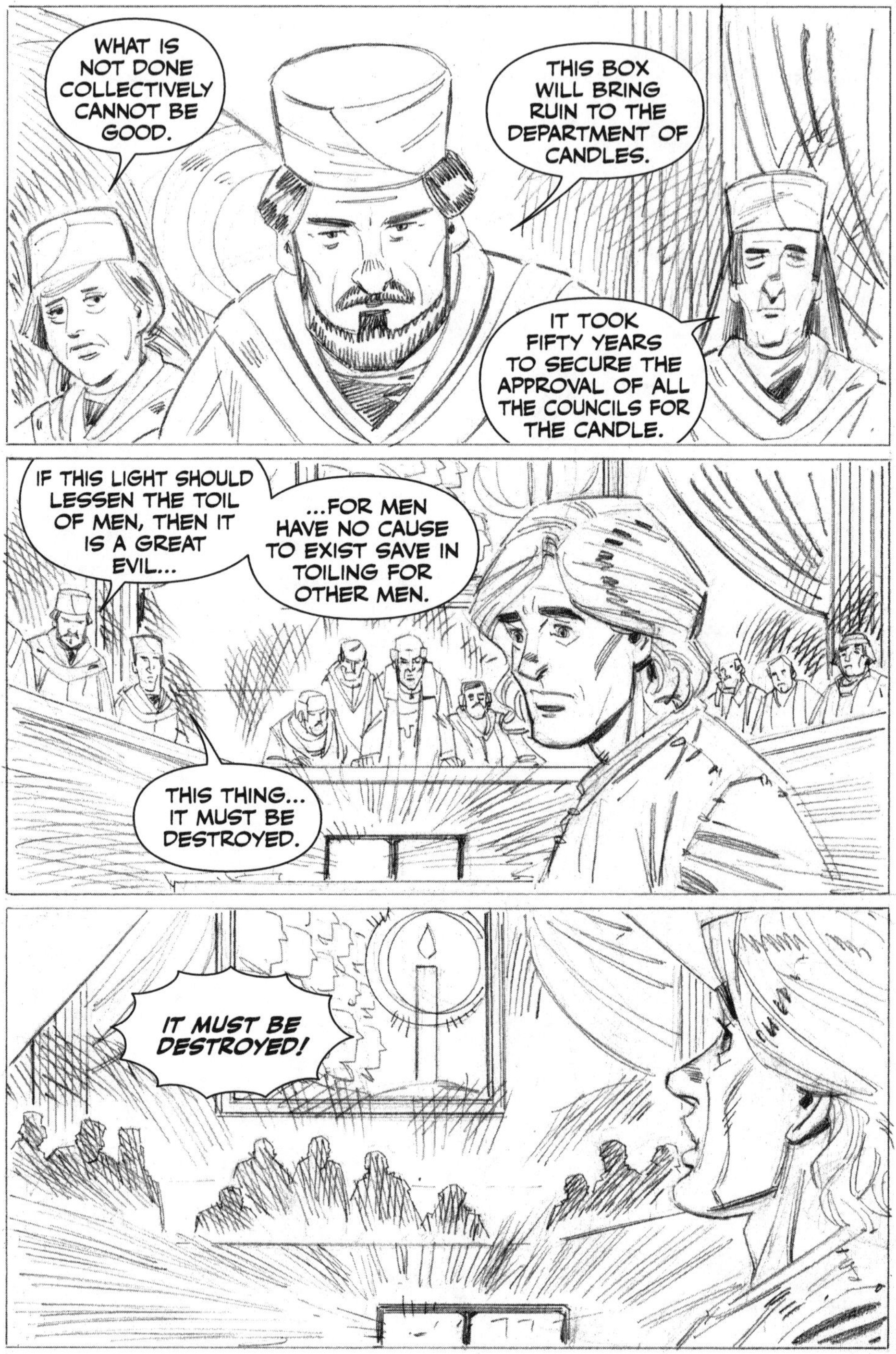
WHAT IS NOT DONE COLLECTIVELY CANNOT BE GOOD.
THIS BOX WILL BRING RUIN TO THE DEPARTMENT OF CANDLES.
IT TOOK FIFTY YEARS TO SECURE THE APPROVAL OF ALL THE COUNCILS FOR THE CANDLE.
IF THIS LIGHT SHOULD LESSEN THE TOIL OF MEN, THEN IT IS A GREAT EVIL...
...FOR MEN HAVE NO CAUSE TO EXIST SAVE IN TOILING FOR OTHER MEN.
THIS THING... IT MUST BE DESTROYED.
IT MUST BE DESTROYED!

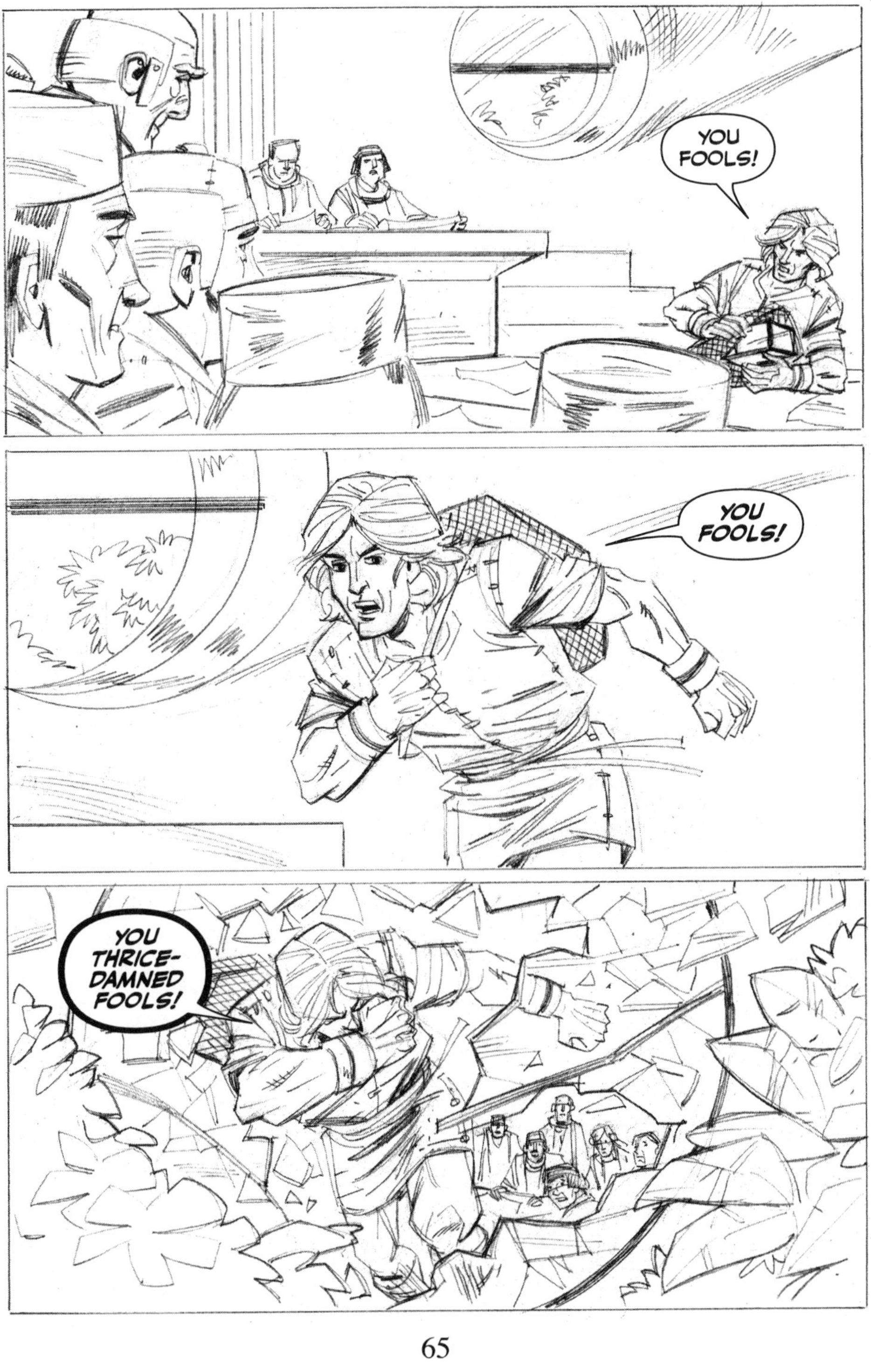
YOU FOOLS!
YOU FOOLS!
YOU THRICE-DAMNED FOOLS!

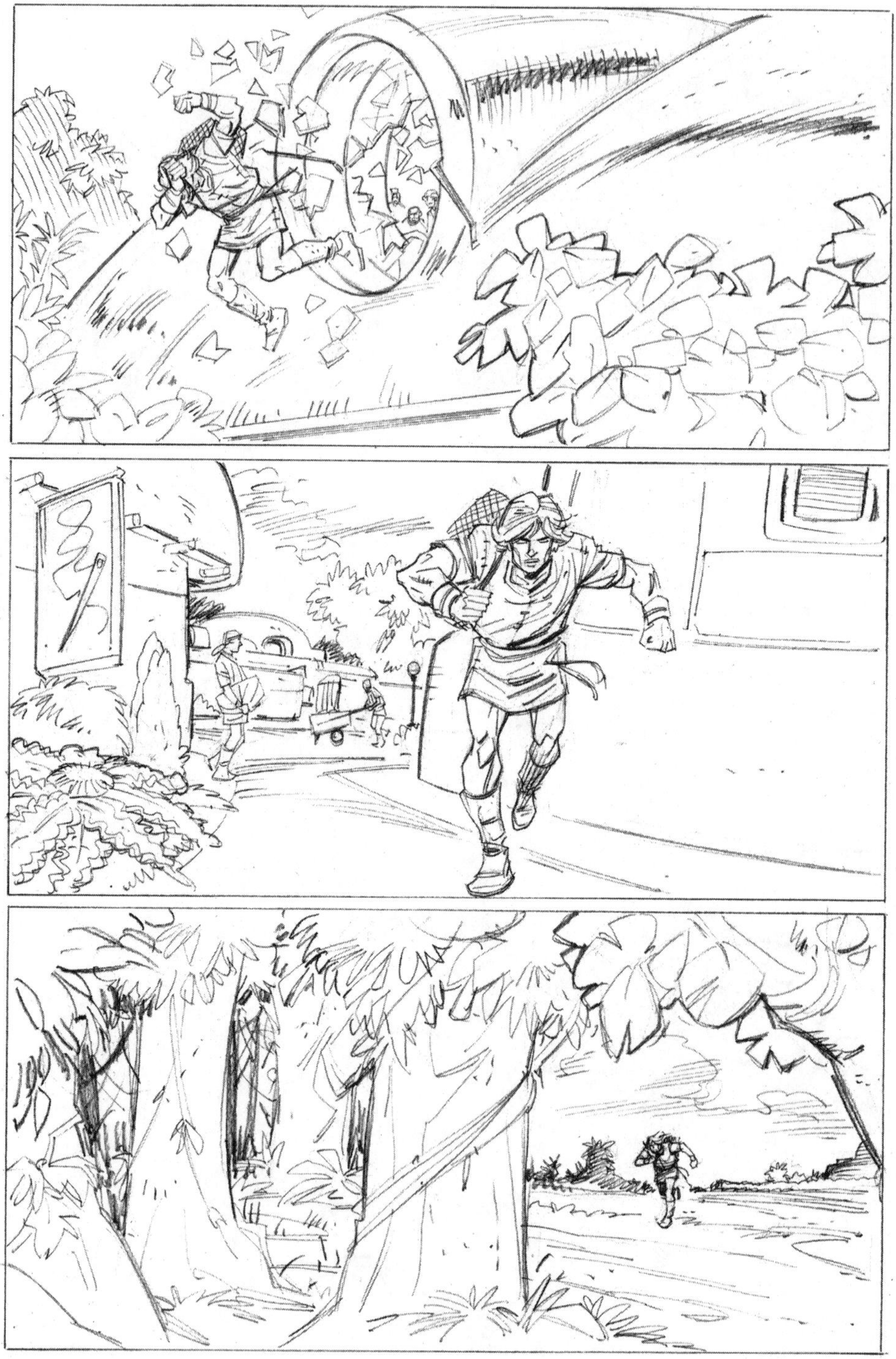

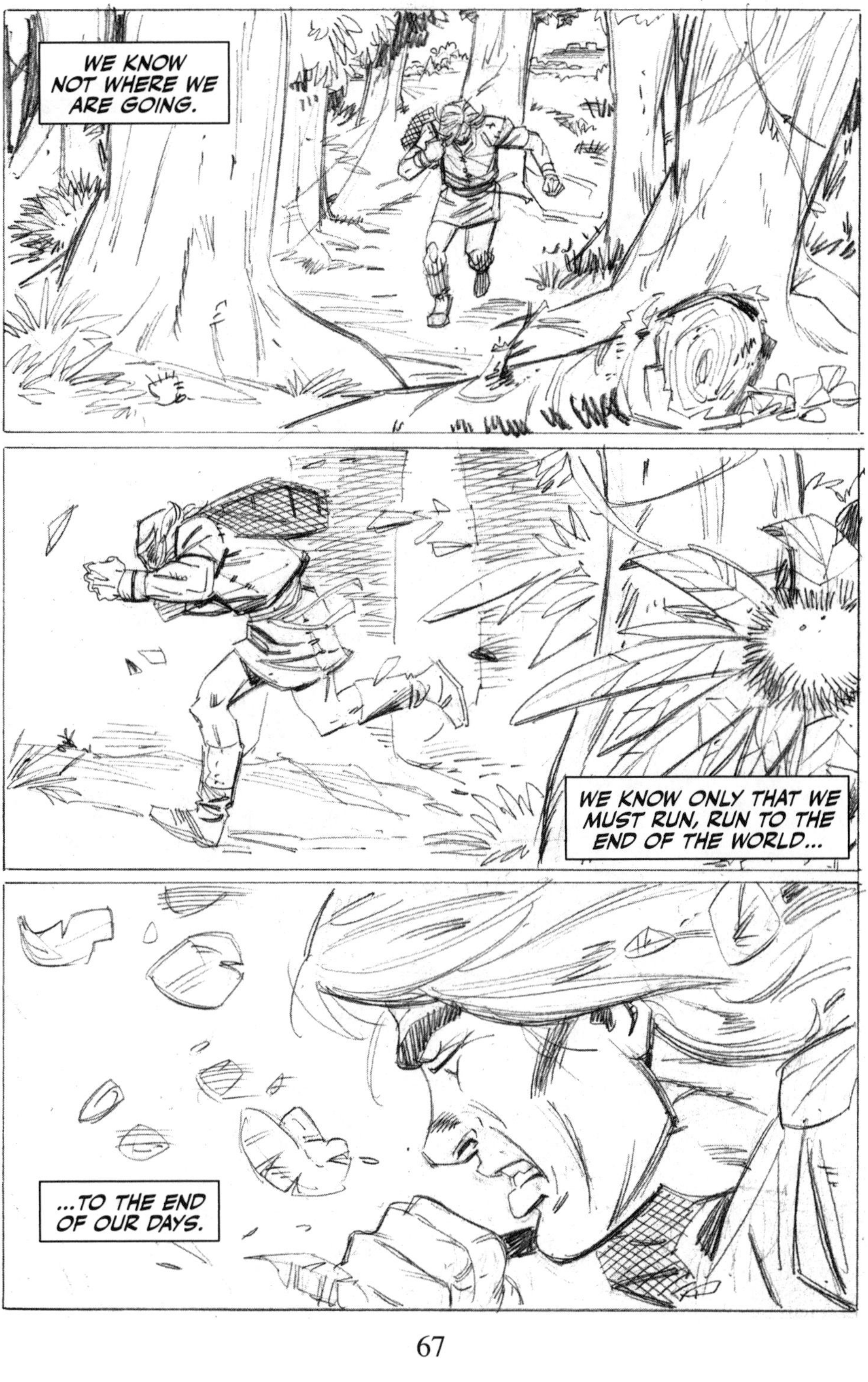
WE KNOW NOT WHERE WE ARE GOING.
WE KNOW ONLY THAT WE MUST RUN, RUN TO THE END OF THE WORLD...
...TO THE END OF OUR DAYS.

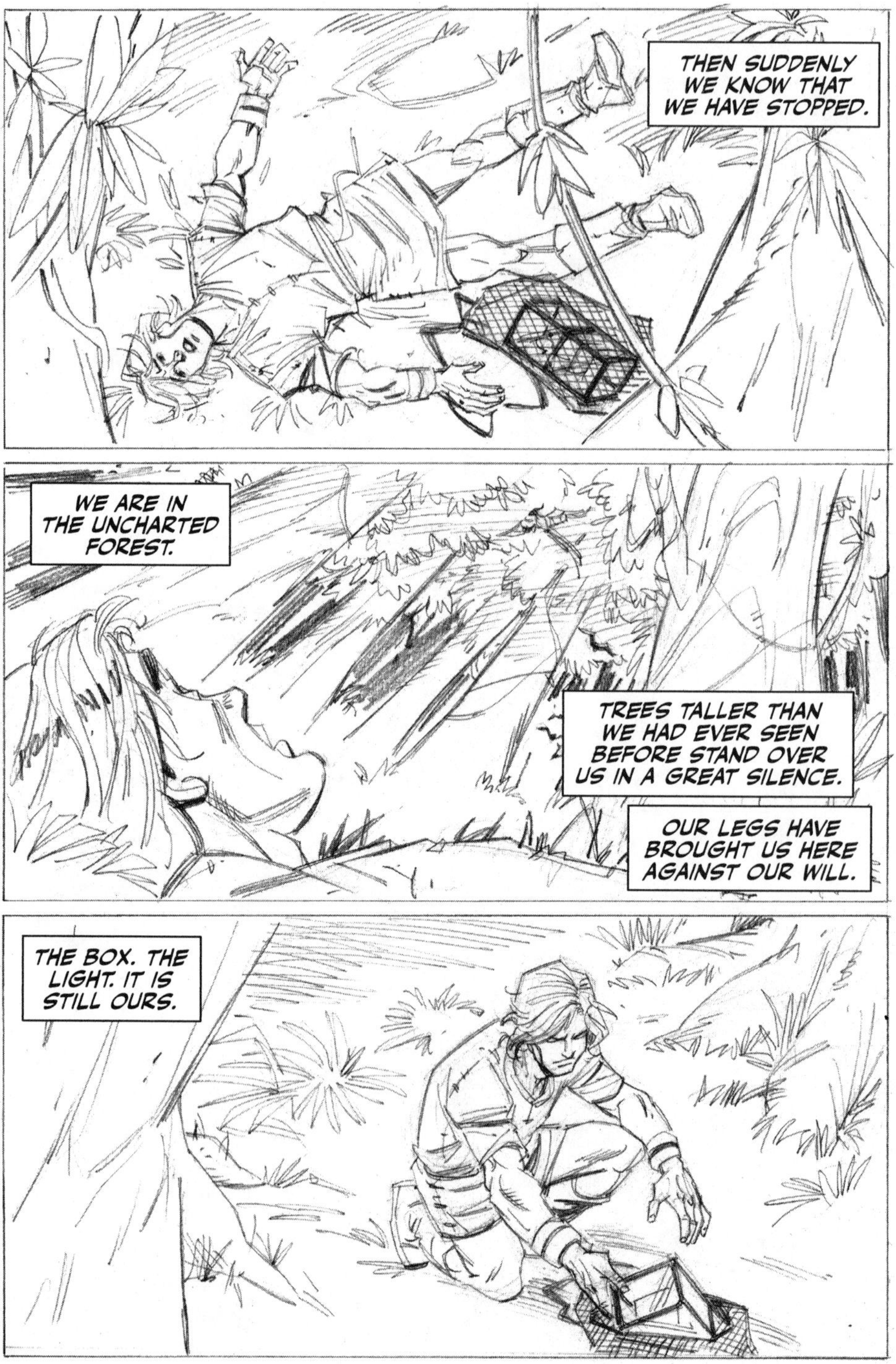
THEN SUDDENLY WE KNOW THAT WE HAVE STOPPED.
WE ARE IN THE UNCHARTED FOREST.
TREES TALLER THAN WE HAD EVER SEEN BEFORE STAND OVER US IN A GREAT SILENCE.
OUR LEGS HAVE BROUGHT US HERE AGAINST OUR WILL.
THE BOX. THE LIGHT. IT IS STILL OURS.

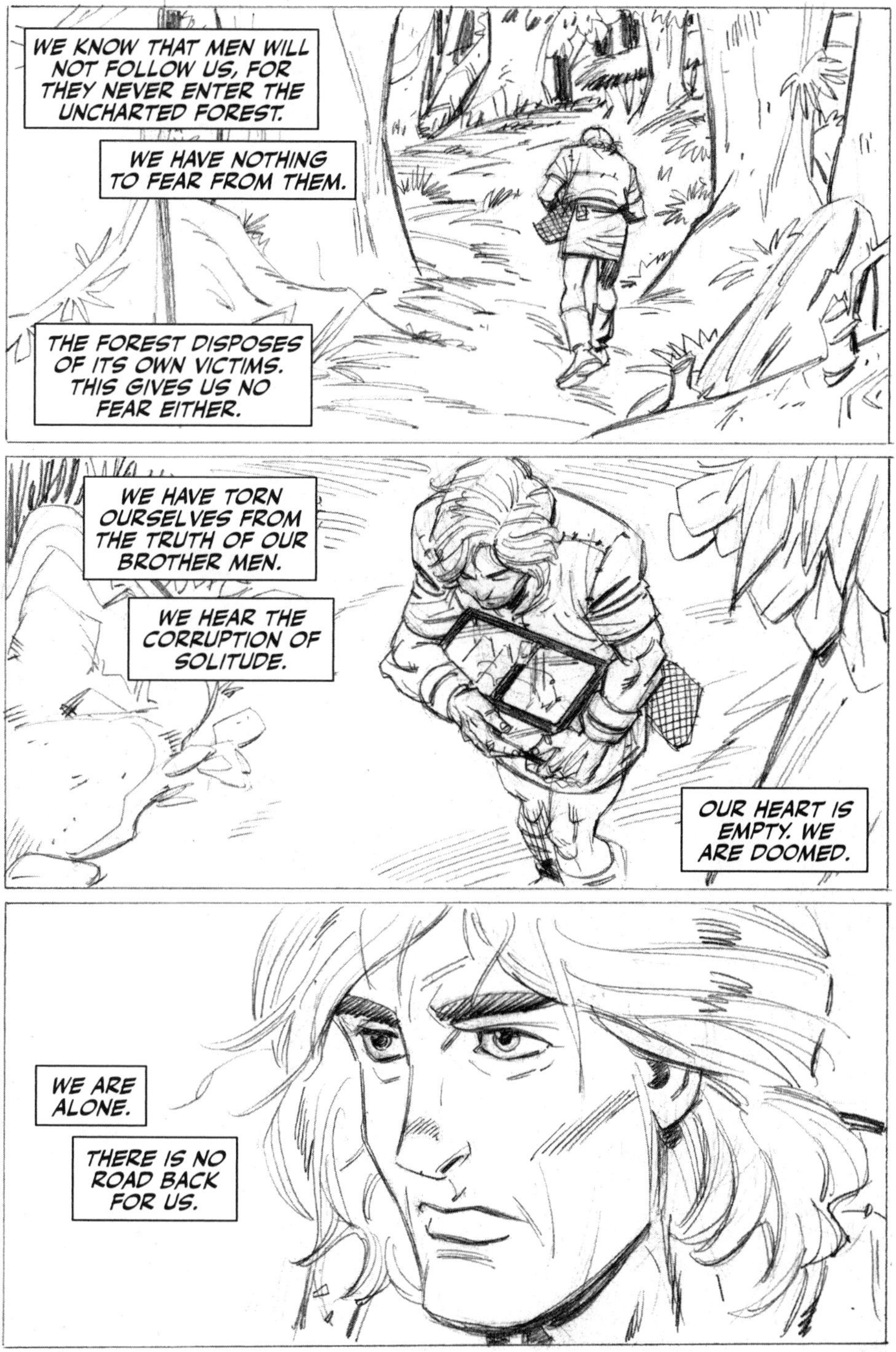
WE KNOW THAT MEN WILL NOT FOLLOW US, FOR THEY NEVER ENTER THE UNCHARTED FOREST.
WE HAVE NOTHING TO FEAR FROM THEM.
THE FOREST DISPOSES OF ITS OWN VICTIMS. THIS GIVES US NO FEAR EITHER.
WE HAVE TORN OURSELVES FROM THE TRUTH OF OUR BROTHER MEN.
WE HEAR THE CORRUPTION OF SOLITUDE.
OUR HEART IS EMPTY. WE ARE DOOMED.
WE ARE ALONE.
THERE IS NO ROAD BACK FOR US.

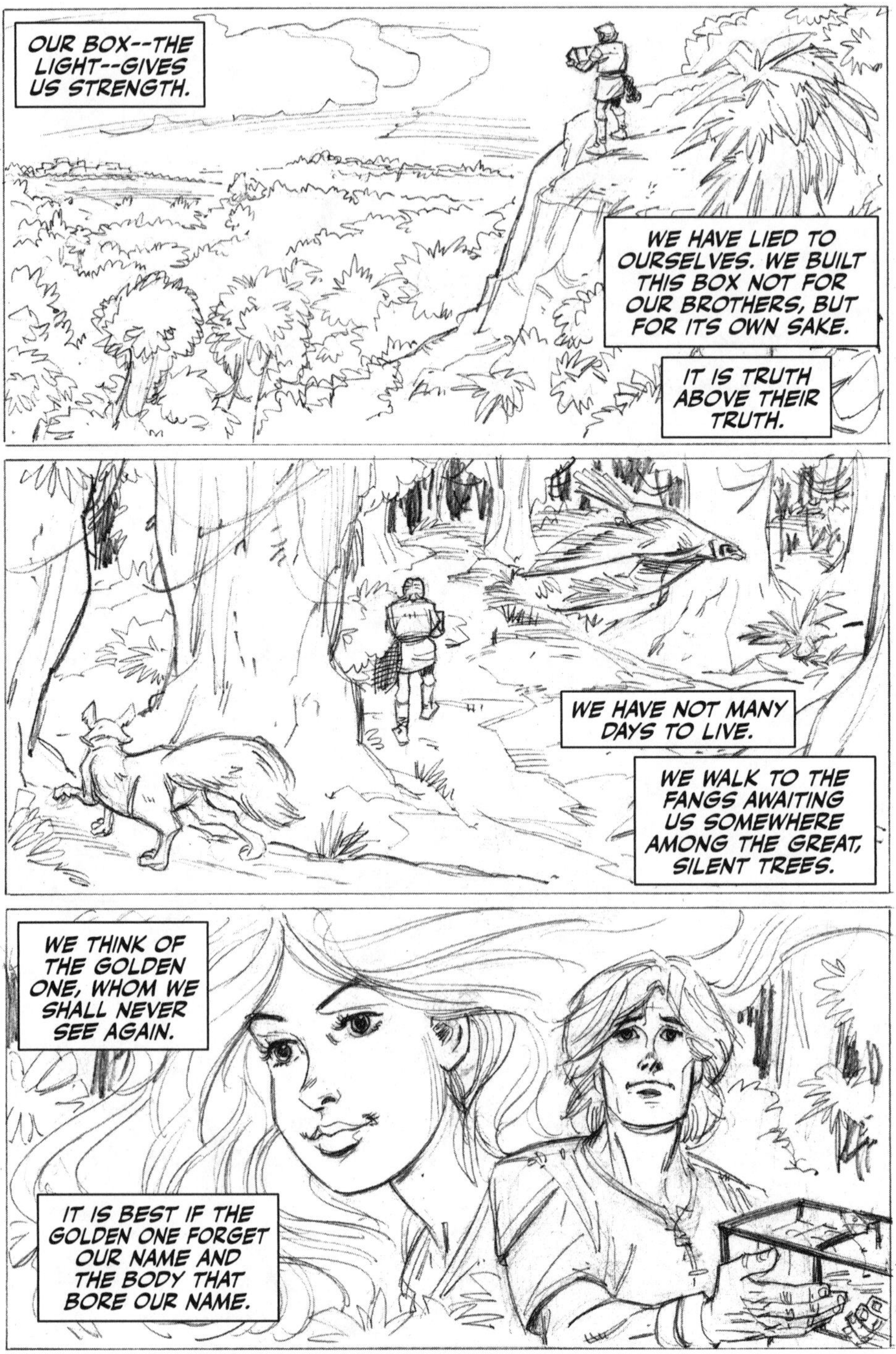
OUR BOX--THE LIGHT--GIVES US STRENGTH.
WE HAVE LIED TO OURSELVES. WE BUILT THIS BOX NOT FOR OUR BROTHERS, BUT FOR ITS OWN SAKE.
IT IS TRUTH ABOVE THEIR TRUTH.
WE HAVE NOT MANY DAYS TO LIVE.
WE WALK TO THE FANGS AWAITING US SOMEWHERE AMONG THE GREAT, SILENT TREES.
WE THINK OF THE GOLDEN ONE, WHOM WE SHALL NEVER SEE AGAIN.
IT IS BEST IF THE GOLDEN ONE FORGET OUR NAME AND THE BODY THAT BORE OUR NAME.

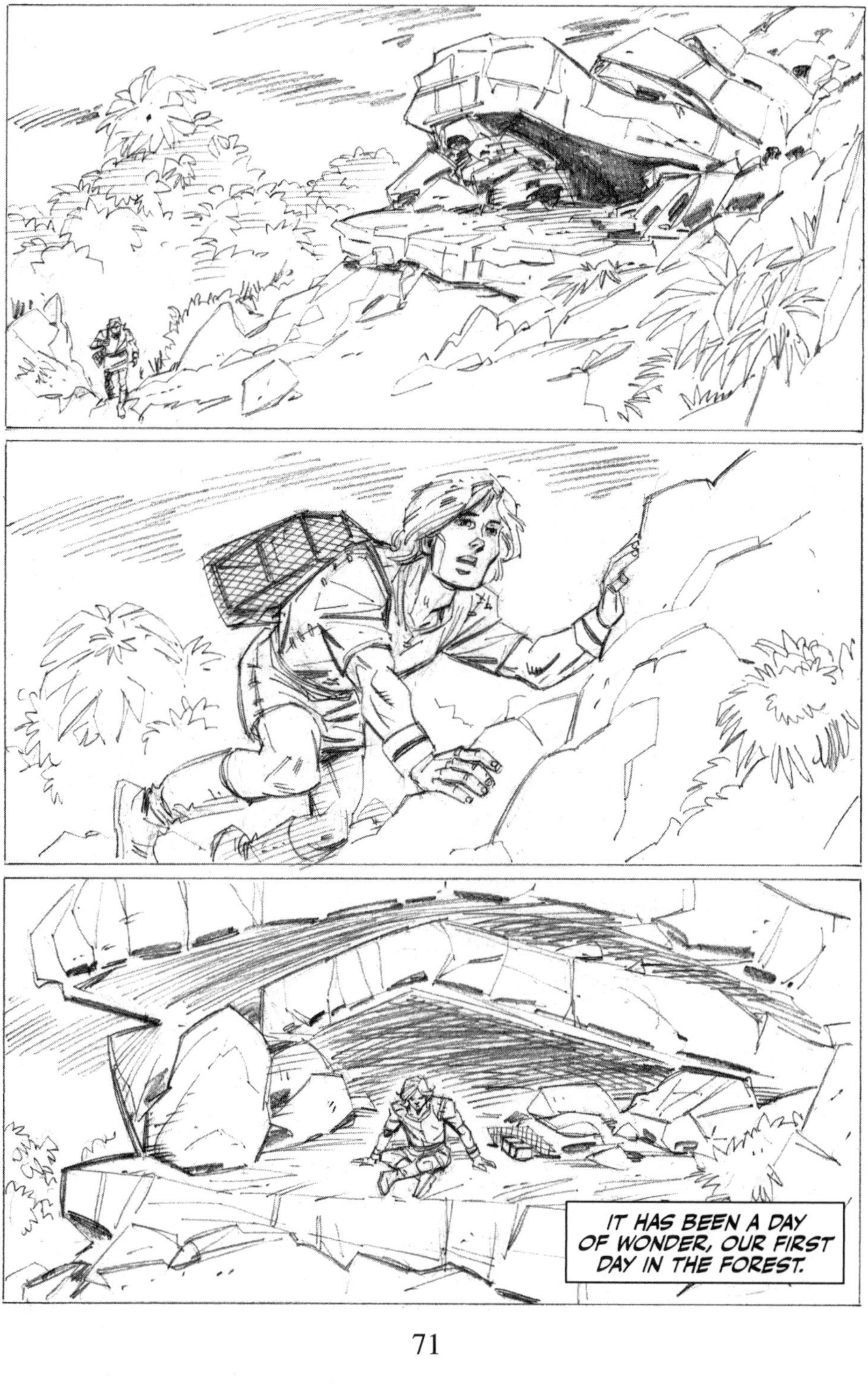
IT HAS BEEN A DAY OF WONDER, OUR FIRST DAY IN THE FOREST.

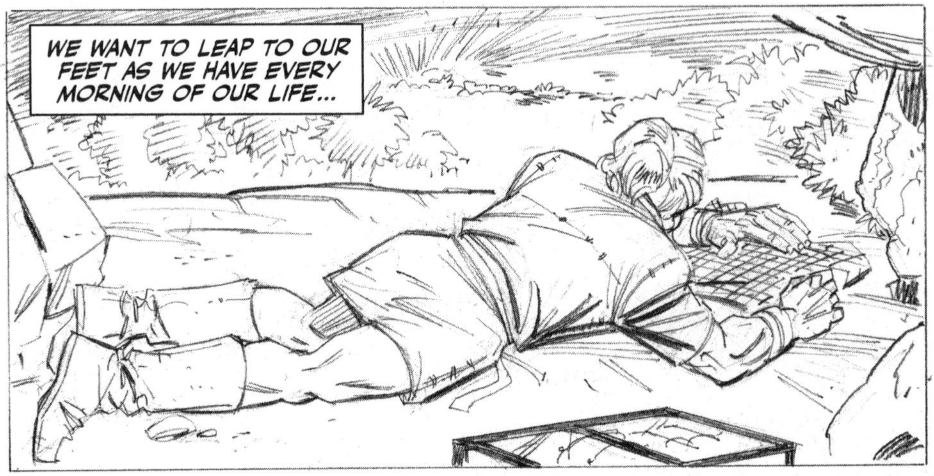
WE WANT TO LEAP TO OUR FEET AS WE HAVE EVERY MORNING OF OUR LIFE...

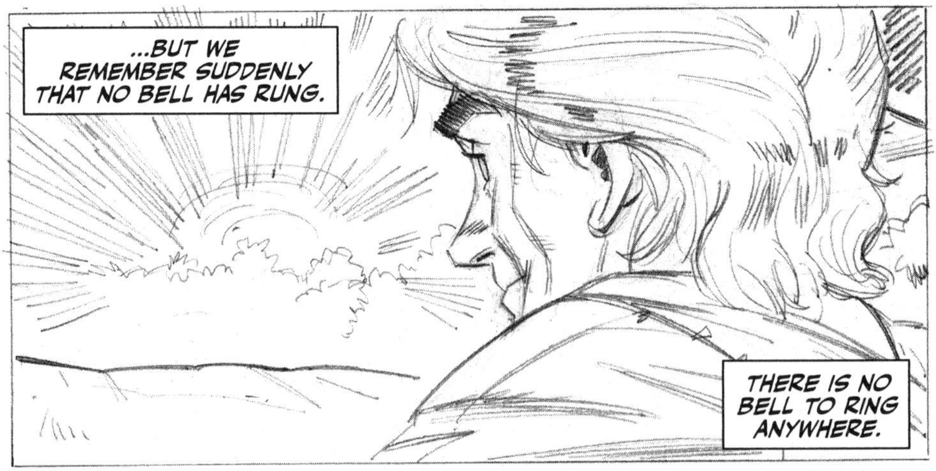
...BUT WE REMEMBER SUDDENLY THAT NO BELL HAS RUNG.
THERE IS NO BELL TO RING ANYWHERE.

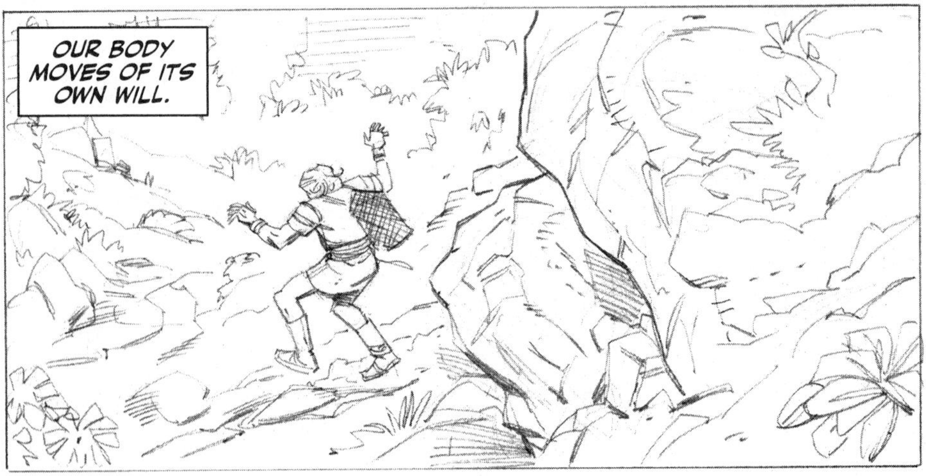
OUR BODY MOVES OF ITS OWN WILL.

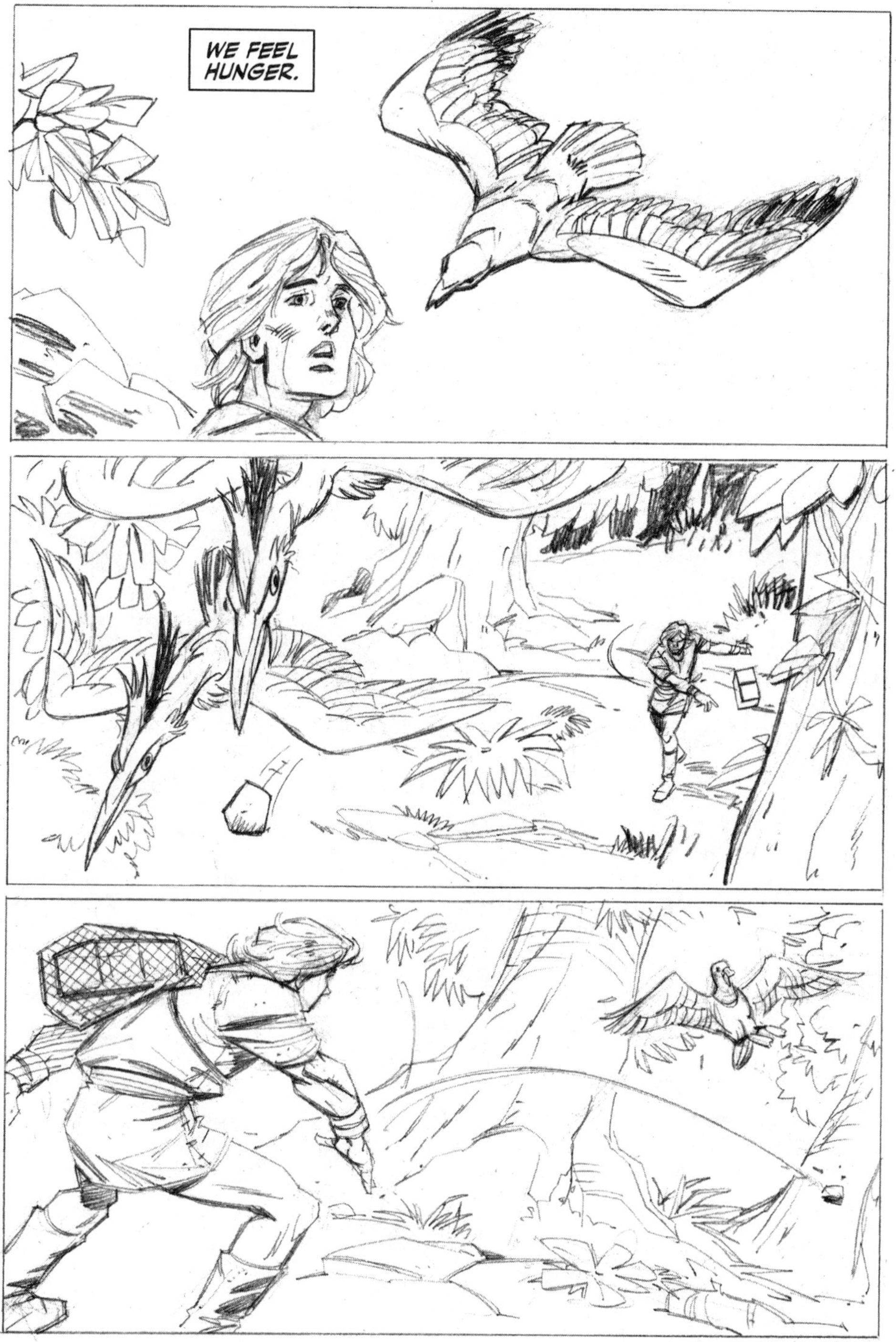
WE FEEL
HUNGER.

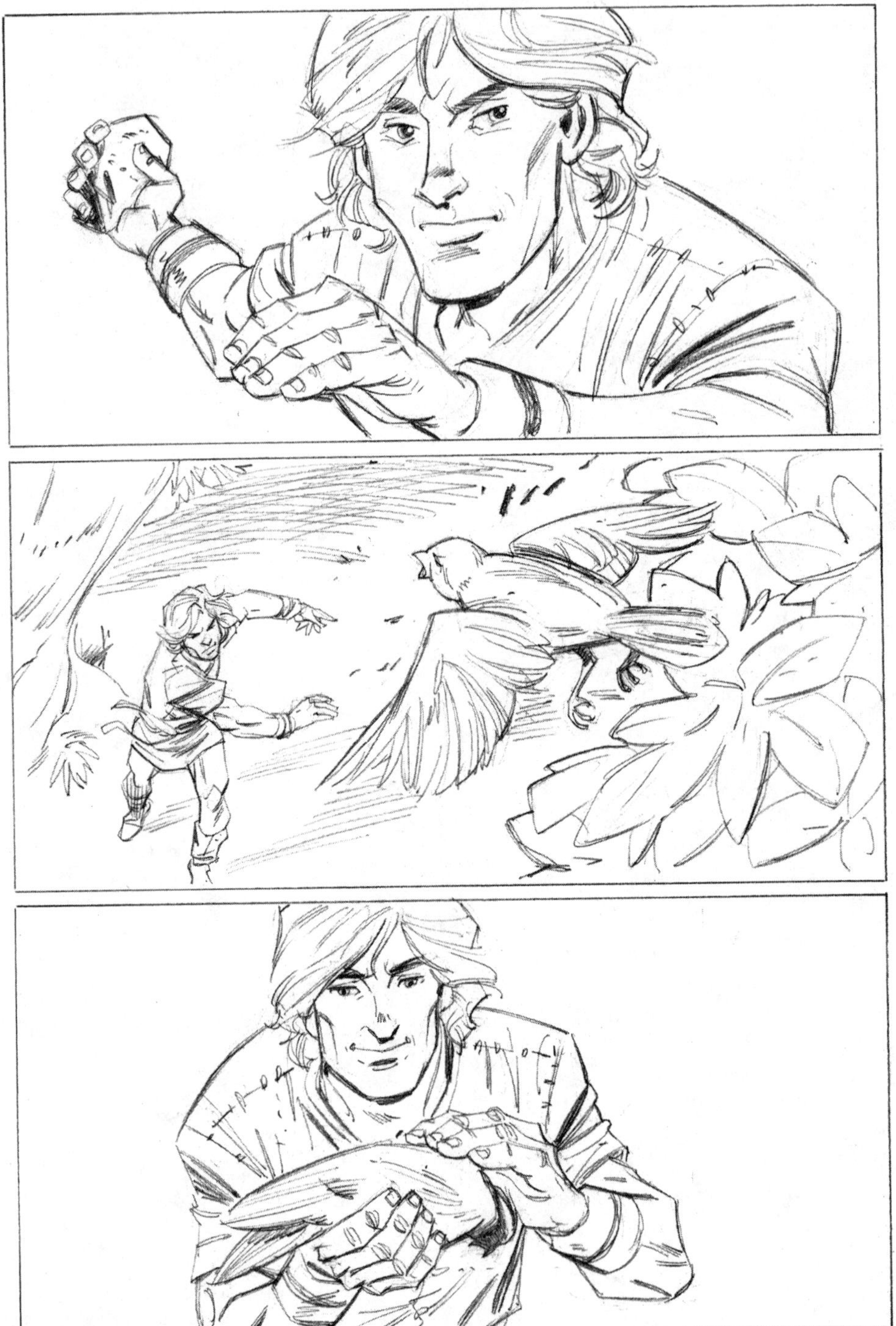

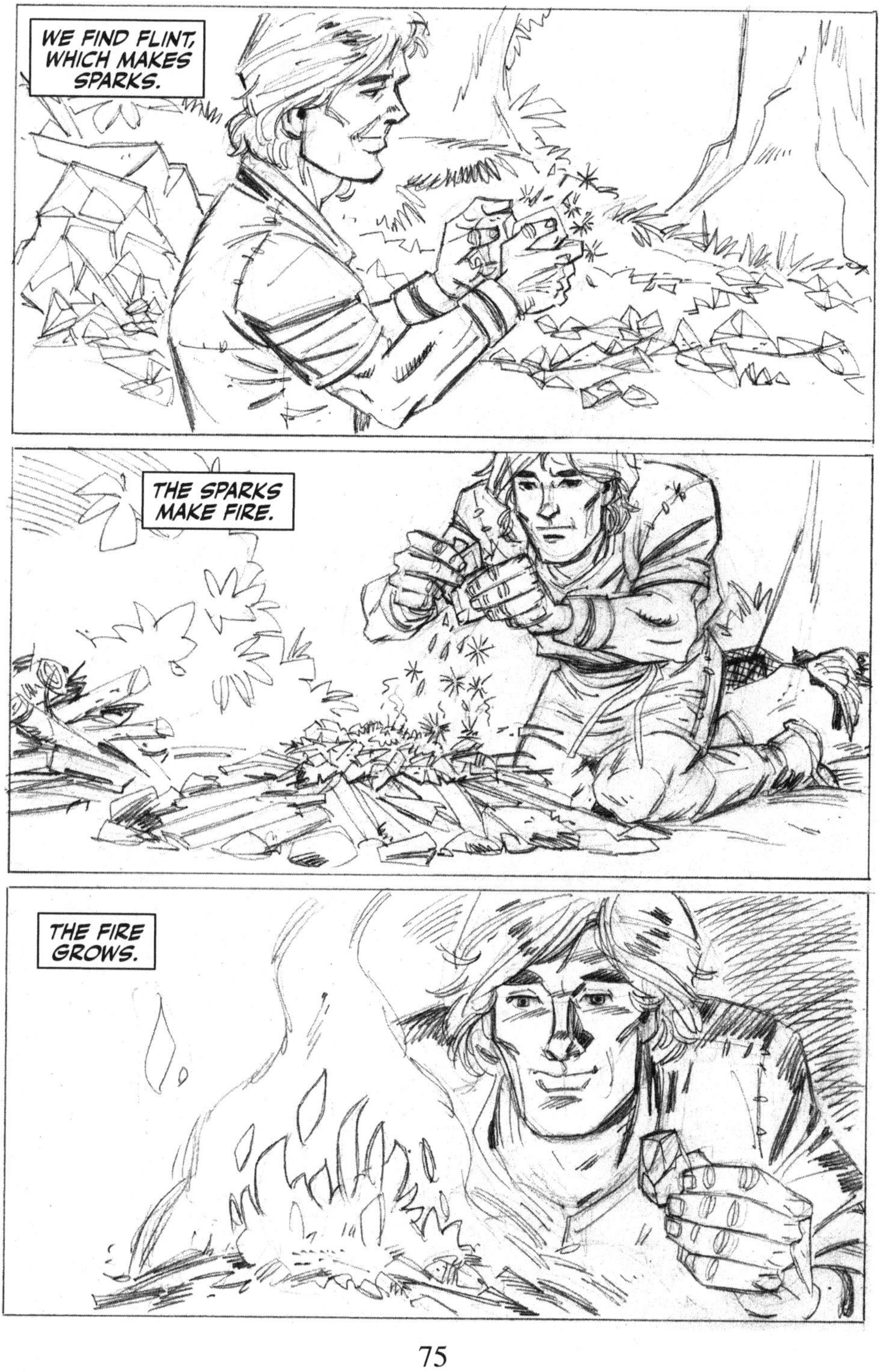
WE FIND FLINT, WHICH MAKES SPARKS.
THE SPARKS MAKE FIRE.
THE FIRE GROWS.

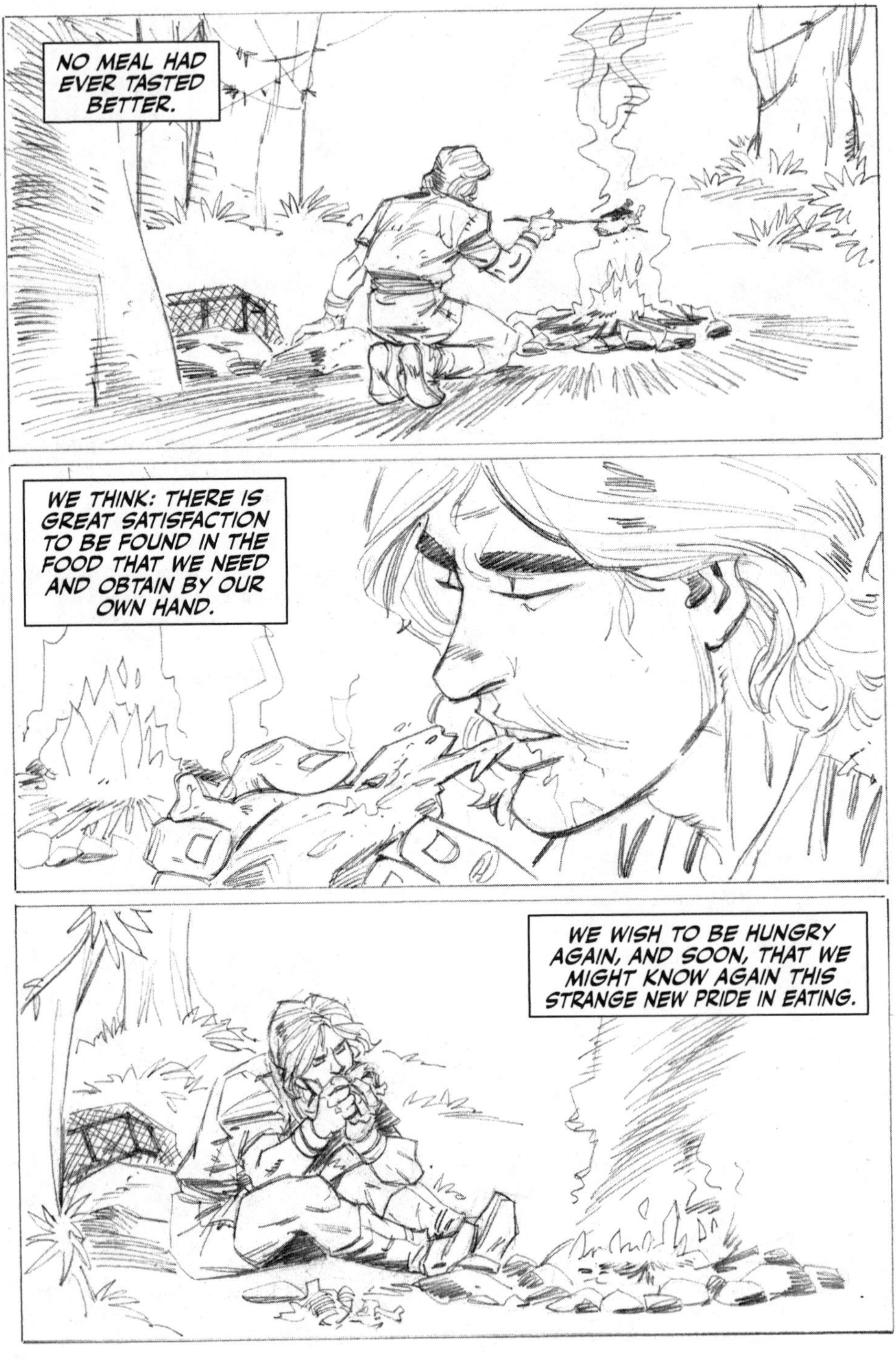
NO MEAL HAD EVER TASTED BETTER.
WE THINK: THERE IS GREAT SATISFACTION TO BE FOUND IN THE FOOD THAT WE NEED AND OBTAIN BY OUR OWN HAND.
WE WISH TO BE HUNGRY AGAIN, AND SOON, THAT WE MIGHT KNOW AGAIN THIS STRANGE NEW PRIDE IN EATING.

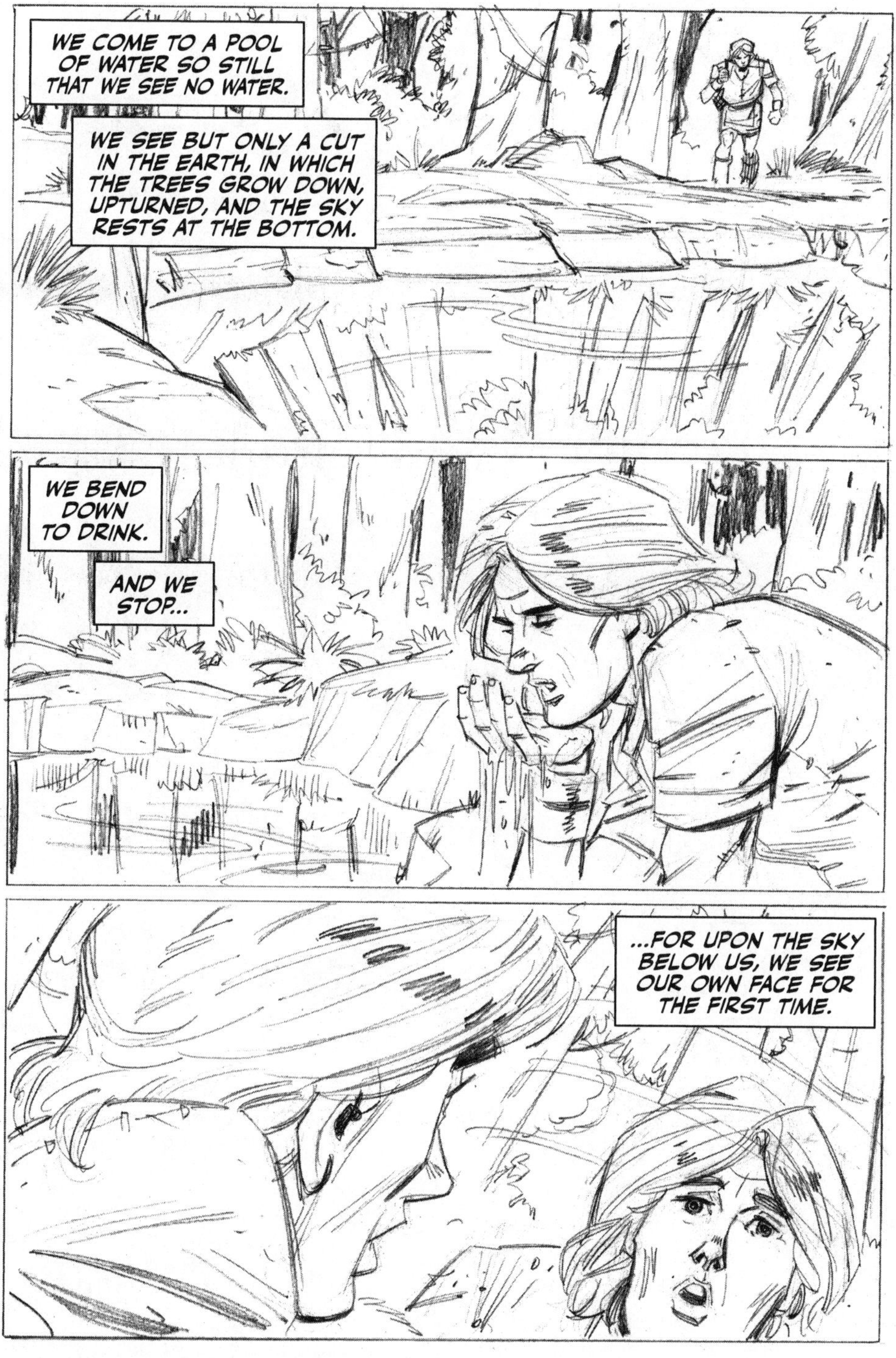
WE COME TO A POOL OF WATER SO STILL THAT WE SEE NO WATER.
WE SEE BUT ONLY A CUT IN THE EARTH, IN WHICH THE TREES GROW DOWN, UPTURNED, AND THE SKY RESTS AT THE BOTTOM.
WE BEND DOWN TO DRINK.
AND WE STOP...
...FOR UPON THE SKY BELOW US, WE SEE OUR OWN FACE FOR THE FIRST TIME.

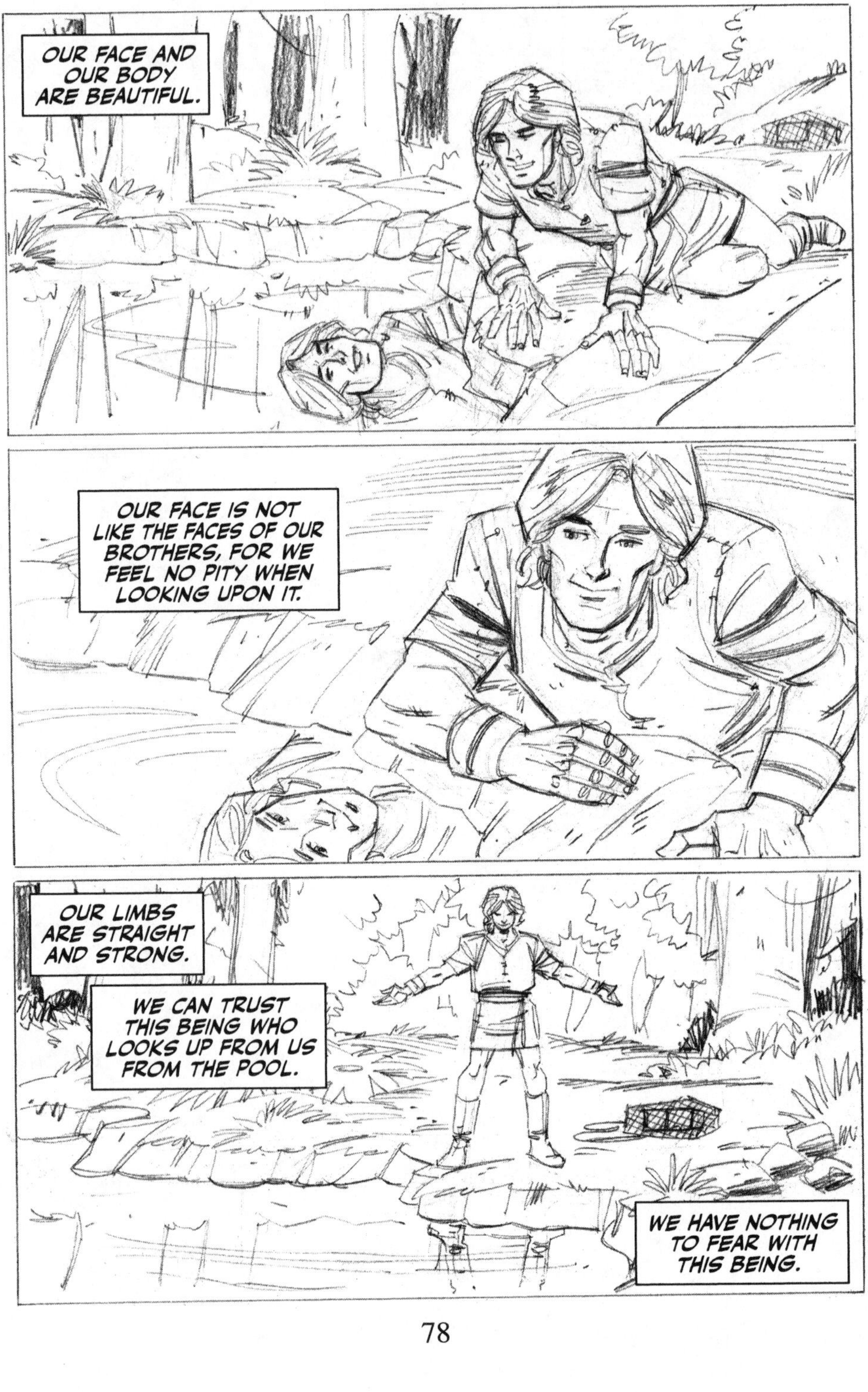
OUR FACE AND OUR BODY ARE BEAUTIFUL.
OUR FACE IS NOT LIKE THE FACES OF OUR BROTHERS, FOR WE FEEL NO PITY WHEN LOOKING UPON IT.
OUR LIMBS ARE STRAIGHT AND STRONG.
WE CAN TRUST THIS BEING WHO LOOKS UP FROM US FROM THE POOL.
WE HAVE NOTHING TO FEAR WITH THIS BEING.

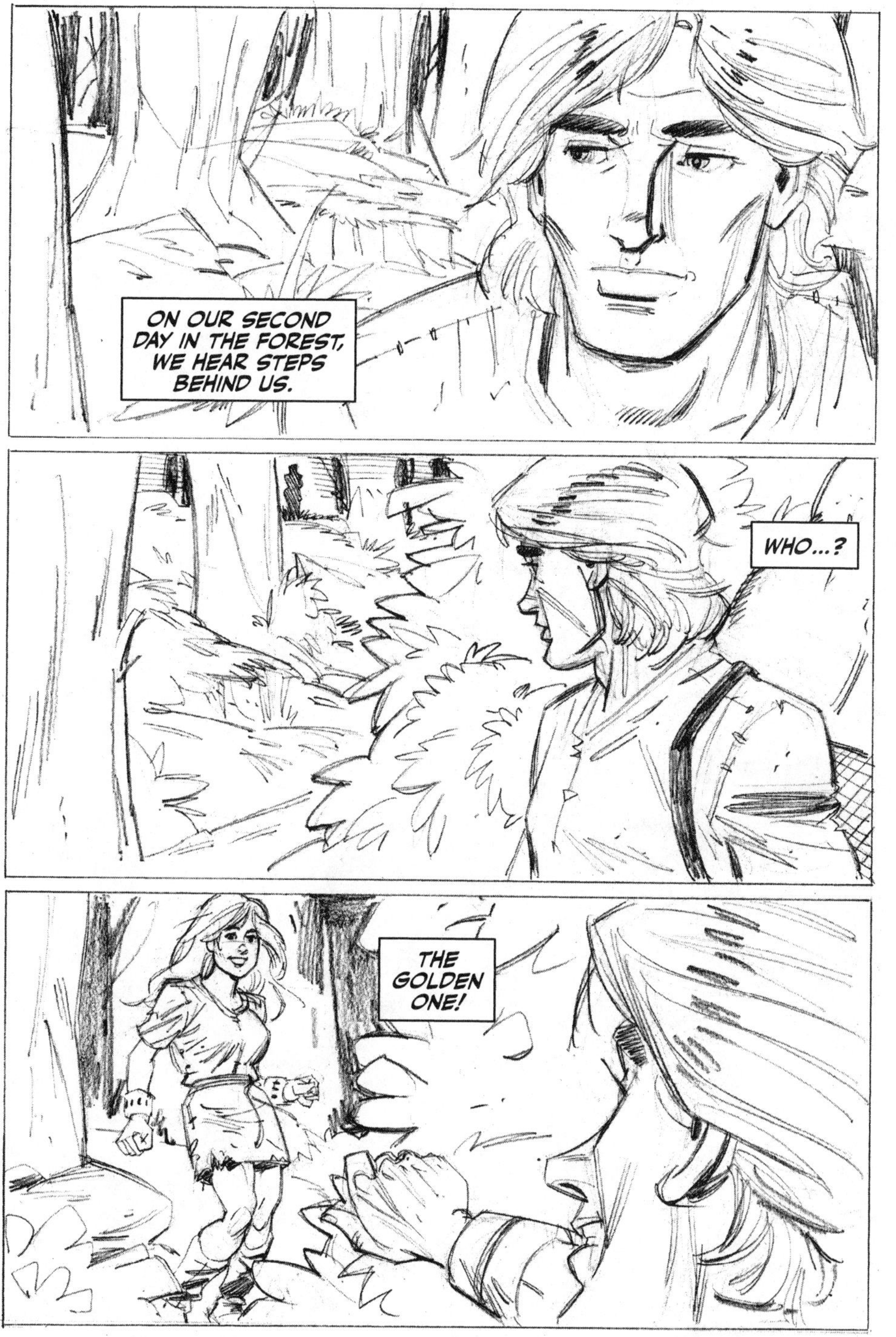
ON OUR SECOND DAY IN THE FOREST, WE HEAR STEPS BEHIND US.
WHO...?
THE GOLDEN ONE!

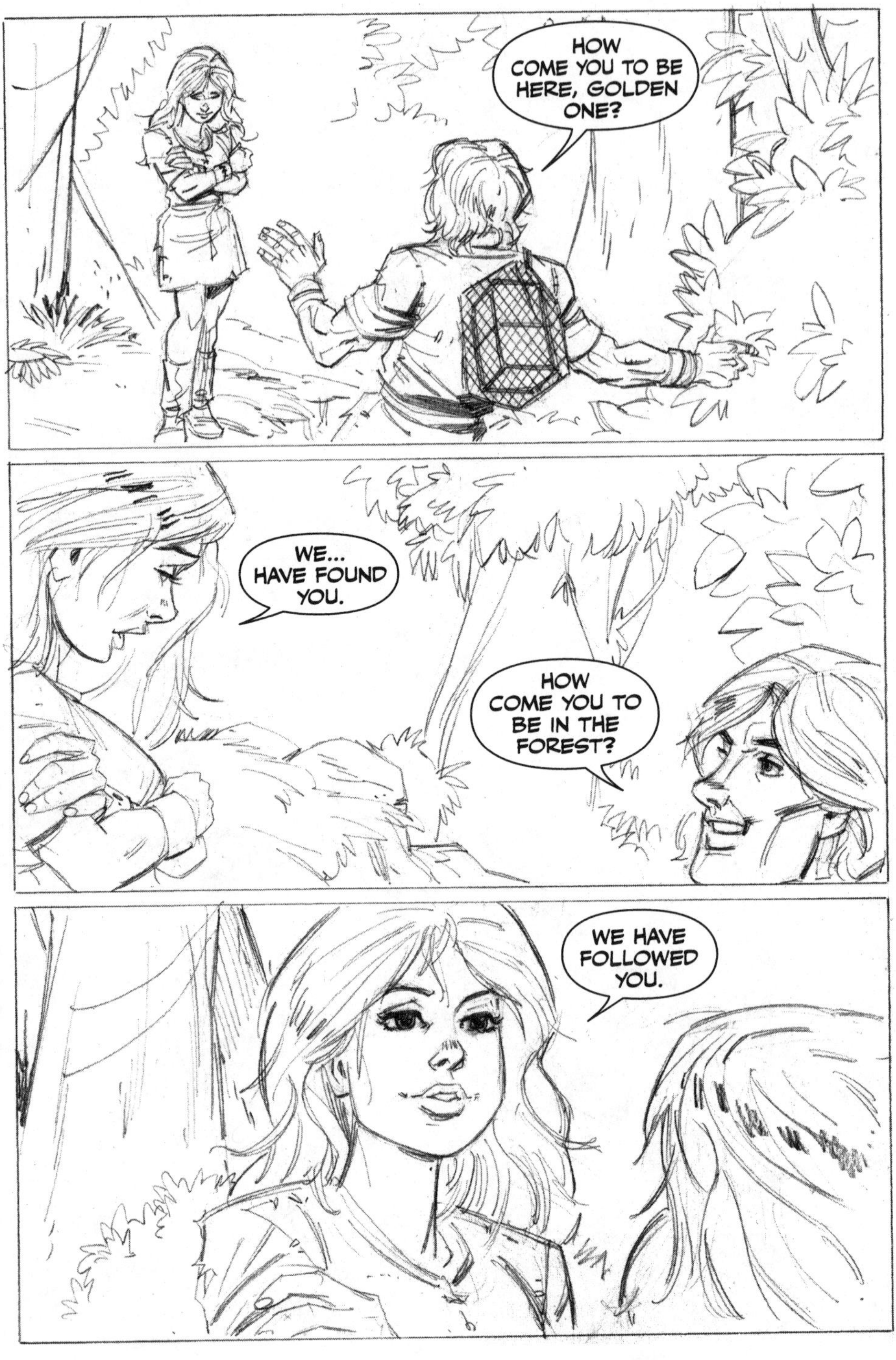
HOW COME YOU TO BE HERE, GOLDEN ONE?
WE... HAVE FOUND YOU.
HOW COME YOU TO BE IN THE FOREST?
WE HAVE FOLLOWED YOU.

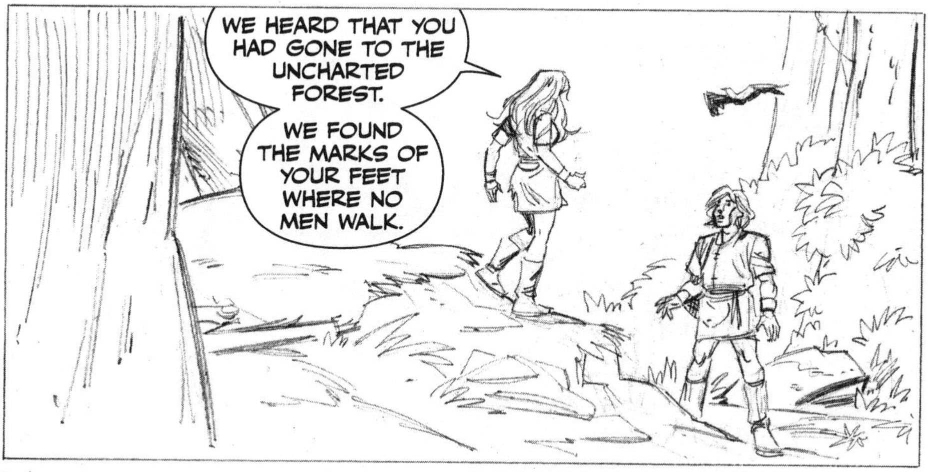
WE HEARD THAT YOU HAD GONE TO THE UNCHARTED FOREST.
WE FOUND THE MARKS OF YOUR FEET WHERE NO MEN WALK.

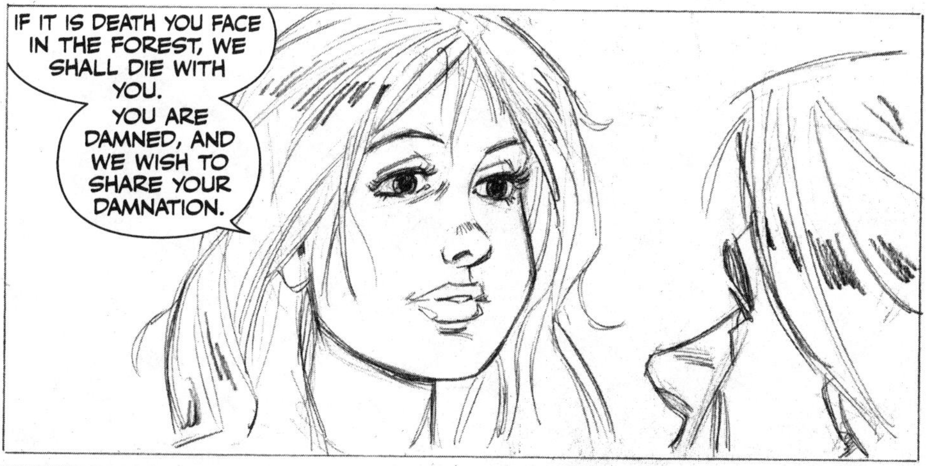
IF IT IS DEATH YOU FACE IN THE FOREST, WE SHALL DIE WITH YOU.
YOU ARE DAMNED, AND WE WISH TO SHARE YOUR DAMNATION.

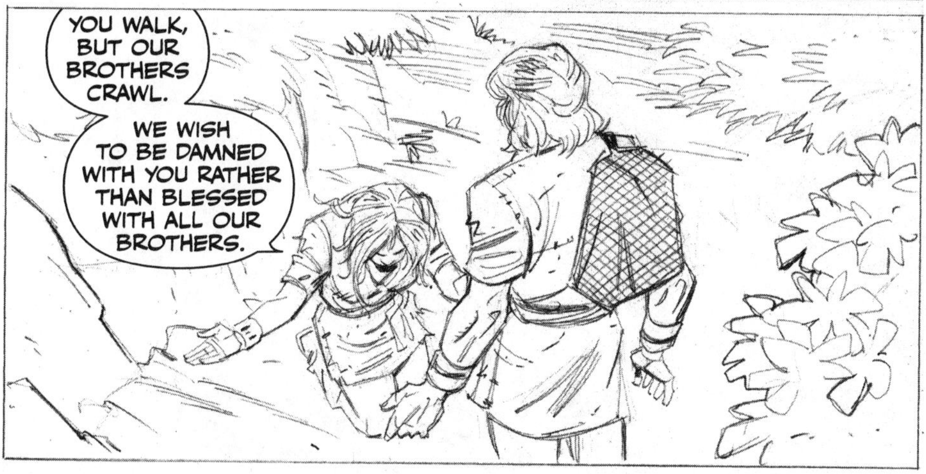
YOU WALK, BUT OUR BROTHERS CRAWL.
WE WISH TO BE DAMNED WITH YOU RATHER THAN BLESSED WITH ALL OUR BROTHERS.

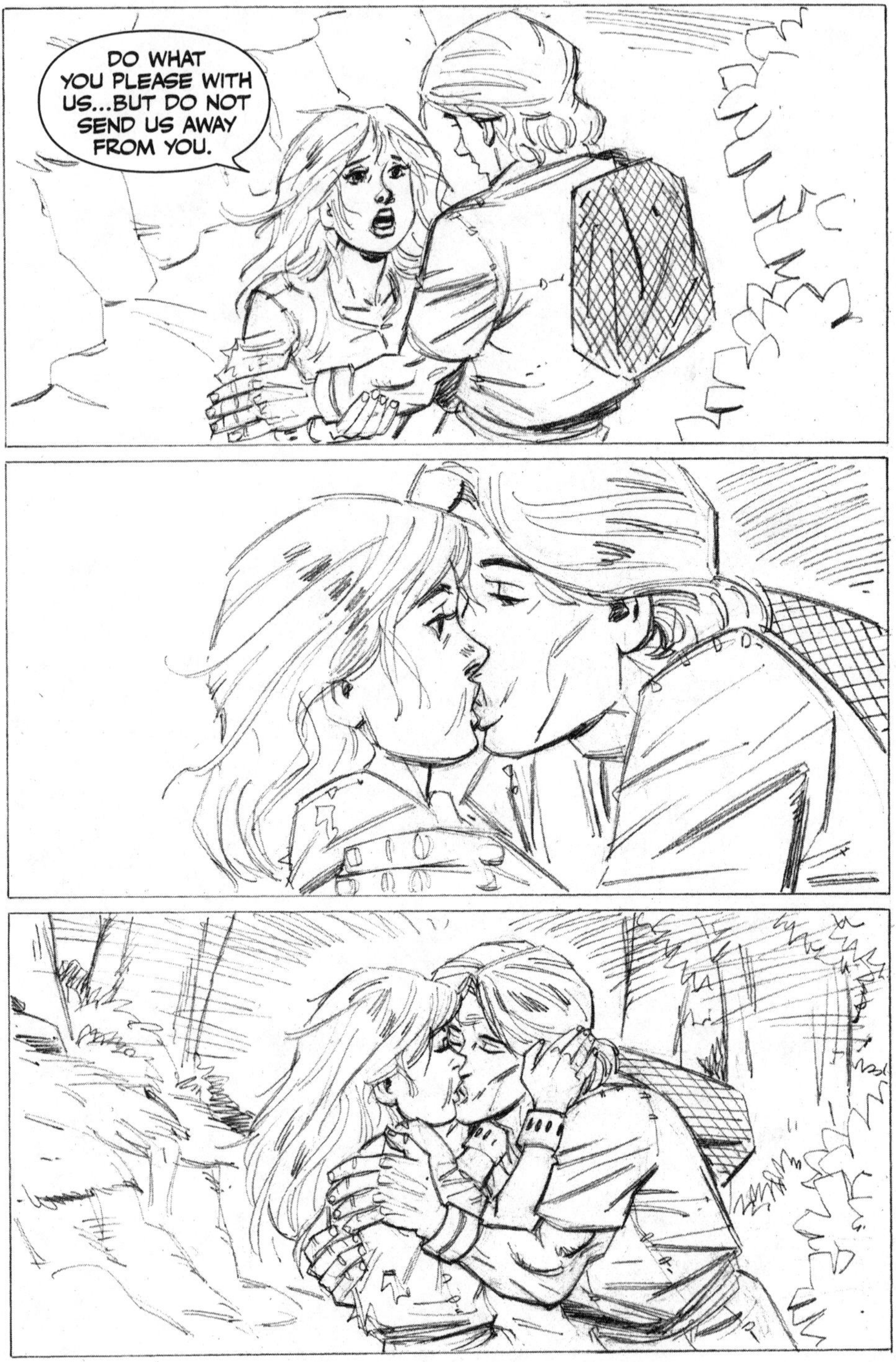
DO WHAT YOU PLEASE WITH US...BUT DO NOT SEND US AWAY FROM YOU.

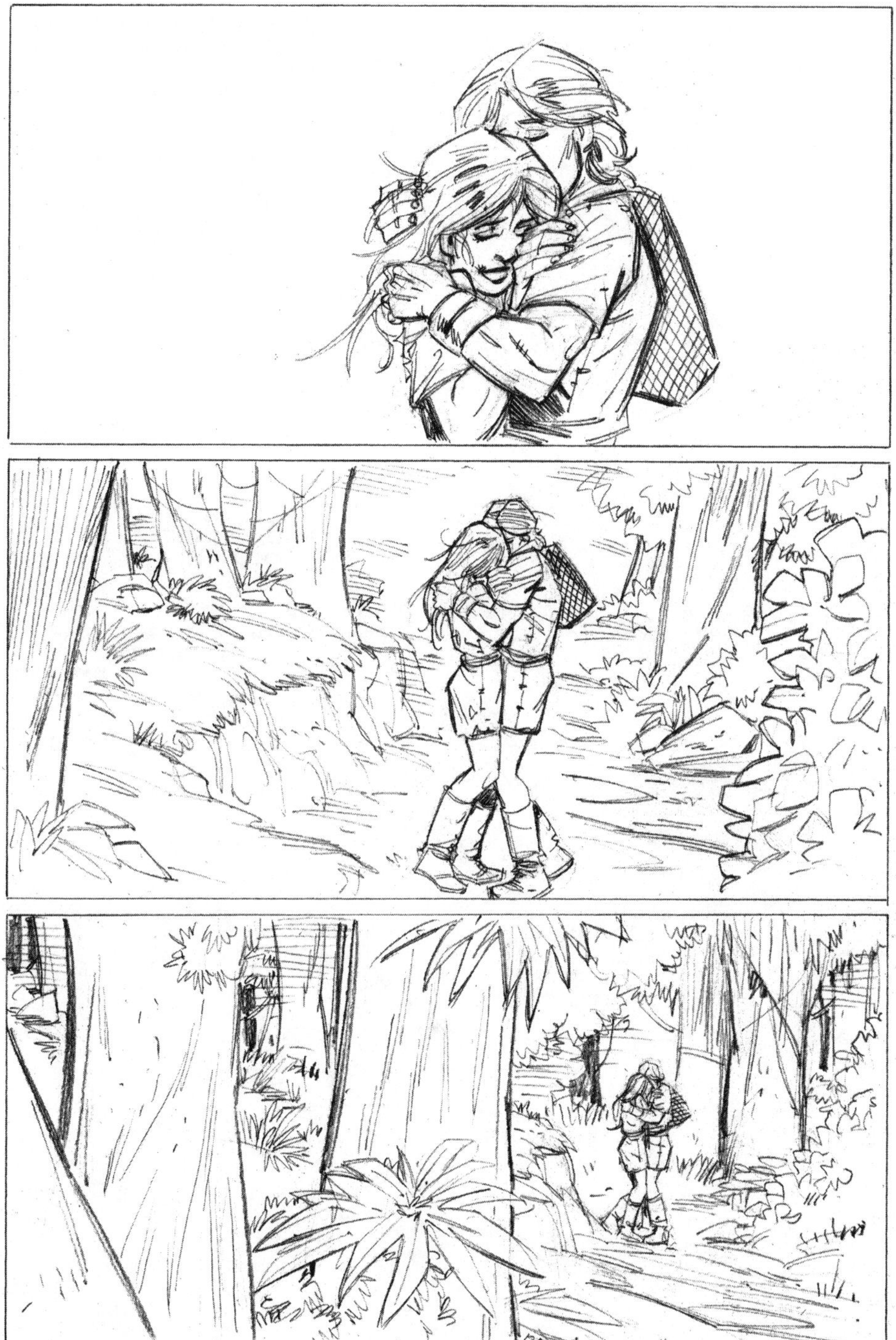

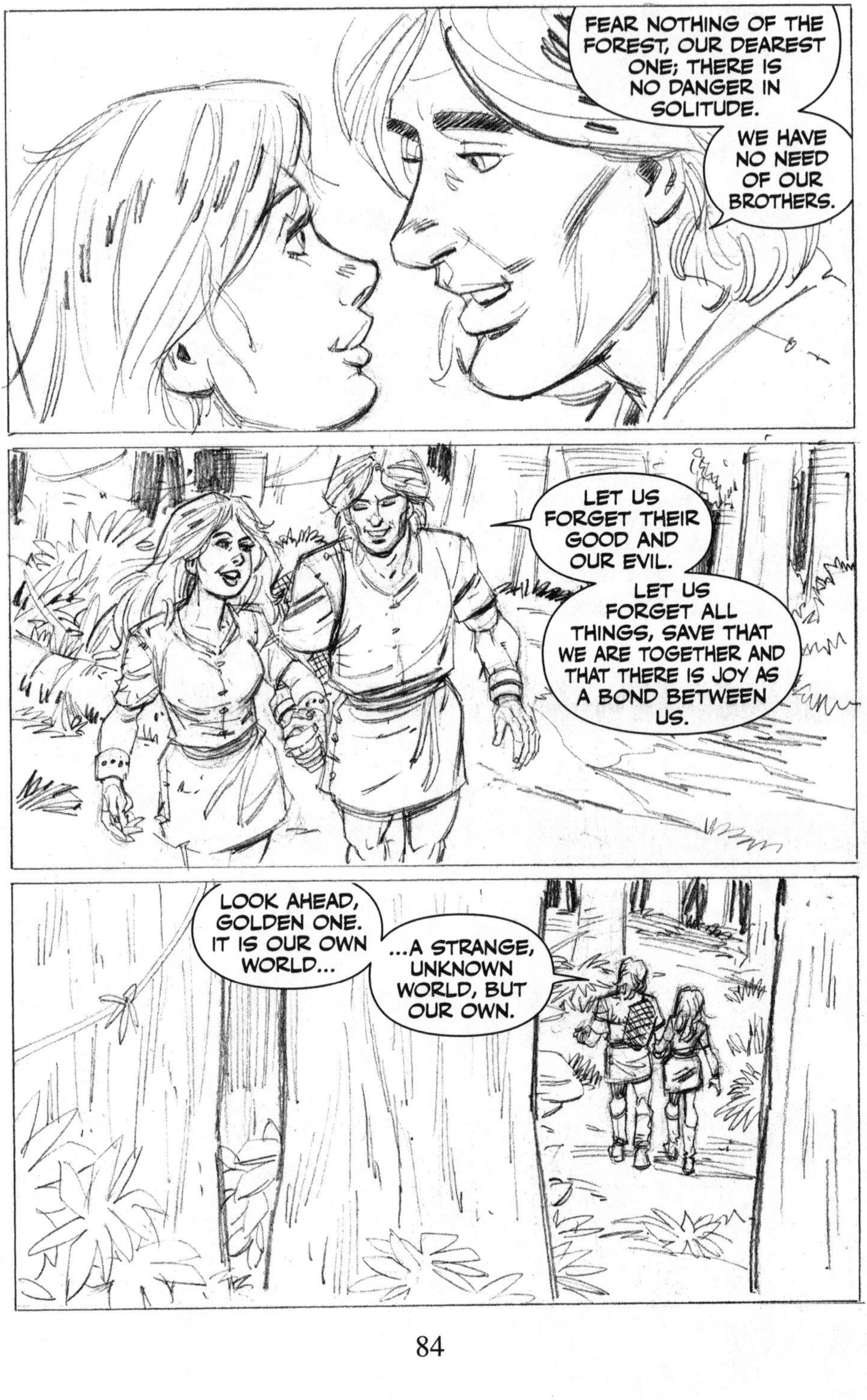
FEAR NOTHING OF THE FOREST, OUR DEAREST ONE; THERE IS NO DANGER IN SOLITUDE.
WE HAVE NO NEED OF OUR BROTHERS.
LET US FORGET THEIR GOOD AND OUR EVIL.
LET US FORGET ALL THINGS, SAVE THAT WE ARE TOGETHER AND THAT THERE IS JOY AS A BOND BETWEEN US.
LOOK AHEAD, GOLDEN ONE. IT IS OUR OWN WORLD...
...A STRANGE, UNKNOWN WORLD, BUT OUR OWN.

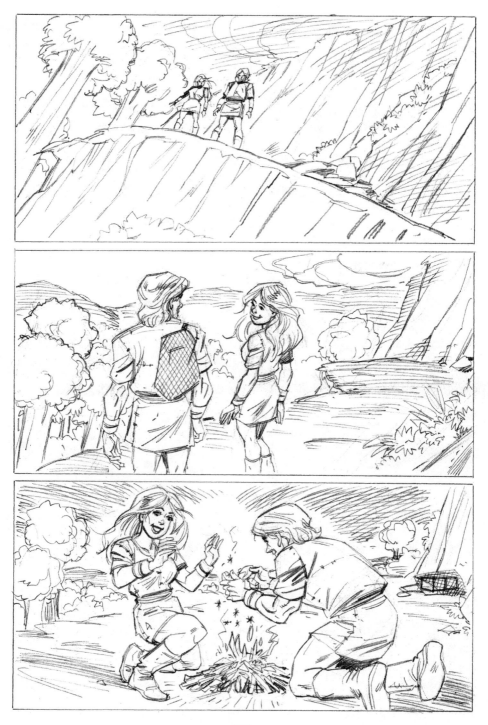

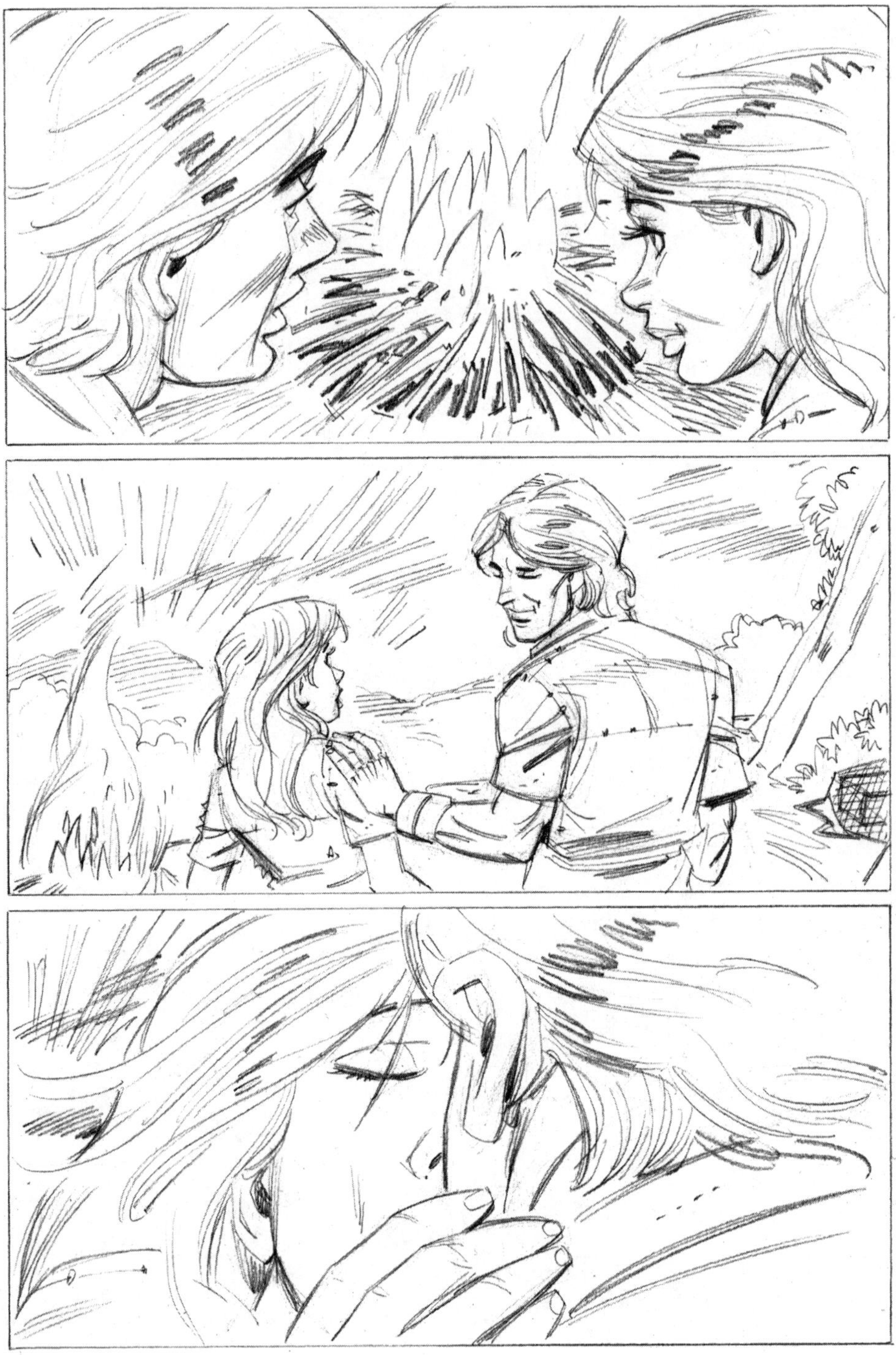

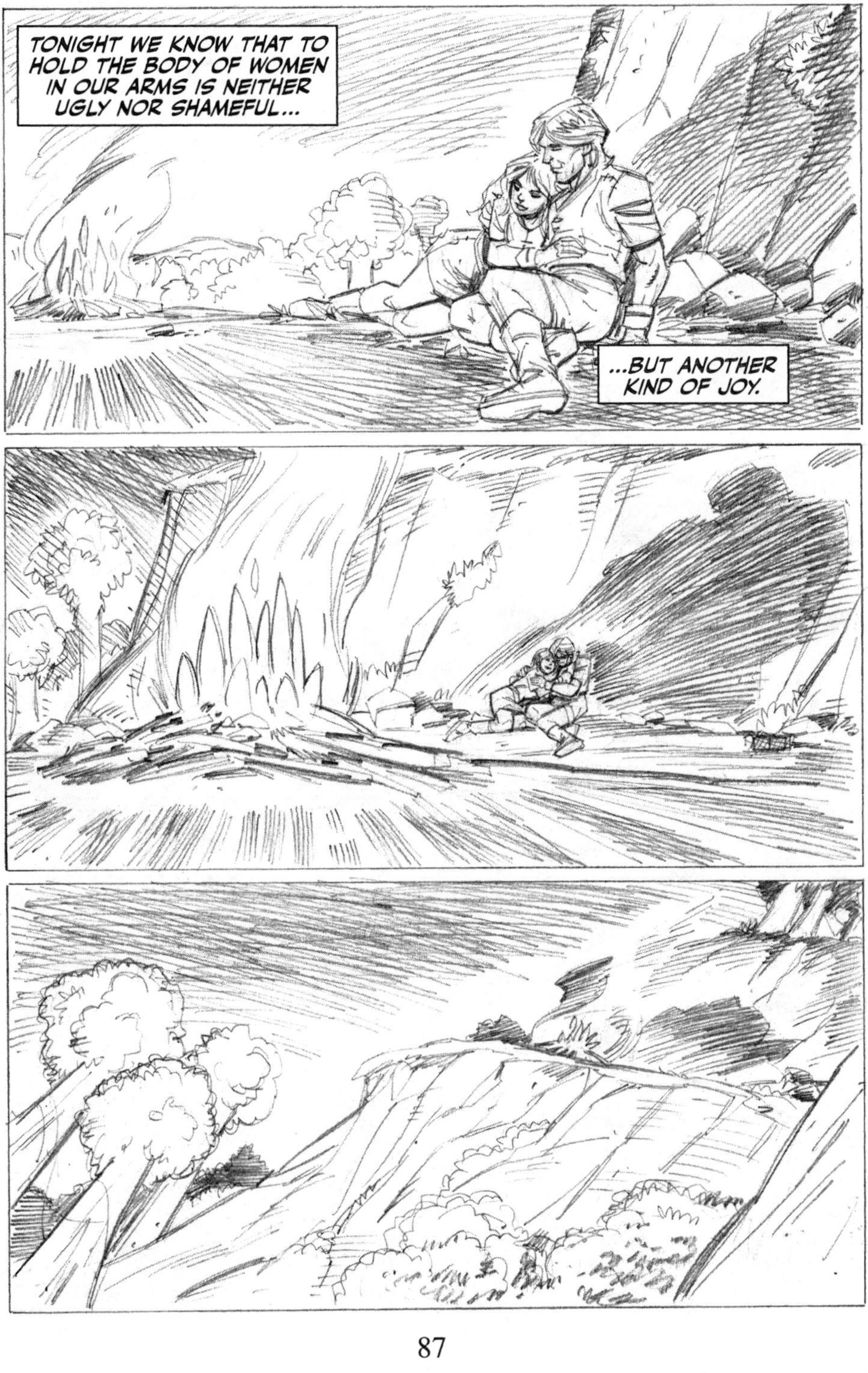
TONIGHT WE KNOW THAT TO HOLD THE BODY OF WOMEN IN OUR ARMS IS NEITHER UGLY NOR SHAMEFUL...
...BUT ANOTHER KIND OF JOY.

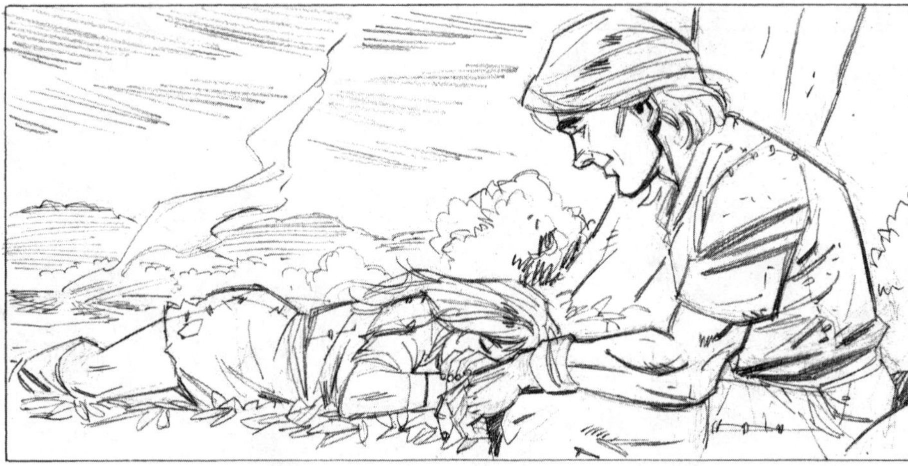

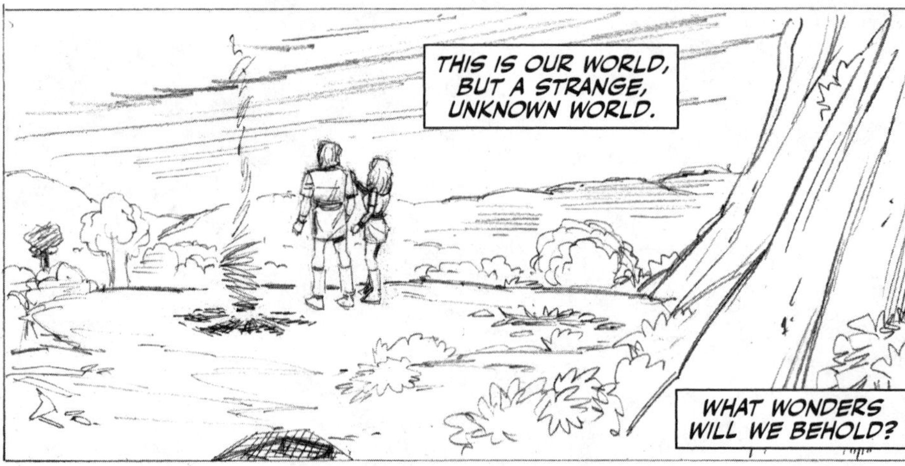
THIS IS OUR WORLD, BUT A STRANGE, UNKNOWN WORLD.
WHAT WONDERS WILL WE BEHOLD?

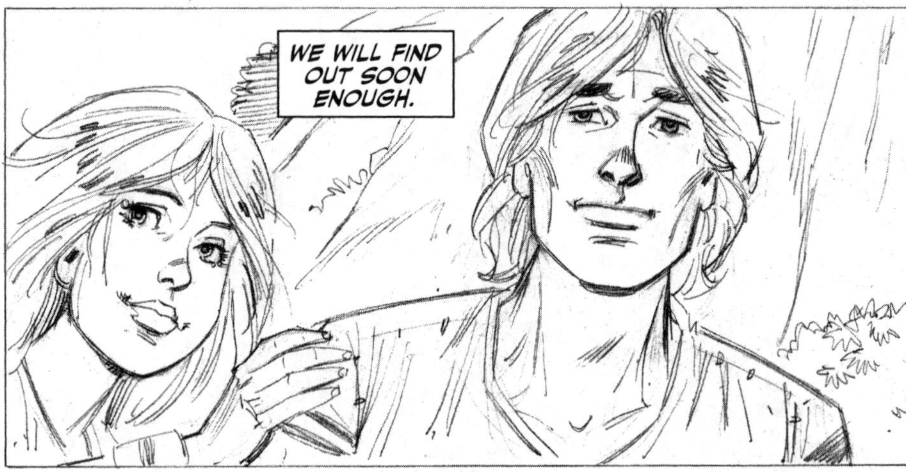
WE WILL FIND OUT SOON ENOUGH.

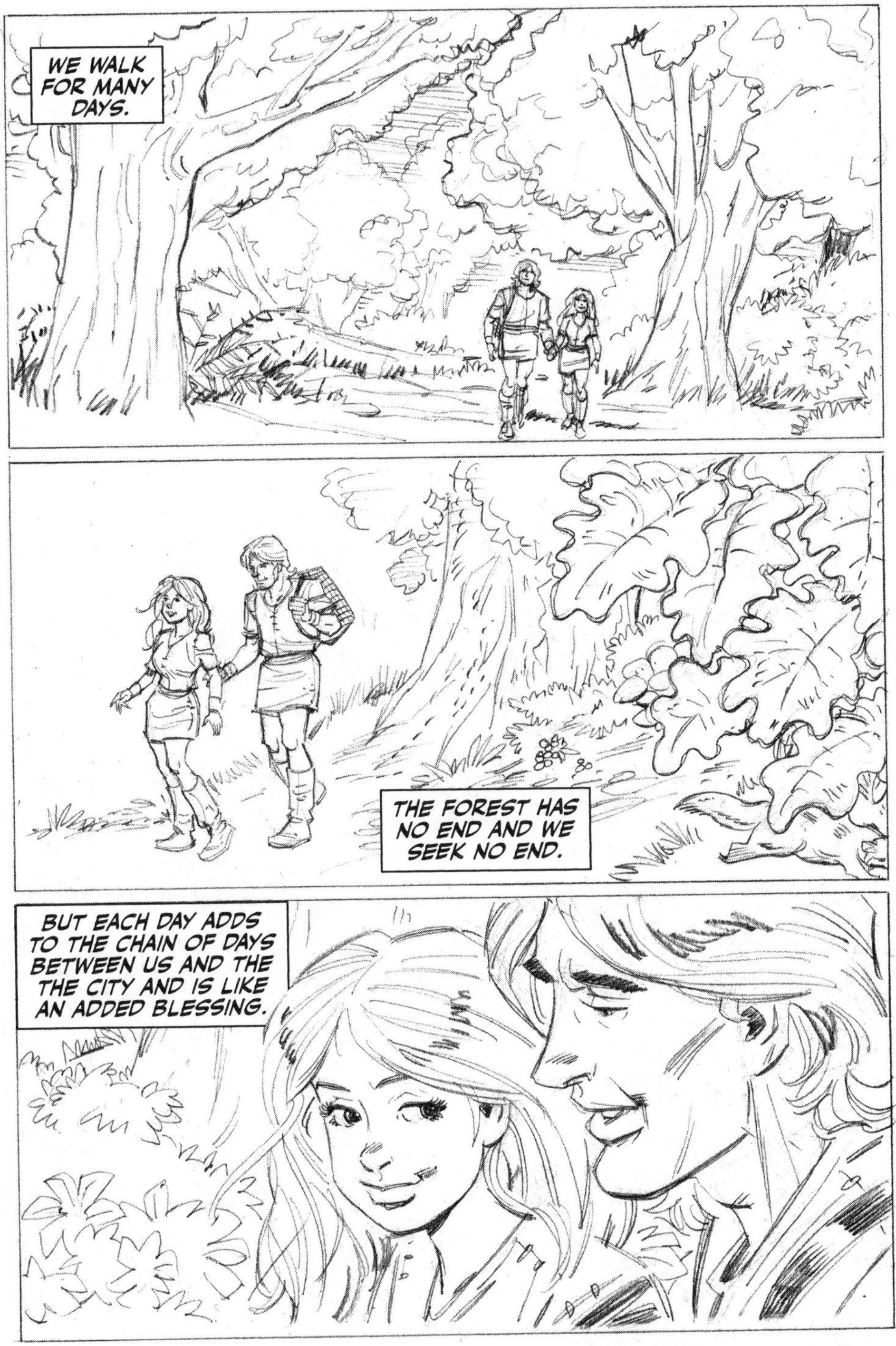
WE WALK FOR MANY DAYS.
THE FOREST HAS NO END AND WE SEEK NO END.
BUT EACH DAY ADDS TO THE CHAIN OF DAYS BETWEEN US AND THE THE CITY AND IS LIKE AN ADDED BLESSING.

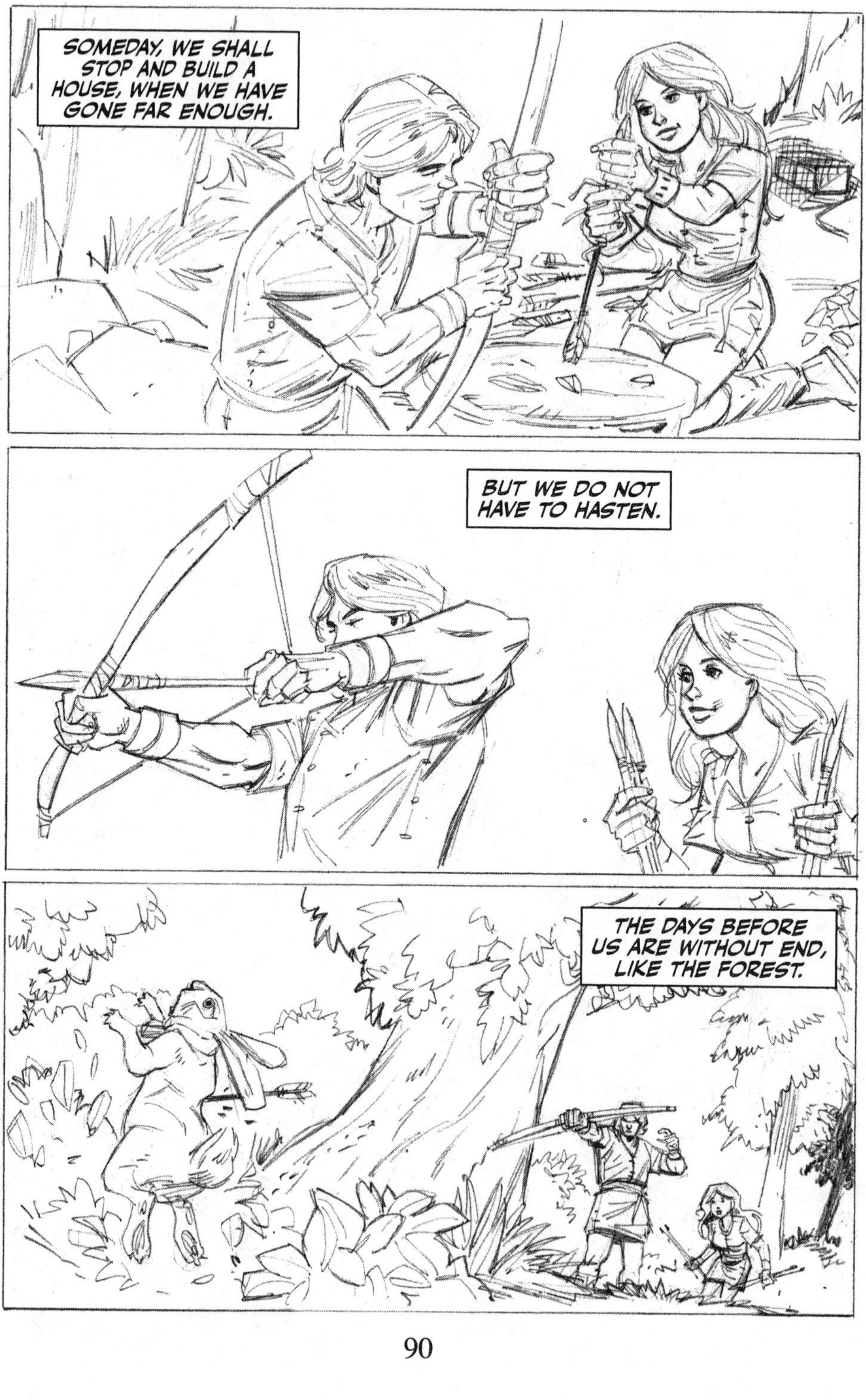
SOMEDAY, WE SHALL STOP AND BUILD A HOUSE, WHEN WE HAVE GONE FAR ENOUGH.
BUT WE DO NOT HAVE TO HASTEN.
THE DAYS BEFORE US ARE WITHOUT END, LIKE THE FOREST.

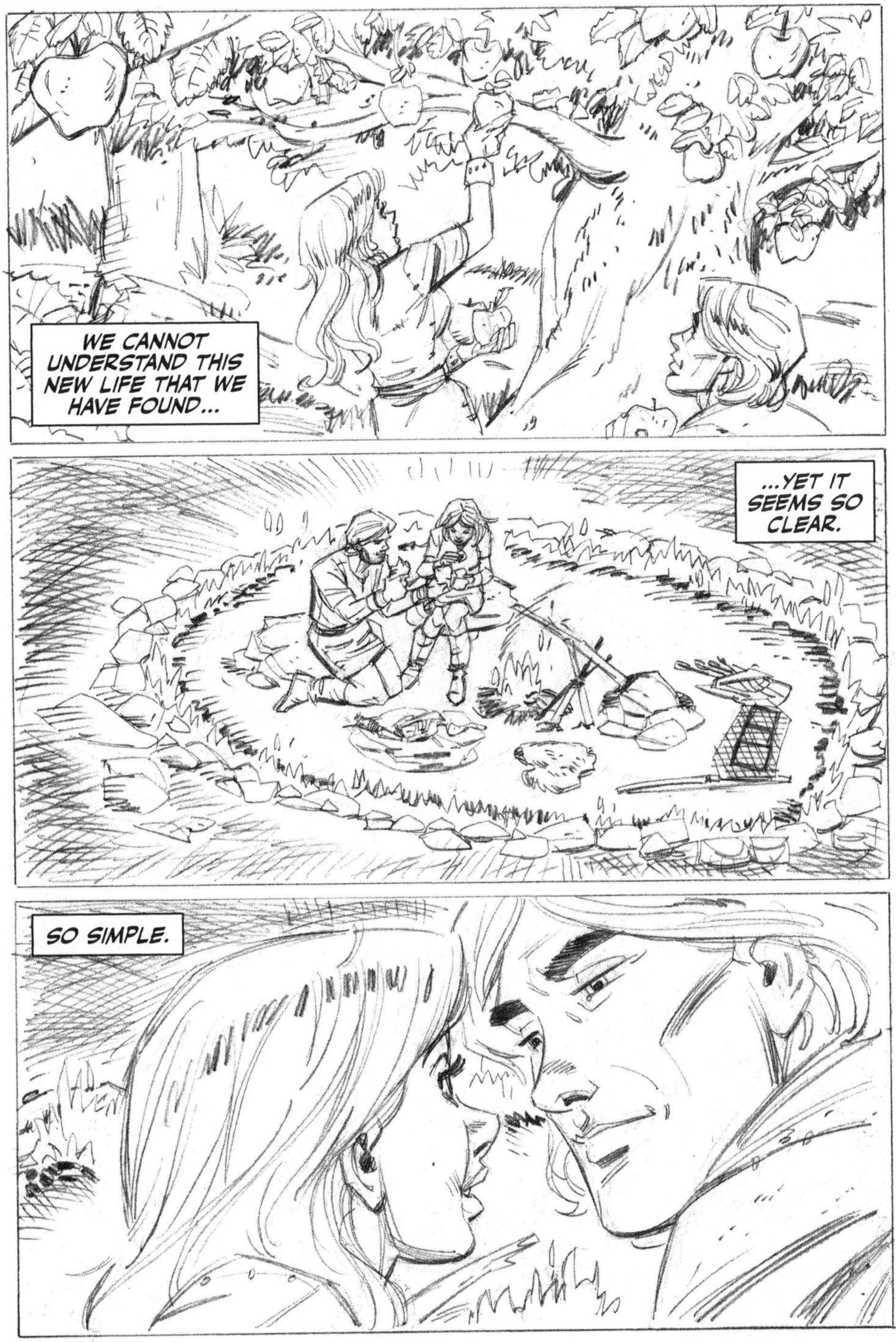
WE CANNOT UNDERSTAND THIS NEW LIFE THAT WE HAVE FOUND...
...YET IT SEEMS SO CLEAR.
SO SIMPLE.

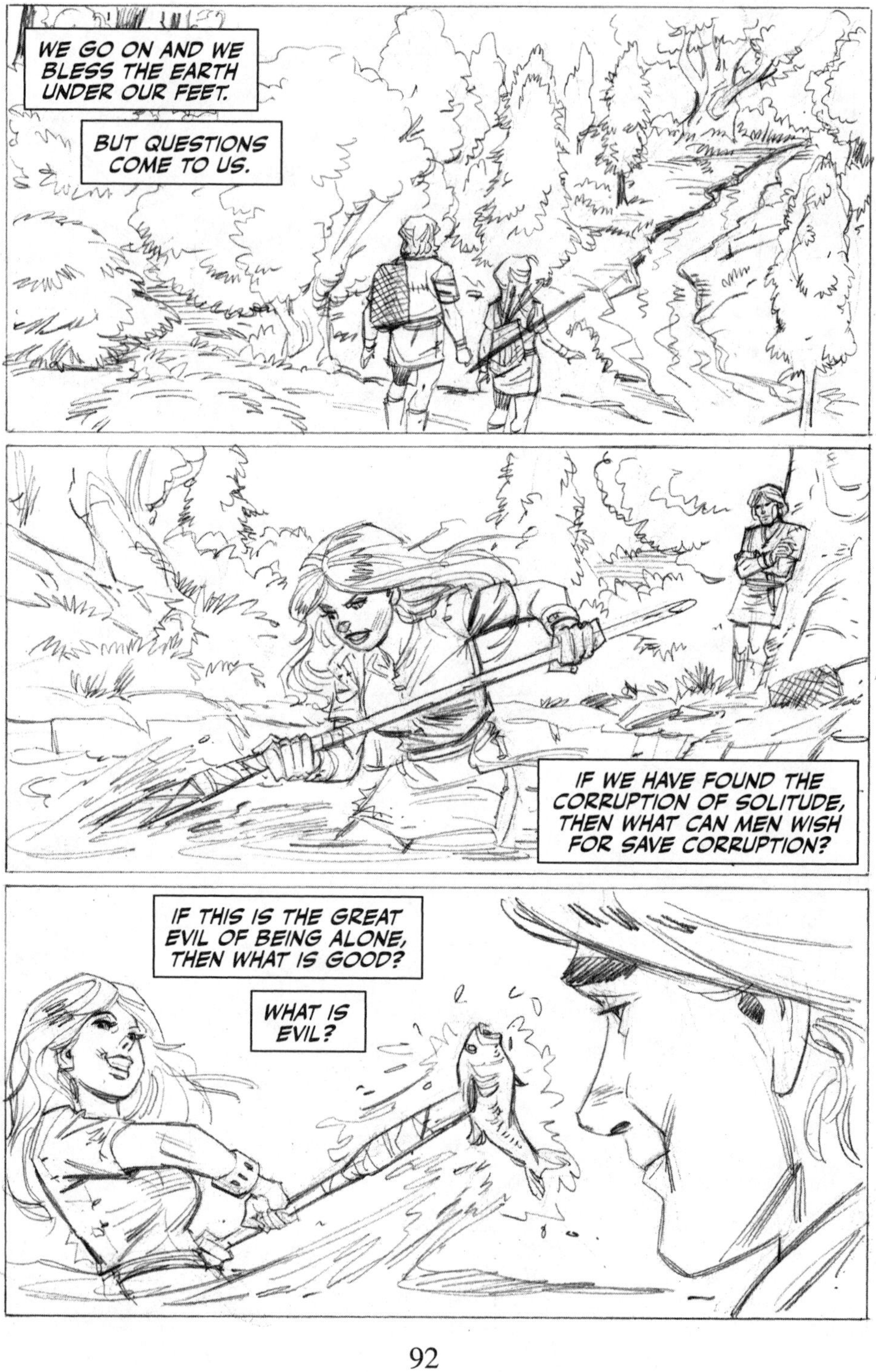
WE GO ON AND WE BLESS THE EARTH UNDER OUR FEET.
BUT QUESTIONS COME TO US.
IF WE HAVE FOUND THE CORRUPTION OF SOLITUDE, THEN WHAT CAN MEN WISH FOR SAVE CORRUPTION?
IF THIS IS THE GREAT EVIL OF BEING ALONE, THEN WHAT IS GOOD?
WHAT IS EVIL?

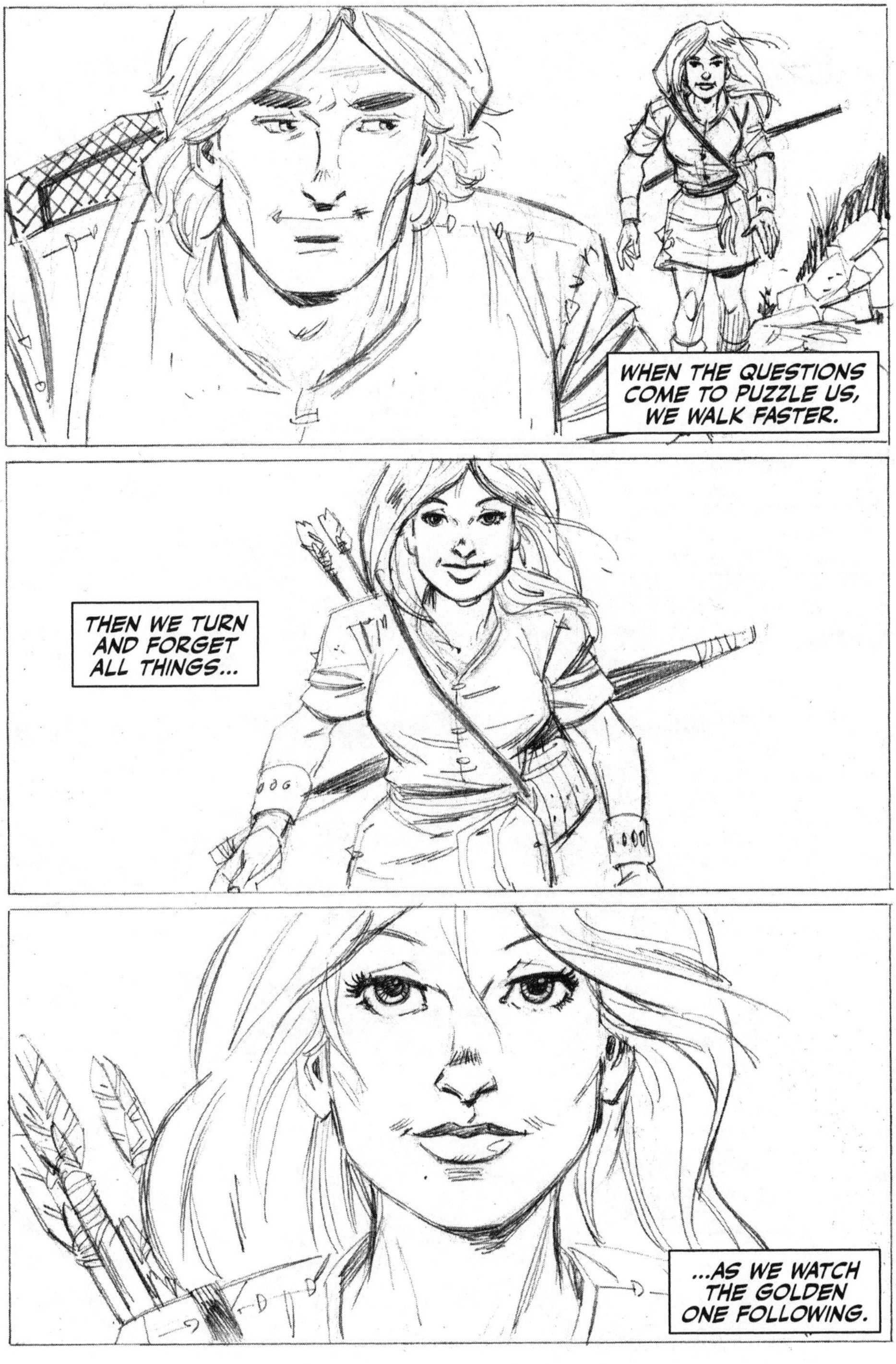
WHEN THE QUESTIONS COME TO PUZZLE US, WE WALK FASTER.
THEN WE TURN AND FORGET ALL THINGS...
...AS WE WATCH THE GOLDEN ONE FOLLOWING.

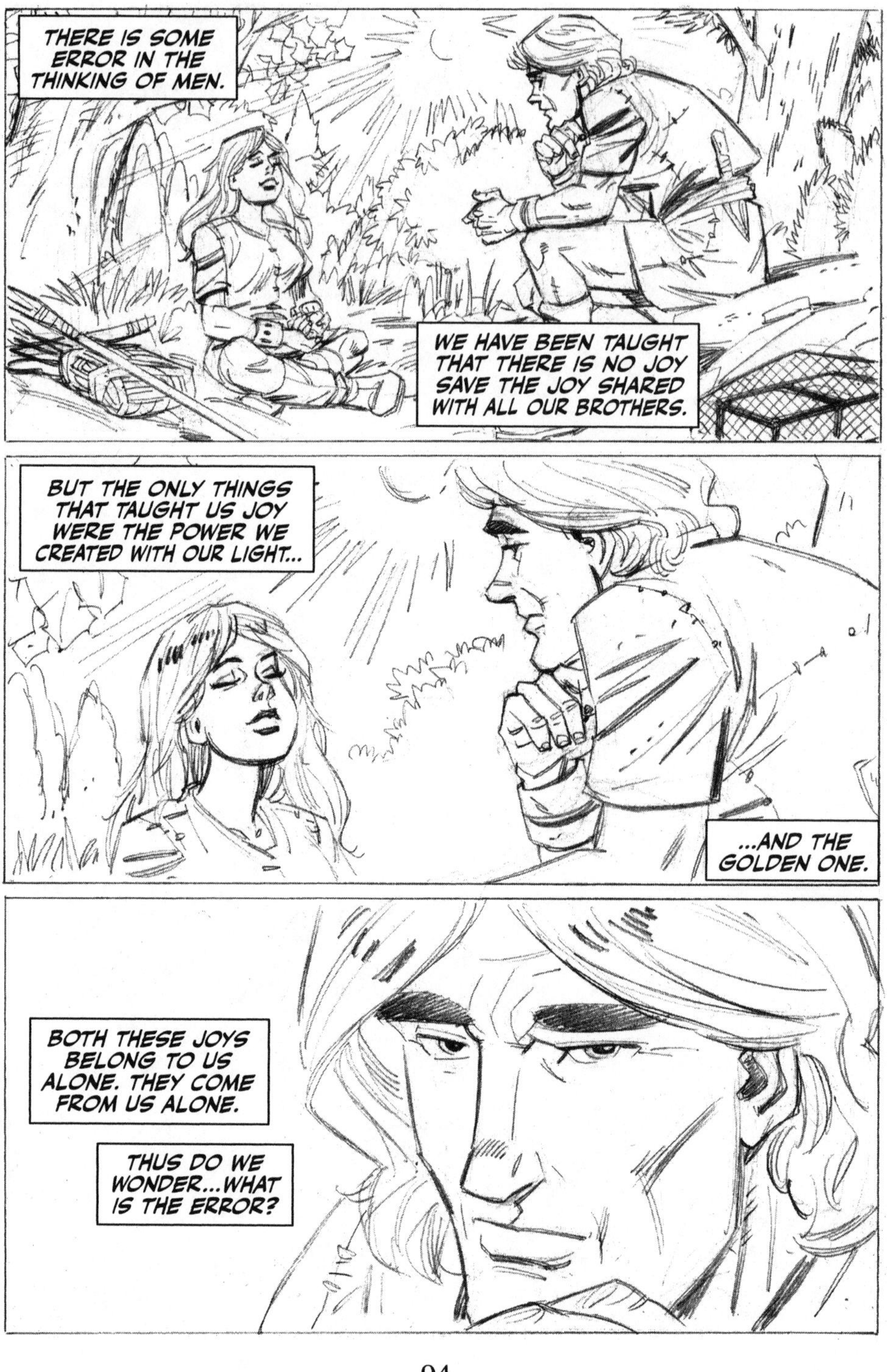
THERE IS SOME ERROR IN THE THINKING OF MEN.
WE HAVE BEEN TAUGHT THAT THERE IS NO JOY SAVE THE JOY SHARED WITH ALL OUR BROTHERS.
BUT THE ONLY THINGS THAT TAUGHT US JOY WERE THE POWER WE CREATED WITH OUR LIGHT...
...AND THE GOLDEN ONE.
BOTH THESE JOYS BELONG TO US ALONE. THEY COME FROM US ALONE.
THUS DO WE WONDER...WHAT IS THE ERROR?

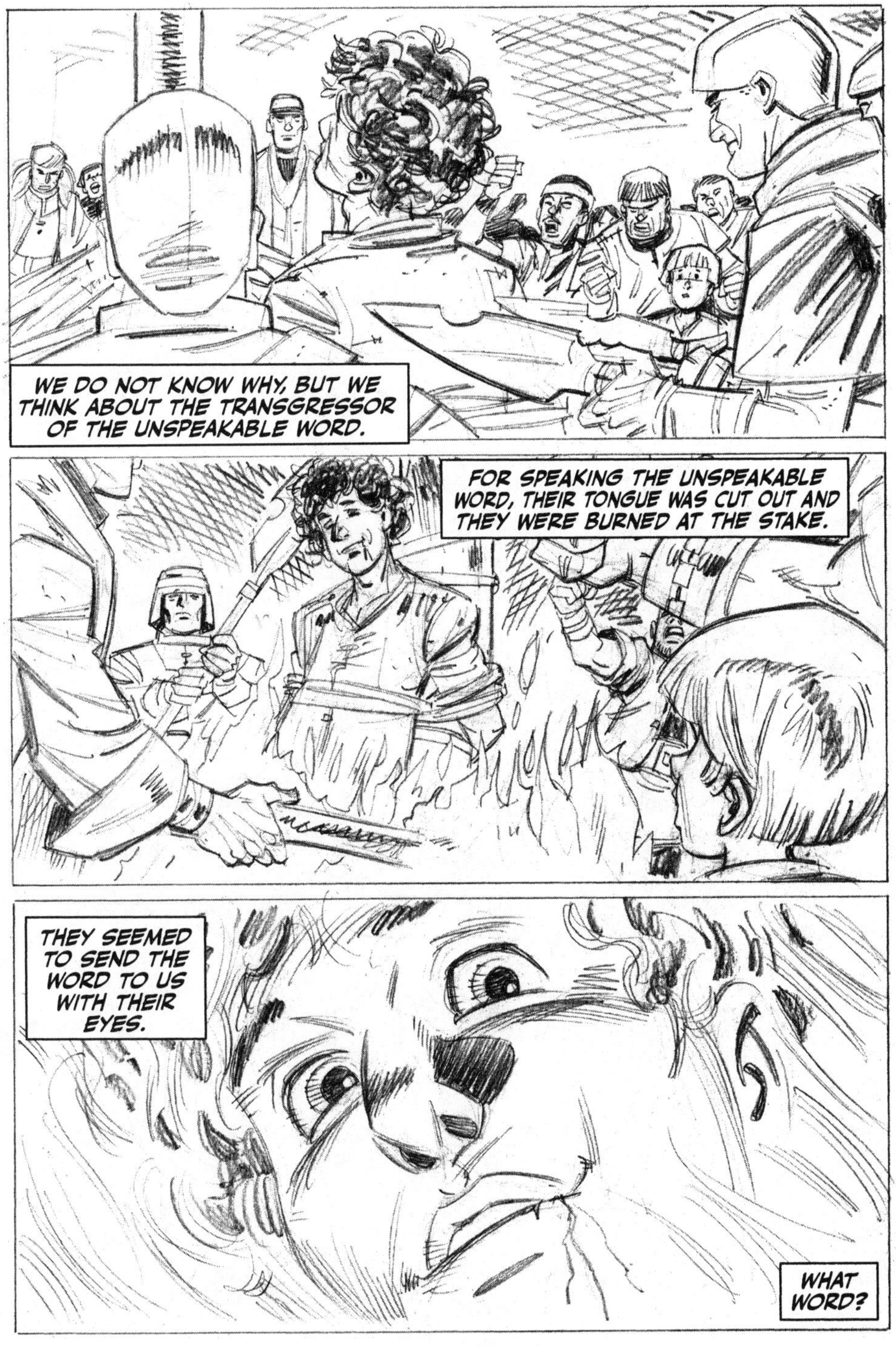
WE DO NOT KNOW WHY, BUT WE THINK ABOUT THE TRANSGRESSOR OF THE UNSPEAKABLE WORD.
FOR SPEAKING THE UNSPEAKABLE WORD, THEIR TONGUE WAS CUT OUT AND THEY WERE BURNED AT THE STAKE.
THEY SEEMED TO SEND THE WORD TO US WITH THEIR EYES.
WHAT WORD?

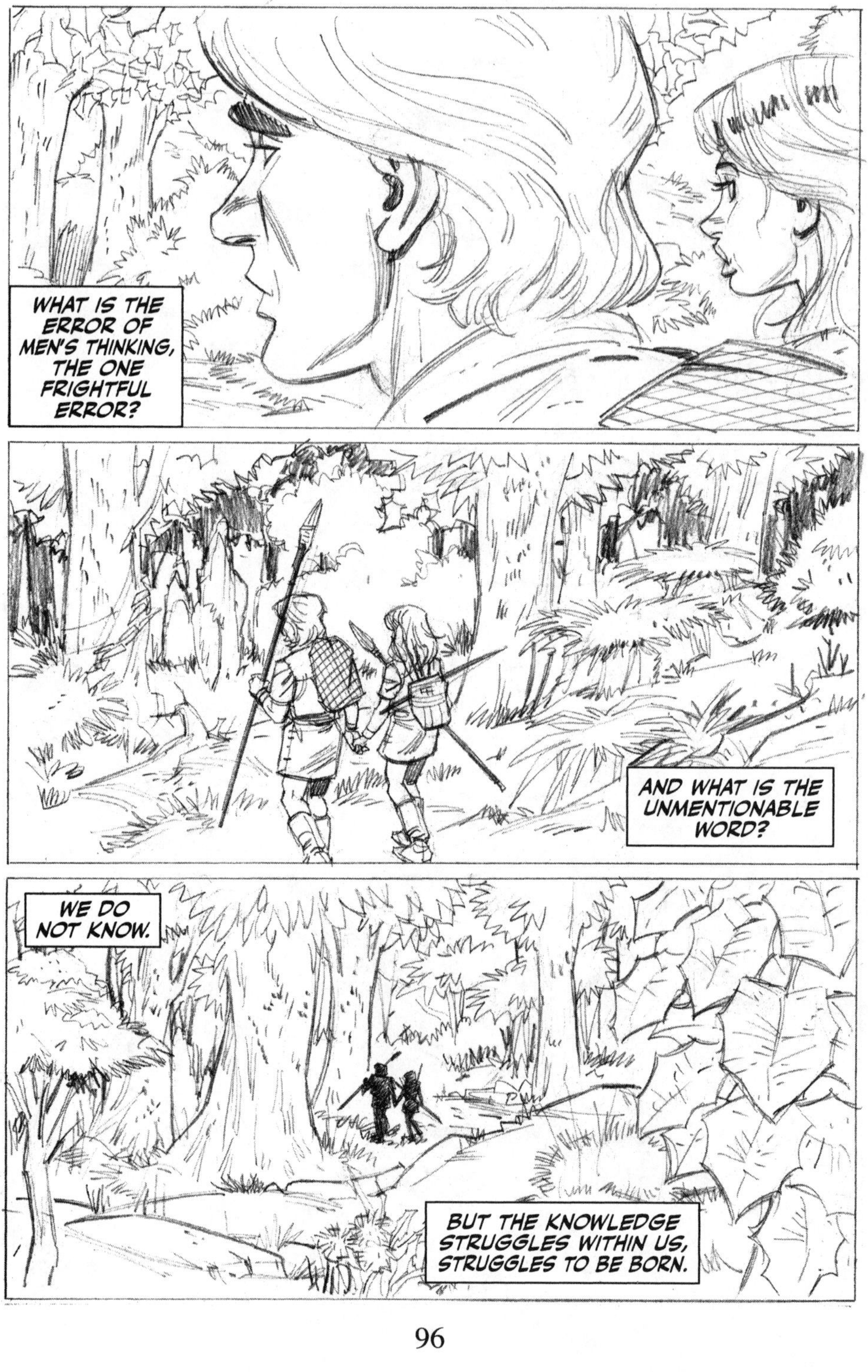
WHAT IS THE ERROR OF MEN'S THINKING, THE ONE FRIGHTFUL ERROR?
AND WHAT IS THE UNMENTIONABLE WORD?
WE DO NOT KNOW.
BUT THE KNOWLEDGE STRUGGLES WITHIN US, STRUGGLES TO BE BORN.

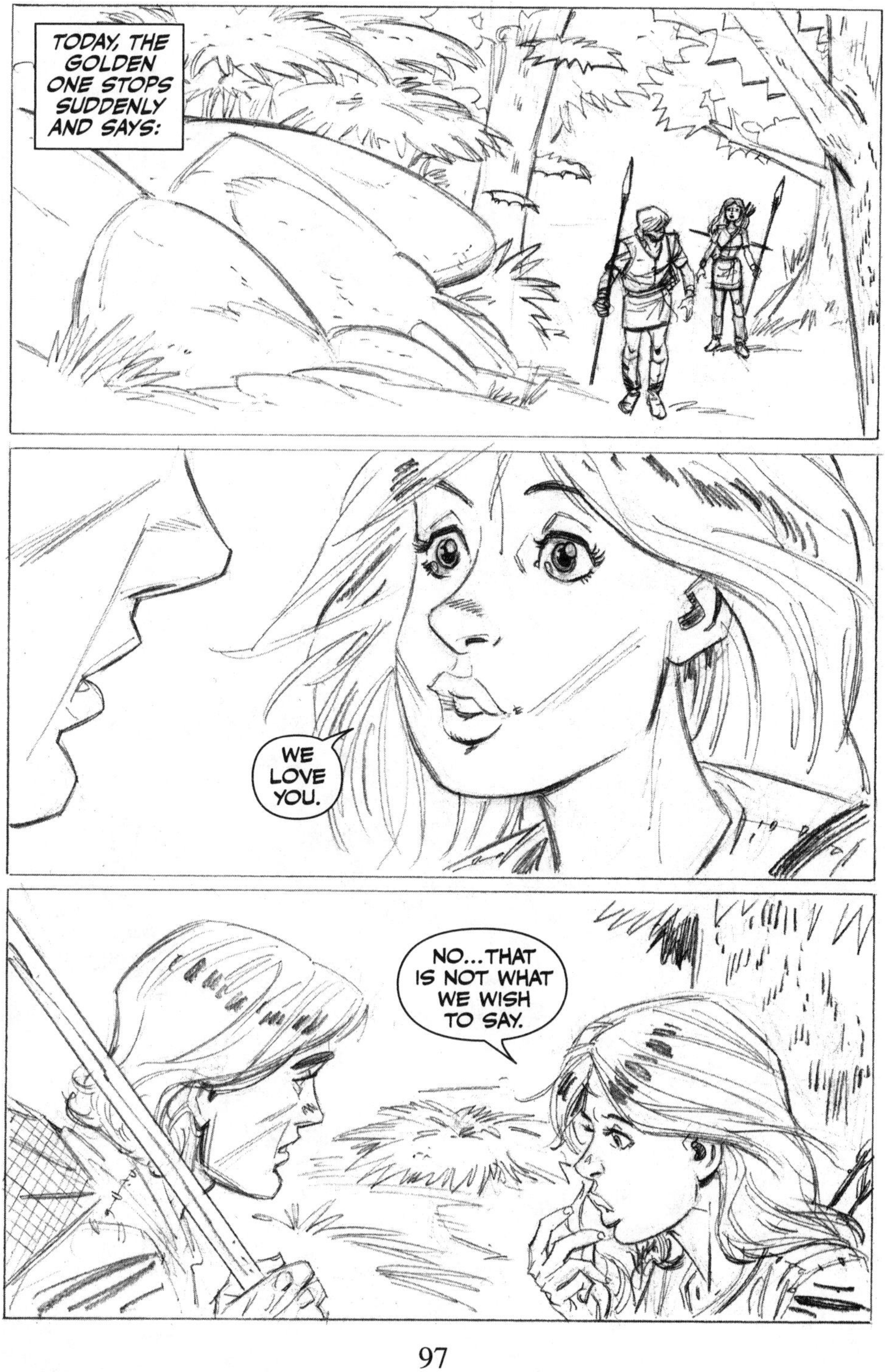
TODAY, THE GOLDEN ONE STOPS SUDDENLY AND SAYS:
WE LOVE YOU.
NO...THAT IS NOT WHAT WE WISH TO SAY.

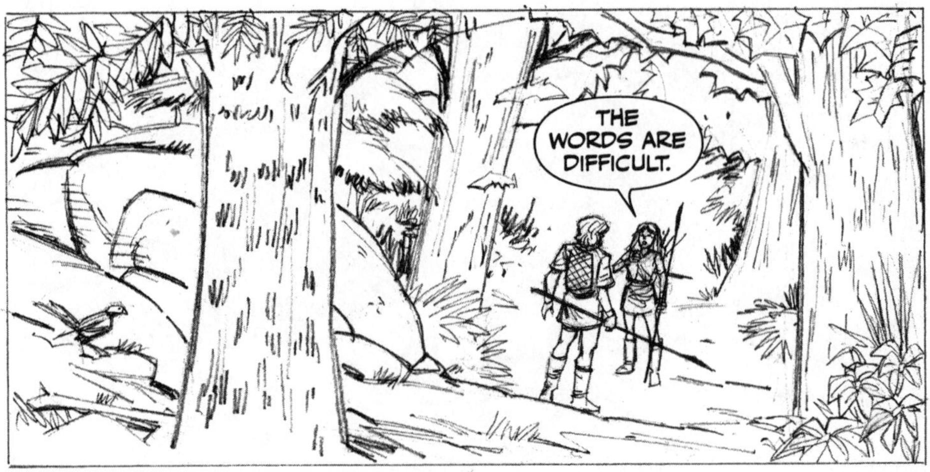
THE WORDS ARE DIFFICULT.

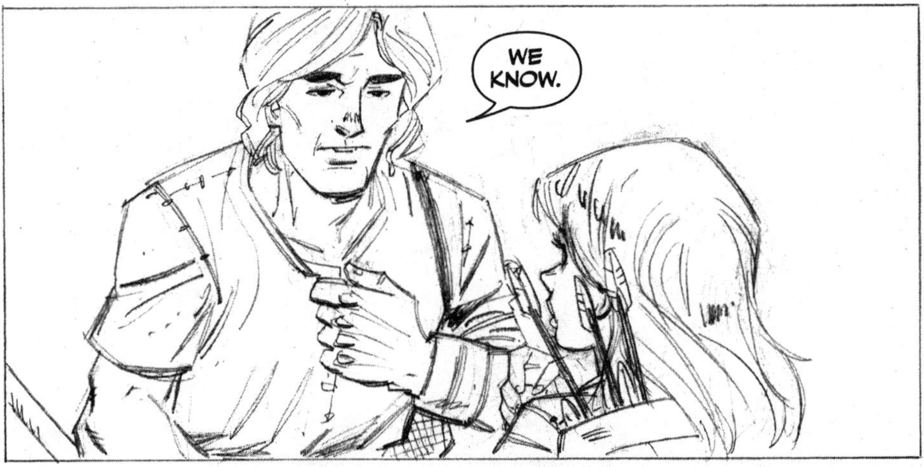
WE KNOW.

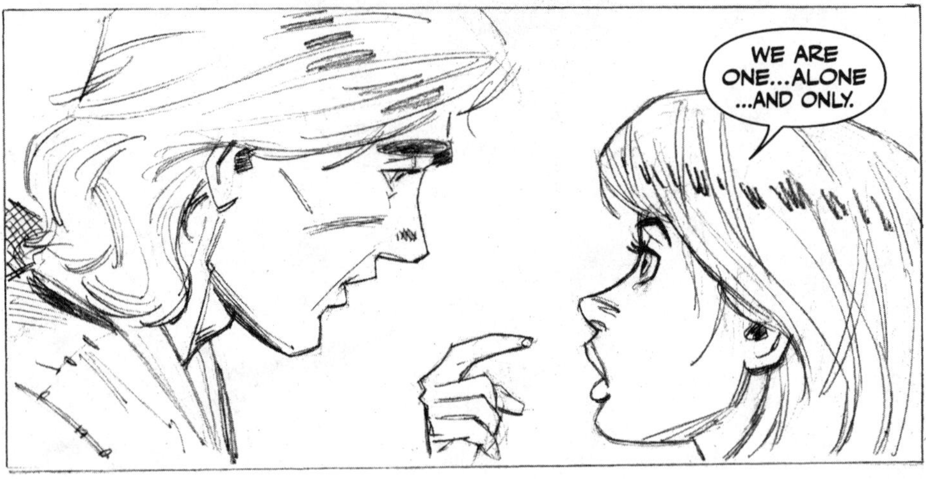
WE ARE ONE...ALONE ...AND ONLY.

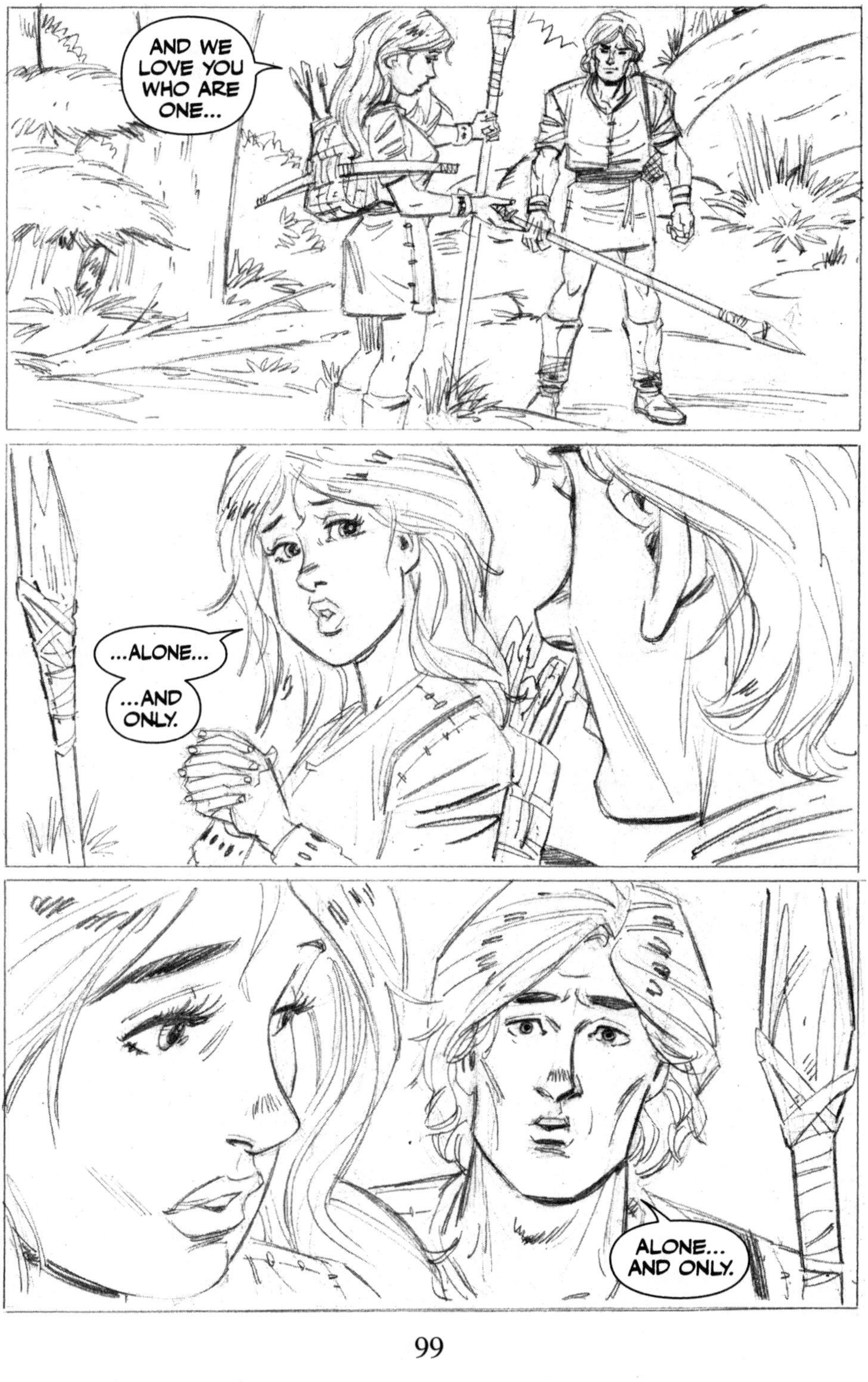
AND WE LOVE YOU WHO ARE ONE...
...ALONE...
...AND ONLY.
ALONE... AND ONLY.

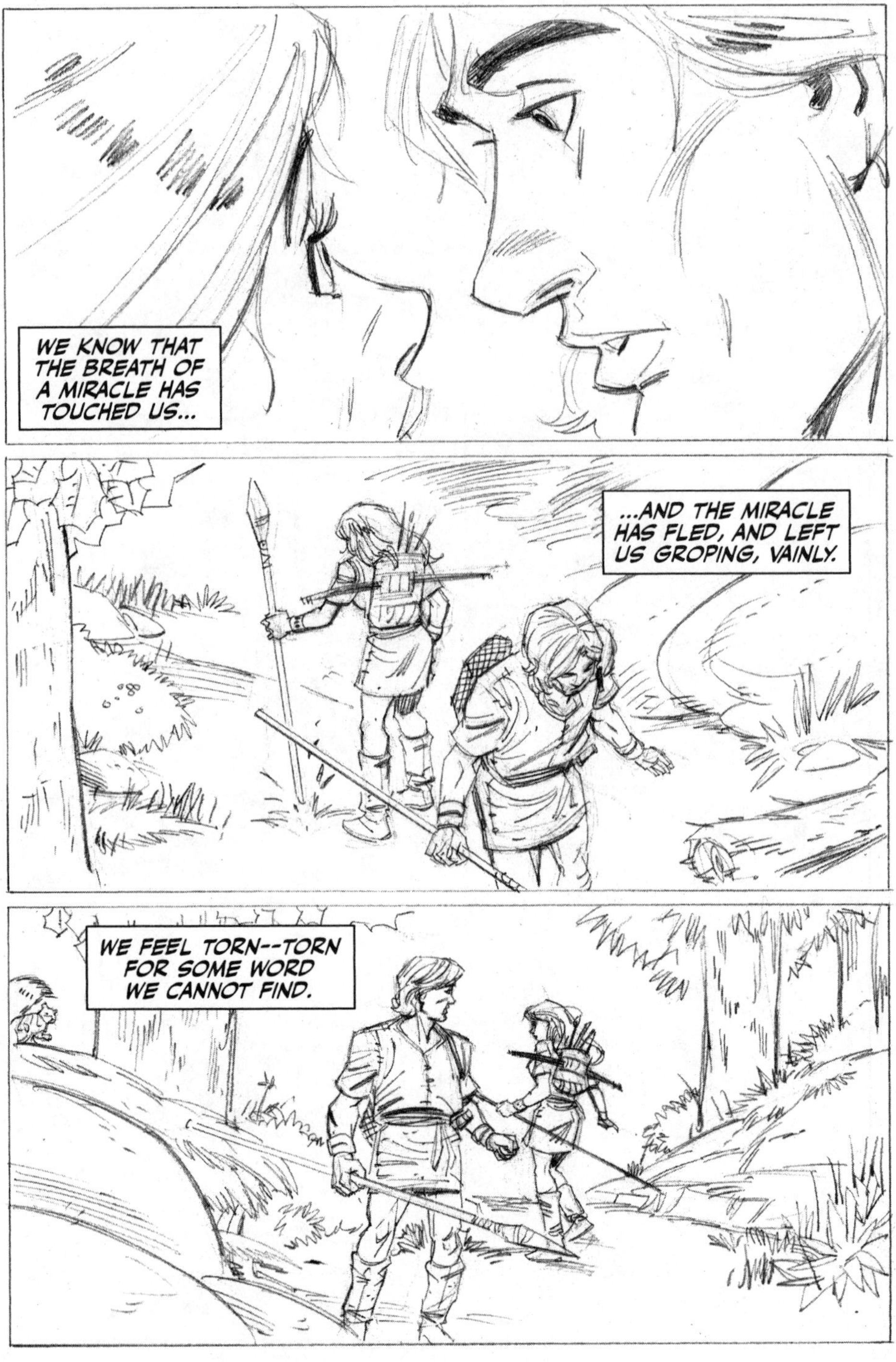
WE KNOW THAT THE BREATH OF A MIRACLE HAS TOUCHED US...
...AND THE MIRACLE HAS FLED, AND LEFT US GROPING, VAINLY.
WE FEEL TORN--TORN FOR SOME WORD WE CANNOT FIND.

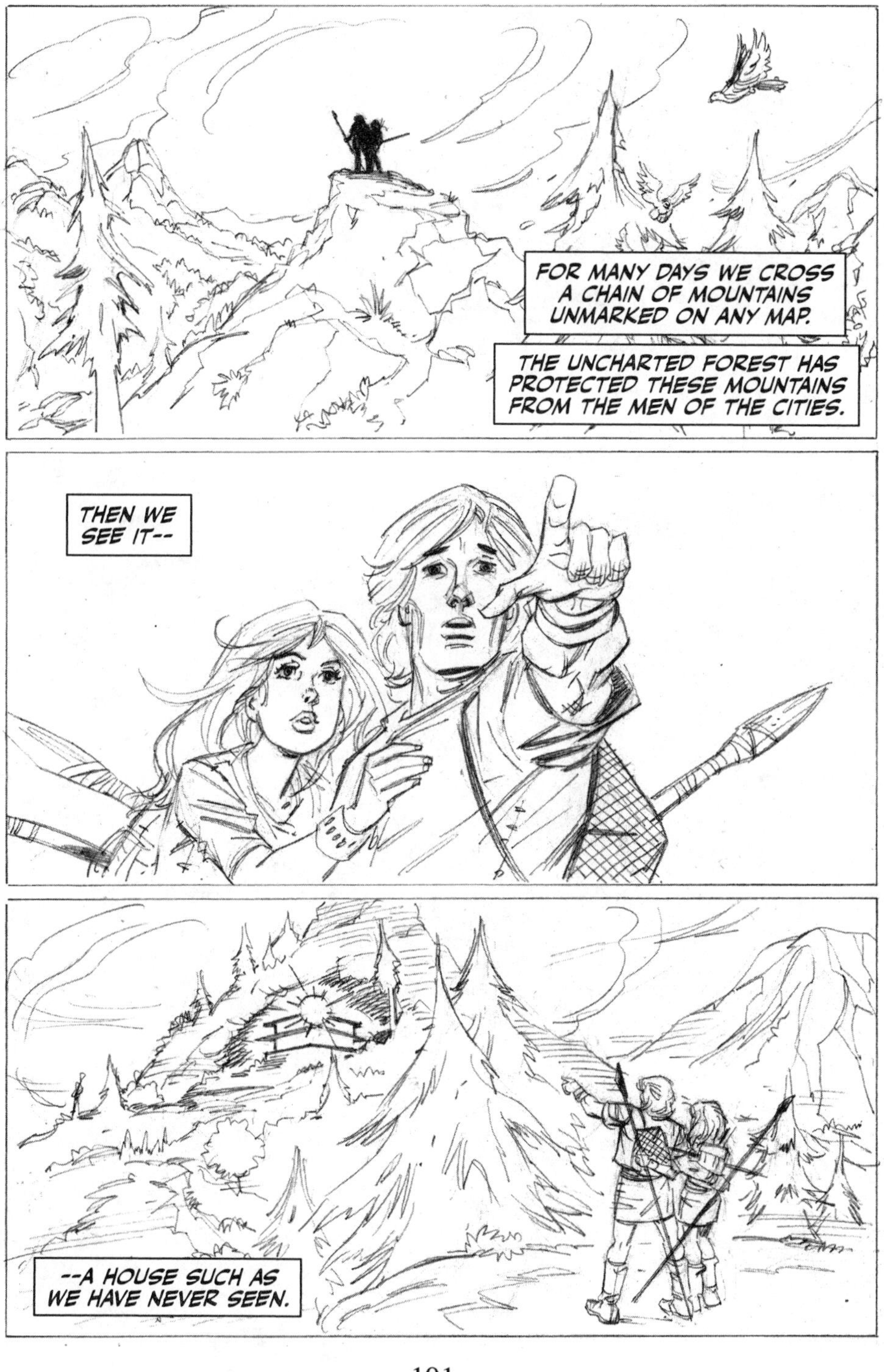
FOR MANY DAYS WE CROSS A CHAIN OF MOUNTAINS UNMARKED ON ANY MAP.
THE UNCHARTED FOREST HAS PROTECTED THESE MOUNTAINS FROM THE MEN OF THE CITIES.
THEN WE SEE IT--
--A HOUSE SUCH AS WE HAVE NEVER SEEN.

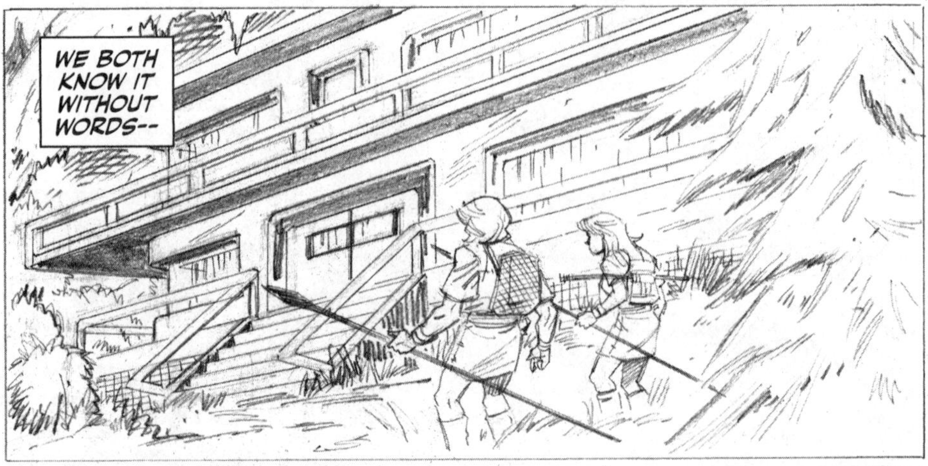
WE BOTH KNOW IT WITHOUT WORDS--

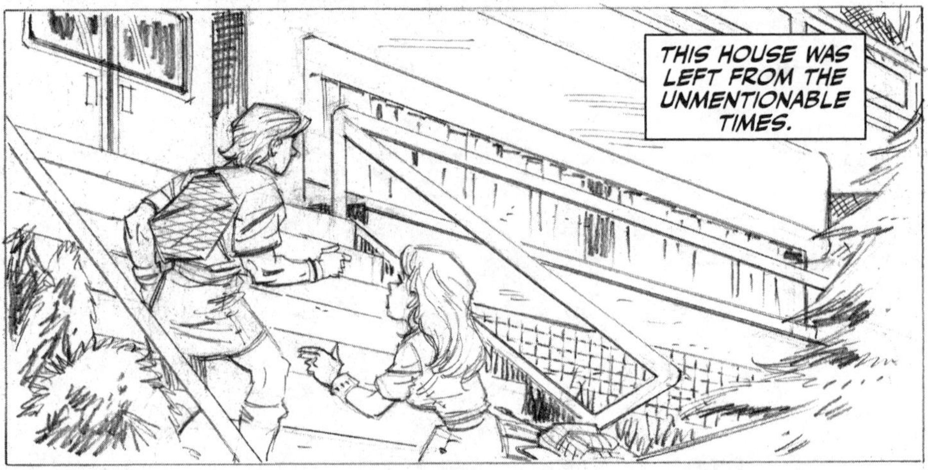
THIS HOUSE WAS LEFT FROM THE UNMENTIONABLE TIMES.

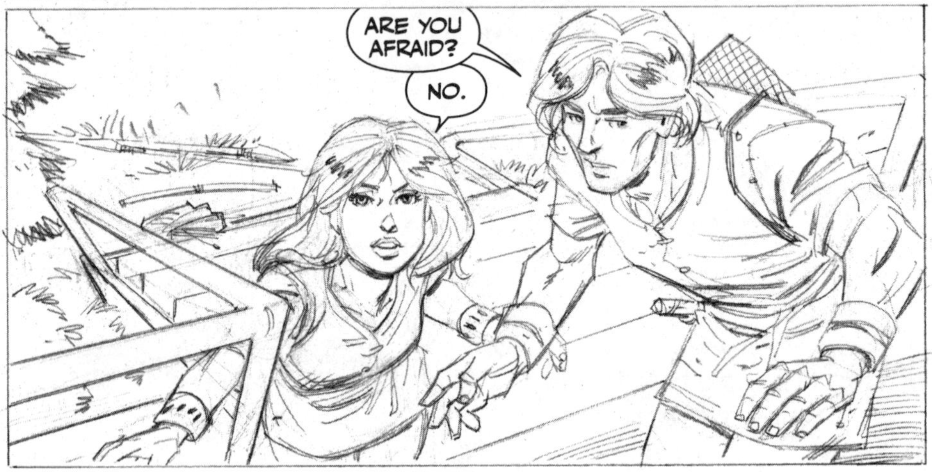
ARE YOU AFRAID?
NO.

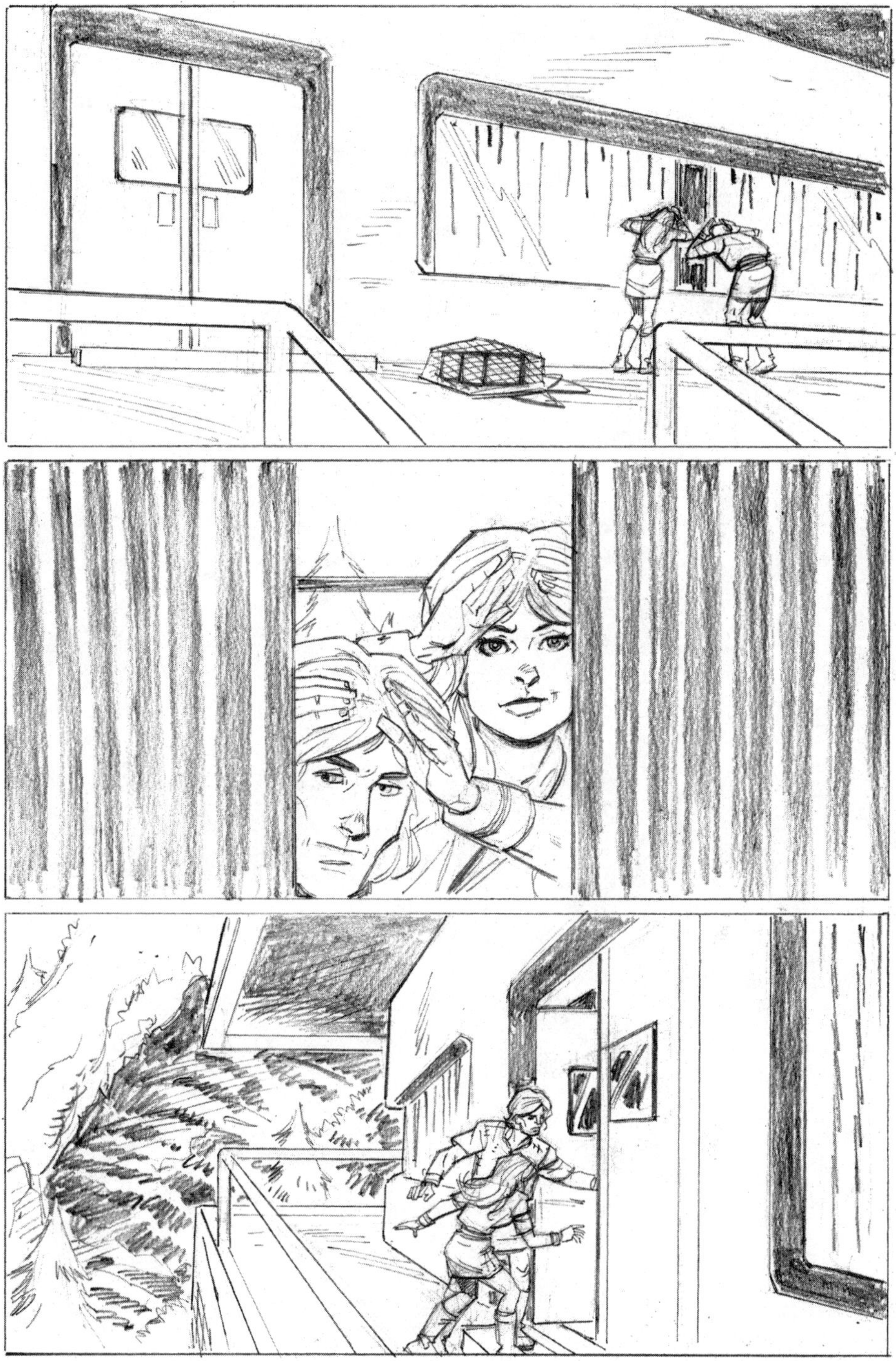

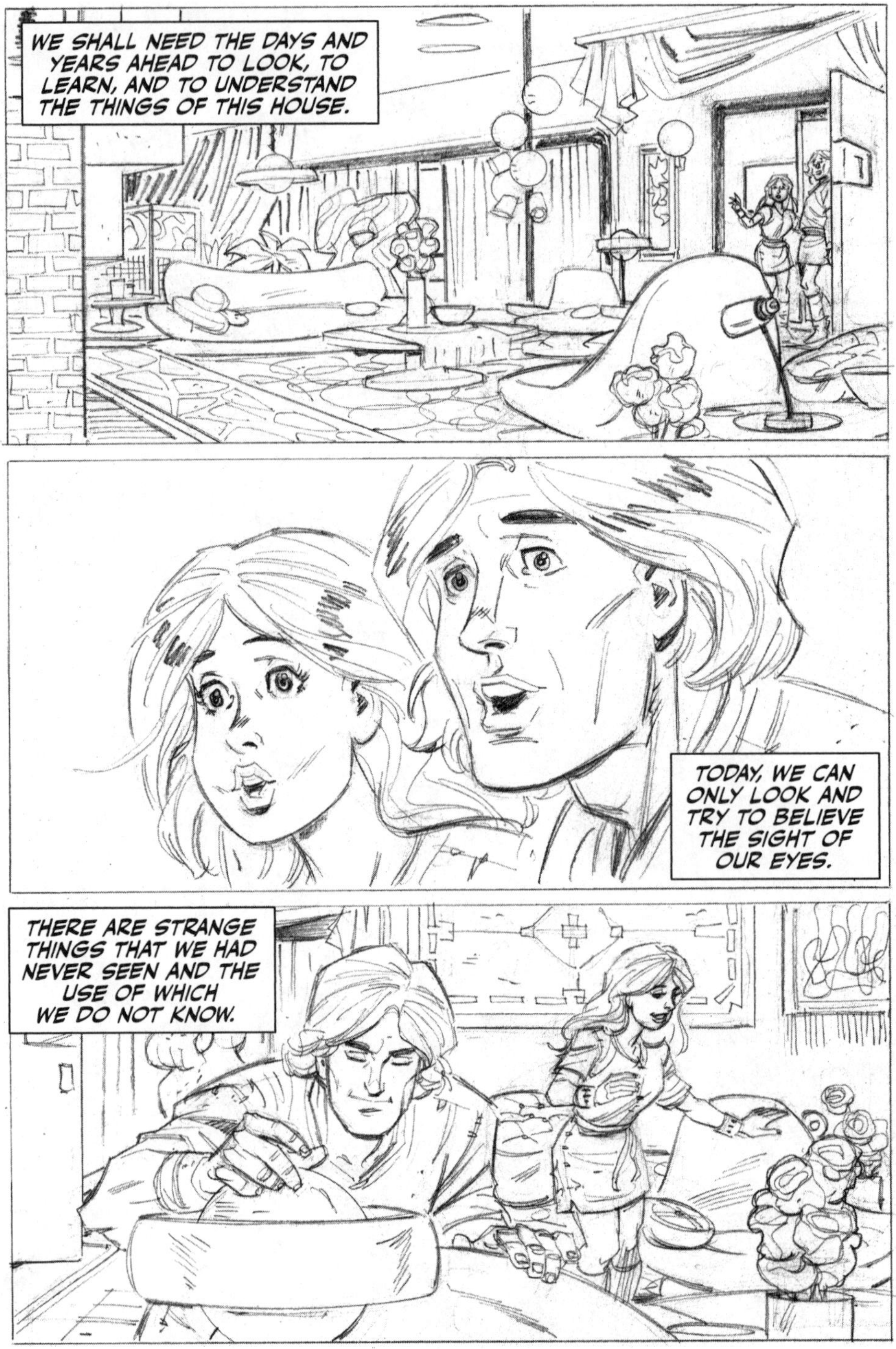
WE SHALL NEED THE DAYS AND YEARS AHEAD TO LOOK, TO LEARN, AND TO UNDERSTAND THE THINGS OF THIS HOUSE.
TODAY, WE CAN ONLY LOOK AND TRY TO BELIEVE THE SIGHT OF OUR EYES.
THERE ARE STRANGE THINGS THAT WE HAD NEVER SEEN AND THE USE OF WHICH WE DO NOT KNOW.

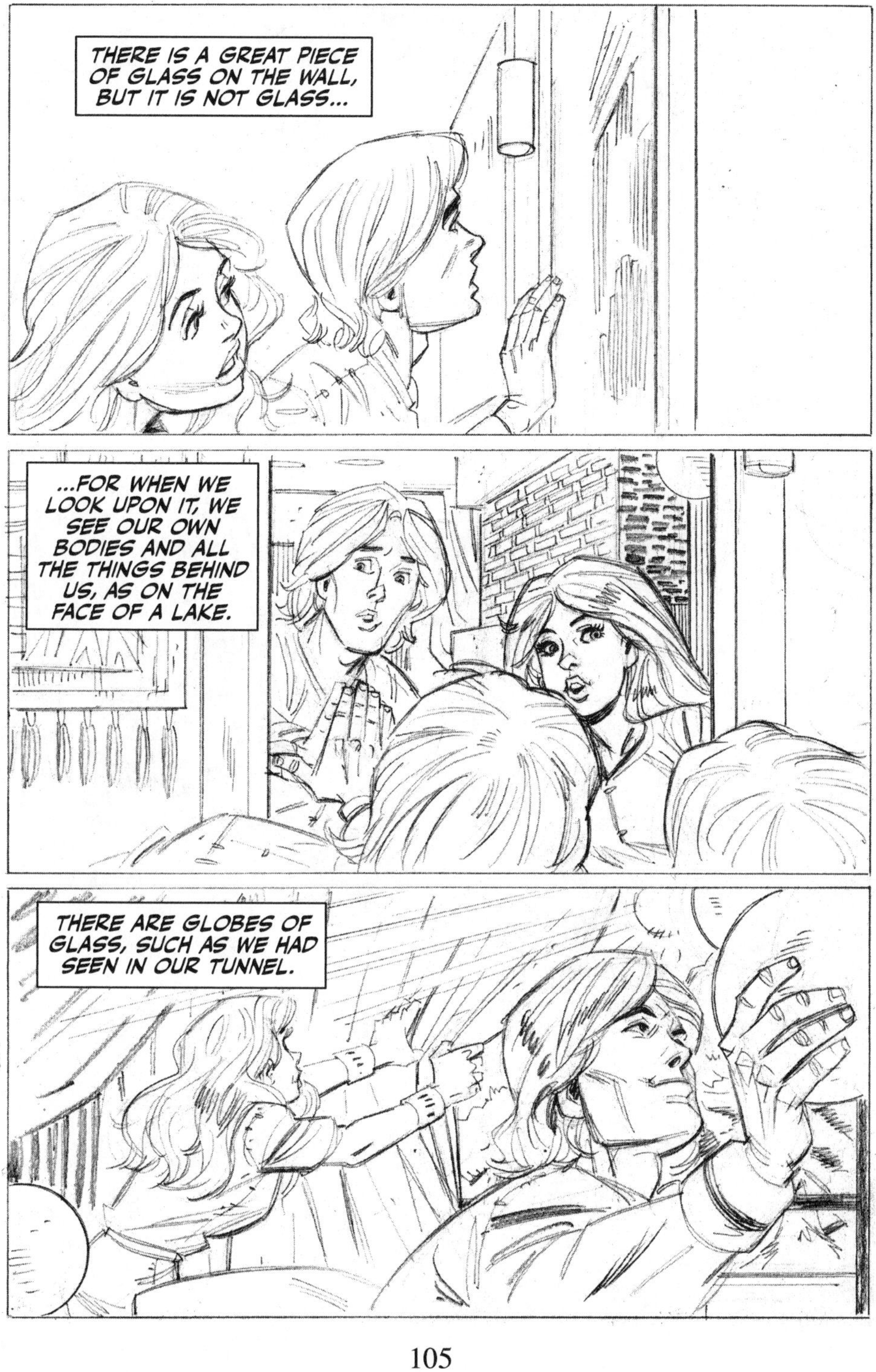
THERE IS A GREAT PIECE OF GLASS ON THE WALL, BUT IT IS NOT GLASS...
...FOR WHEN WE LOOK UPON IT, WE SEE OUR OWN BODIES AND ALL THE THINGS BEHIND US, AS ON THE FACE OF A LAKE.
THERE ARE GLOBES OF GLASS, SUCH AS WE HAD SEEN IN OUR TUNNEL.

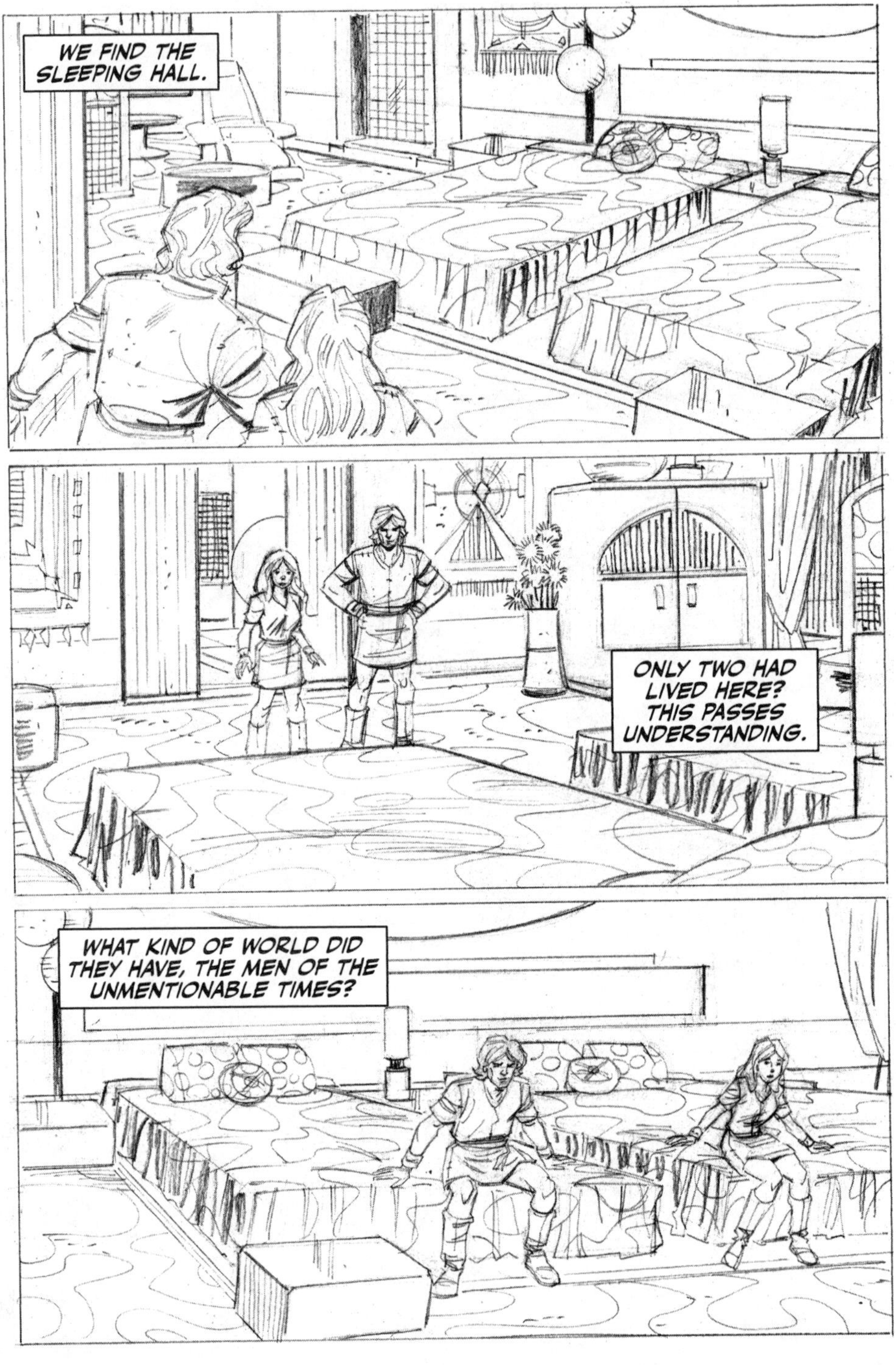
WE FIND THE SLEEPING HALL.
ONLY TWO HAD LIVED HERE? THIS PASSES UNDERSTANDING.
WHAT KIND OF WORLD DID THEY HAVE, THE MEN OF THE UNMENTIONABLE TIMES?

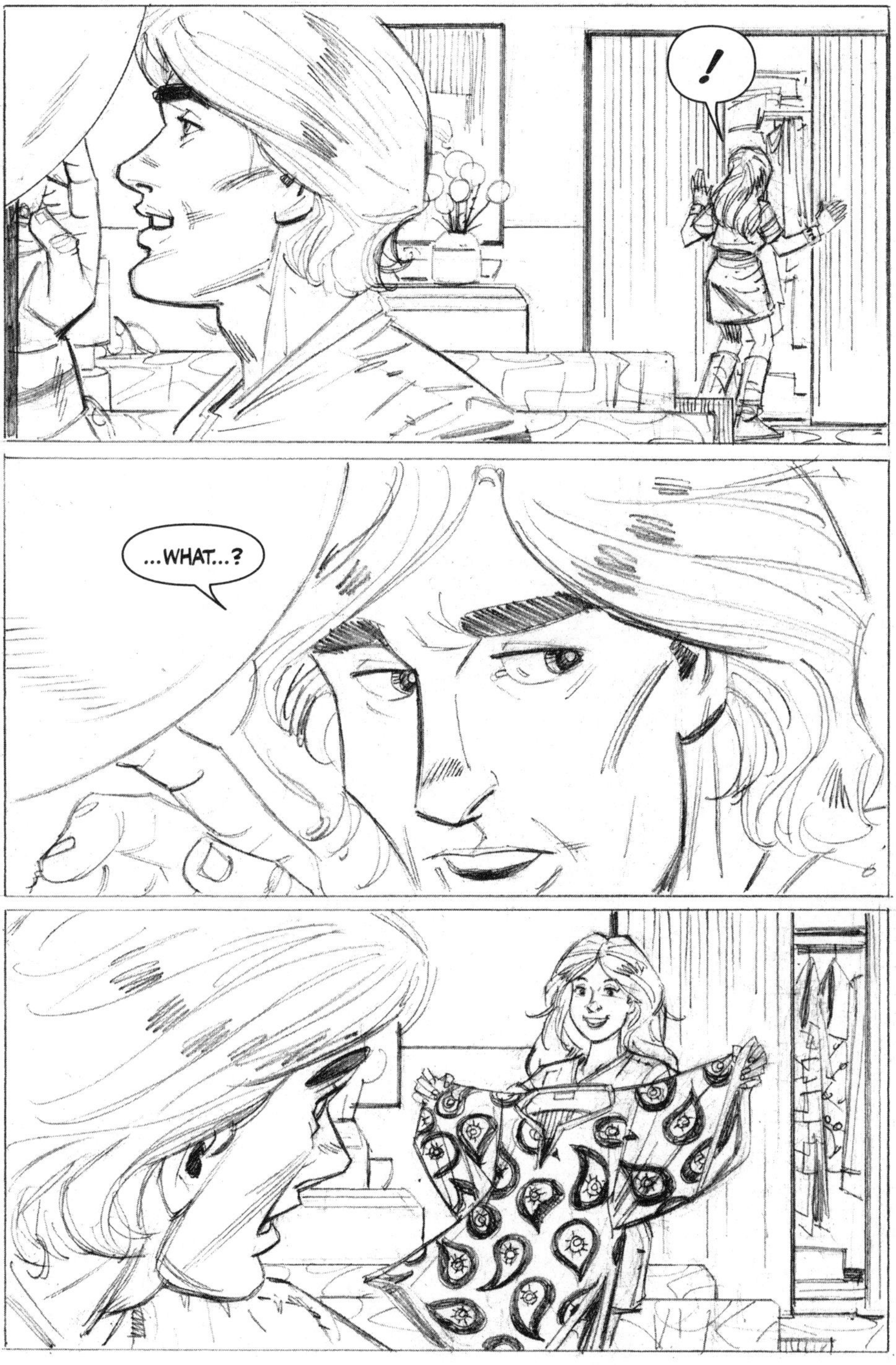
!
...WHAT...?

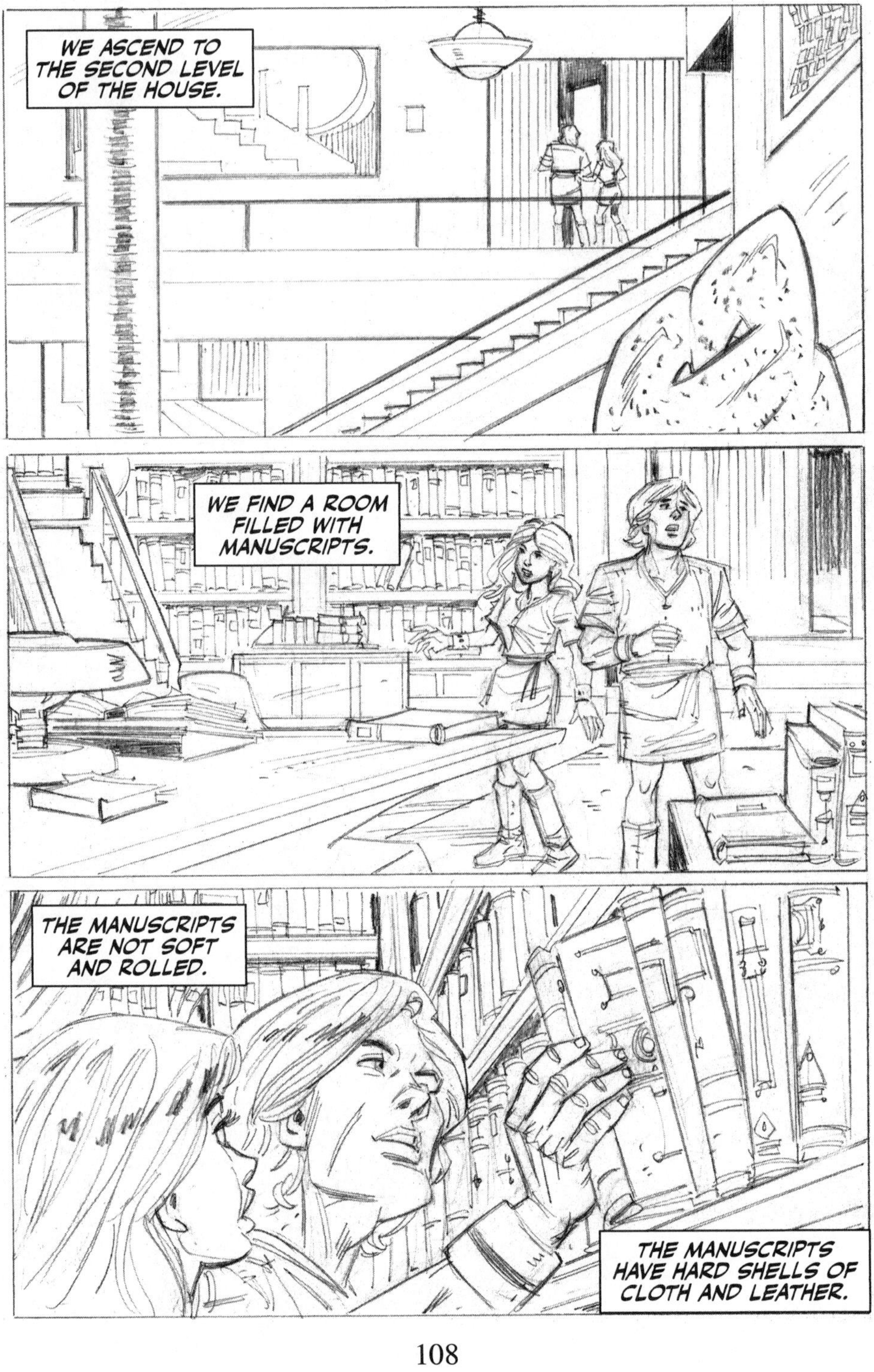
WE ASCEND TO THE SECOND LEVEL OF THE HOUSE.
WE FIND A ROOM FILLED WITH MANUSCRIPTS.
THE MANUSCRIPTS ARE NOT SOFT AND ROLLED.
THE MANUSCRIPTS HAVE HARD SHELLS OF CLOTH AND LEATHER.

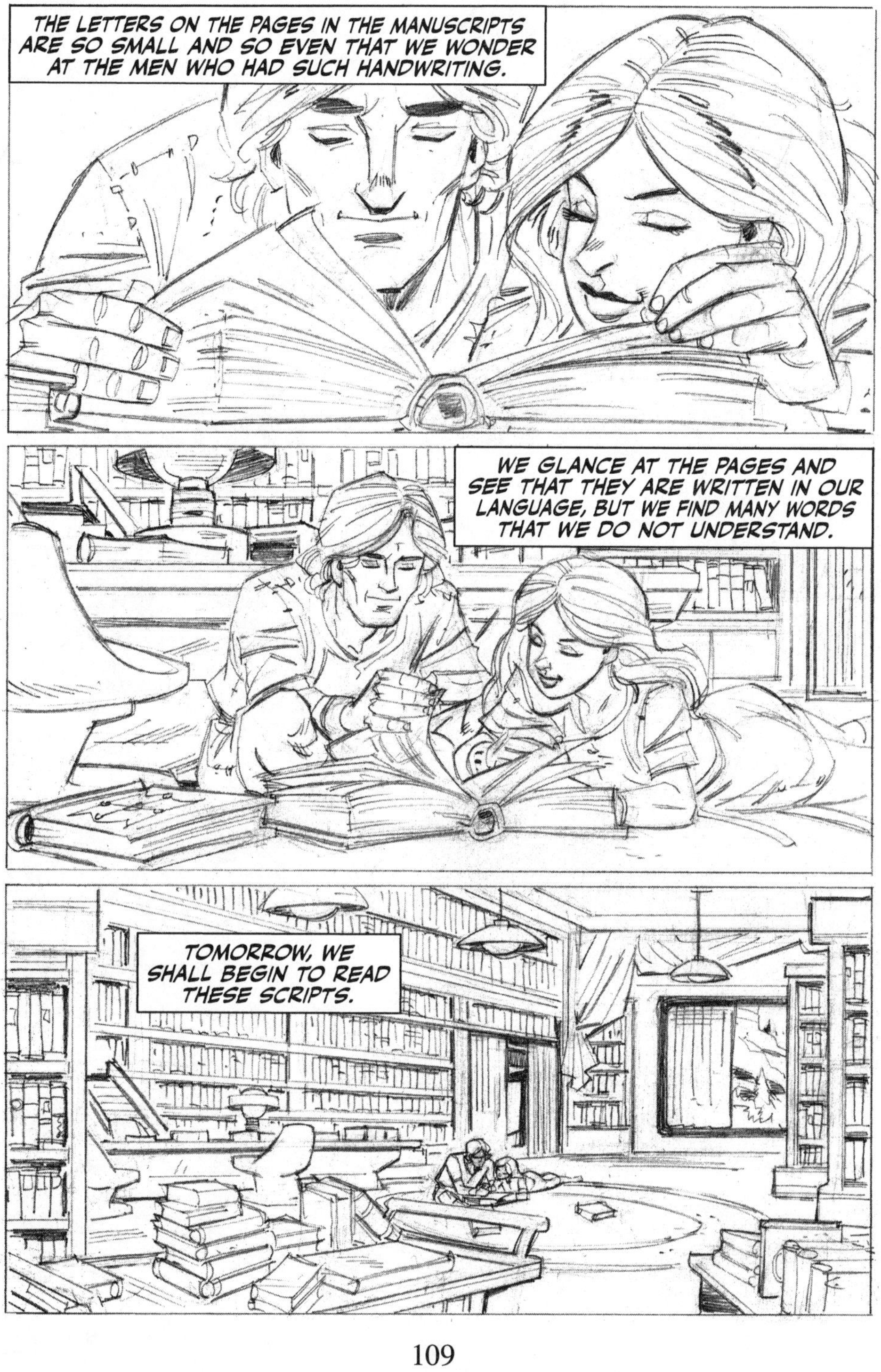
THE LETTERS ON THE PAGES IN THE MANUSCRIPTS ARE SO SMALL AND SO EVEN THAT WE WONDER AT THE MEN WHO HAD SUCH HANDWRITING.
WE GLANCE AT THE PAGES AND SEE THAT THEY ARE WRITTEN IN OUR LANGUAGE, BUT WE FIND MANY WORDS THAT WE DO NOT UNDERSTAND.
TOMORROW, WE SHALL BEGIN TO READ THESE SCRIPTS.

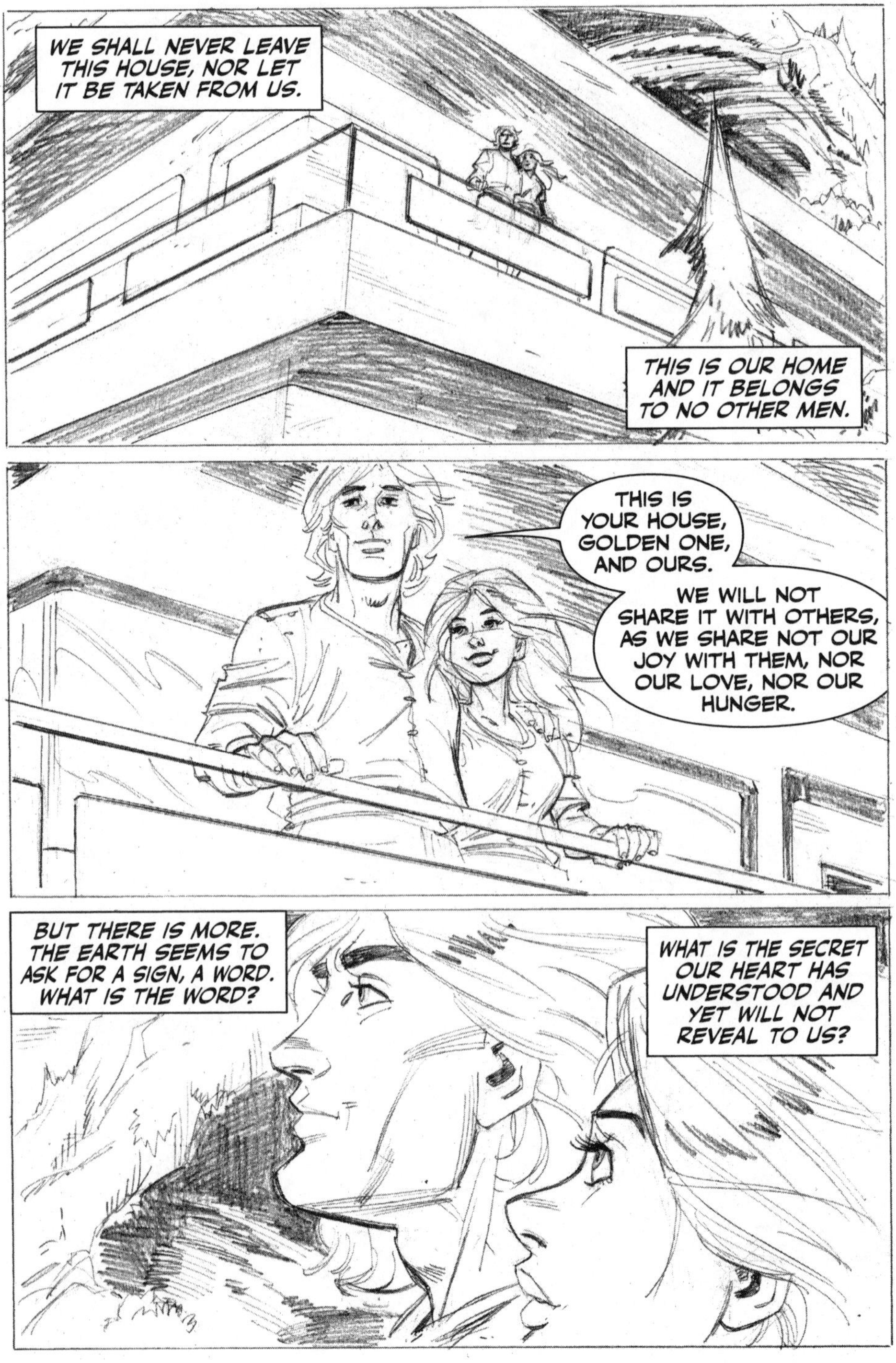
WE SHALL NEVER LEAVE THIS HOUSE, NOR LET IT BE TAKEN FROM US.
THIS IS OUR HOME AND IT BELONGS TO NO OTHER MEN.
THIS IS YOUR HOUSE, GOLDEN ONE, AND OURS.
WE WILL NOT SHARE IT WITH OTHERS, AS WE SHARE NOT OUR JOY WITH THEM, NOR OUR LOVE, NOR OUR HUNGER.
BUT THERE IS MORE. THE EARTH SEEMS TO ASK FOR A SIGN, A WORD. WHAT IS THE WORD?
WHAT IS THE SECRET OUR HEART HAS UNDERSTOOD AND YET WILL NOT REVEAL TO US?

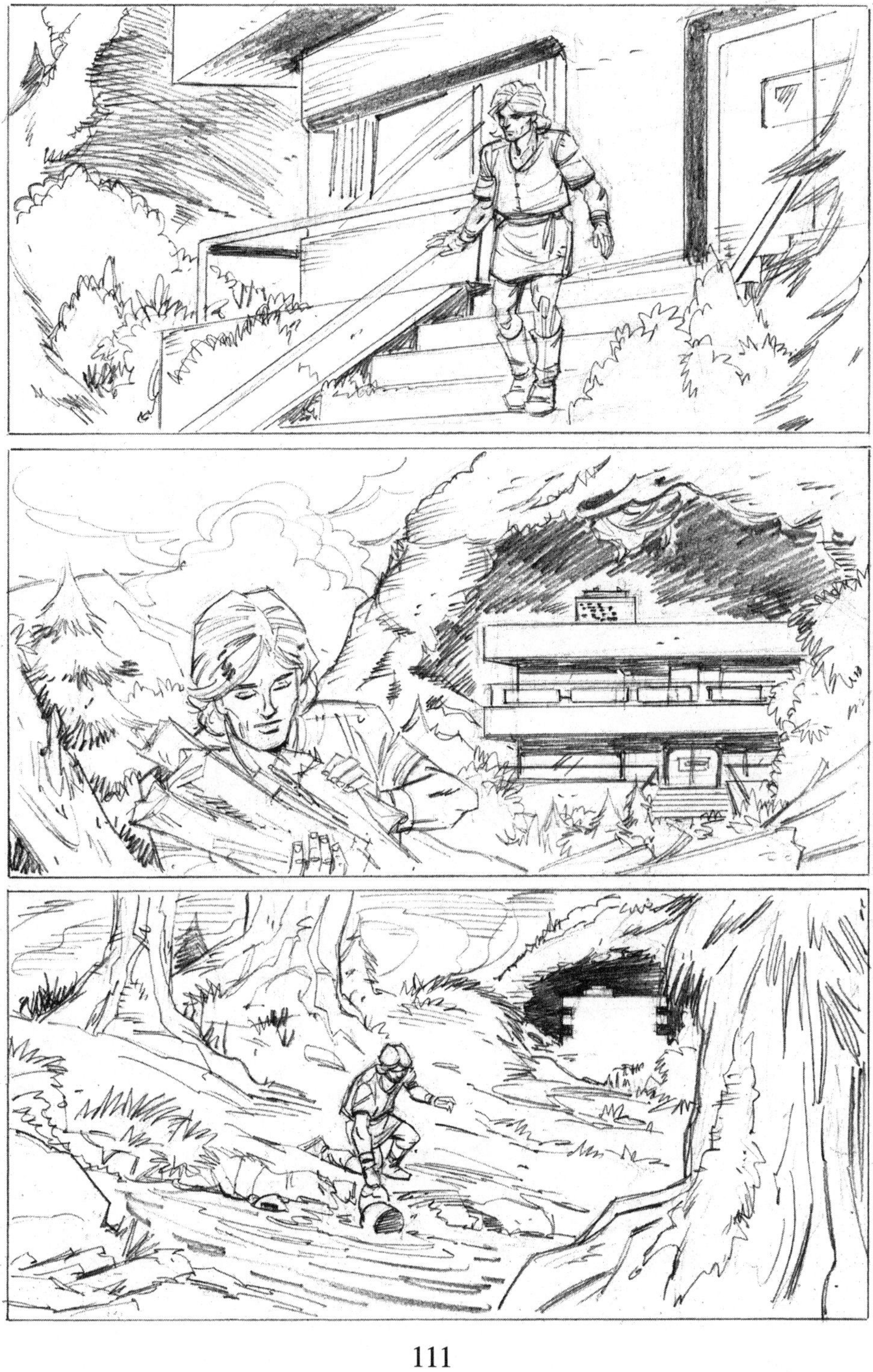

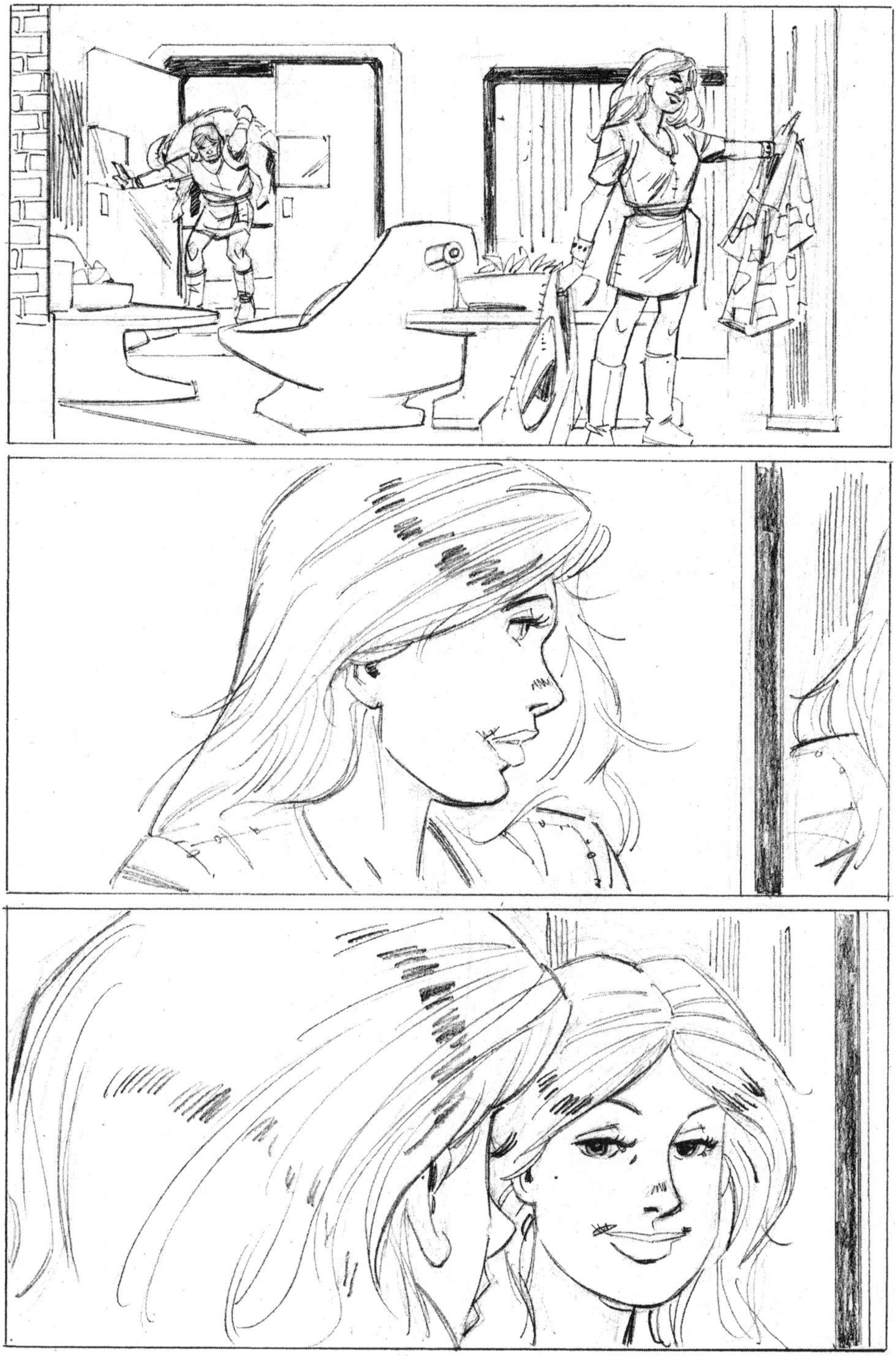

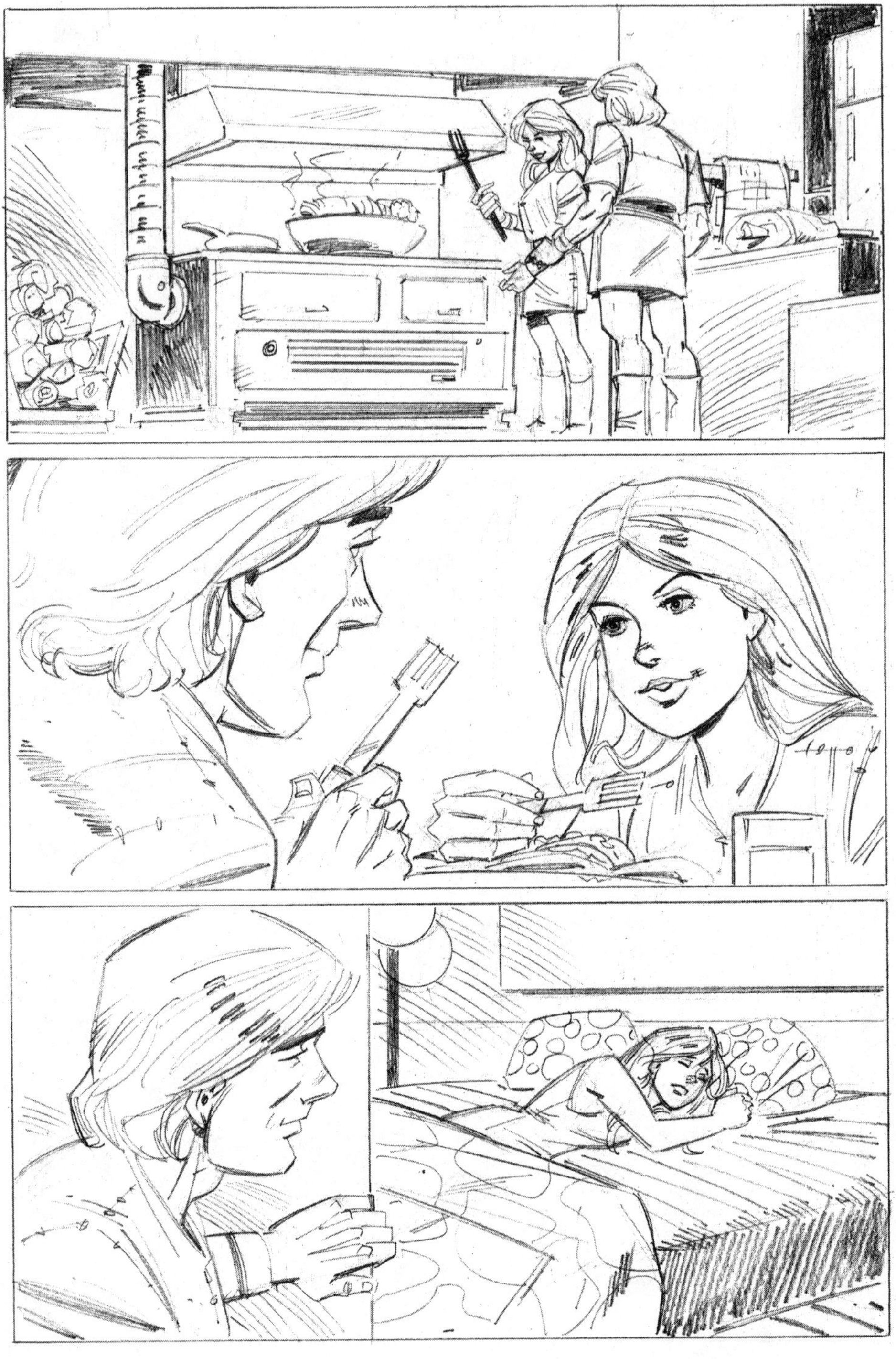

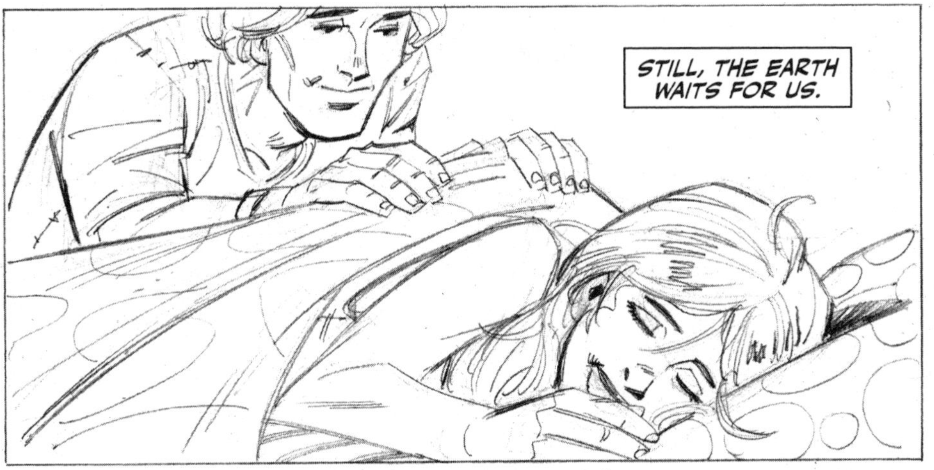
STILL, THE EARTH WAITS FOR US.

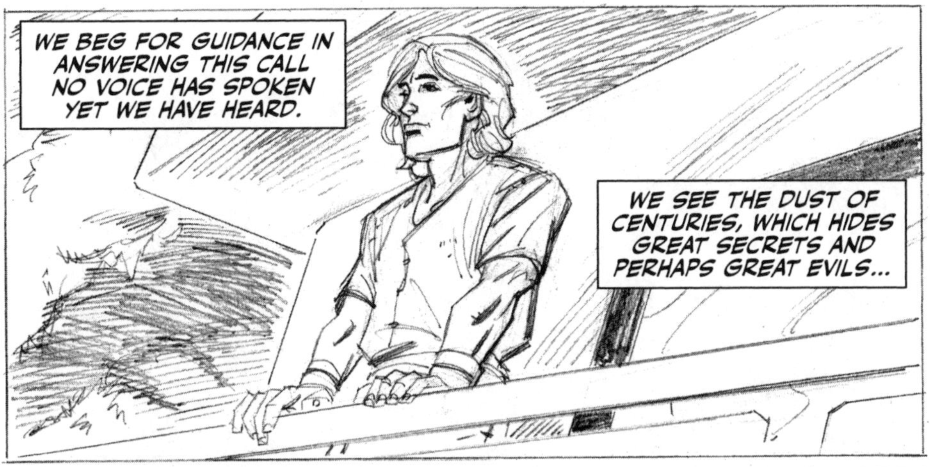
WE BEG FOR GUIDANCE IN ANSWERING THIS CALL NO VOICE HAS SPOKEN YET WE HAVE HEARD.
WE SEE THE DUST OF CENTURIES, WHICH HIDES GREAT SECRETS AND PERHAPS GREAT EVILS...

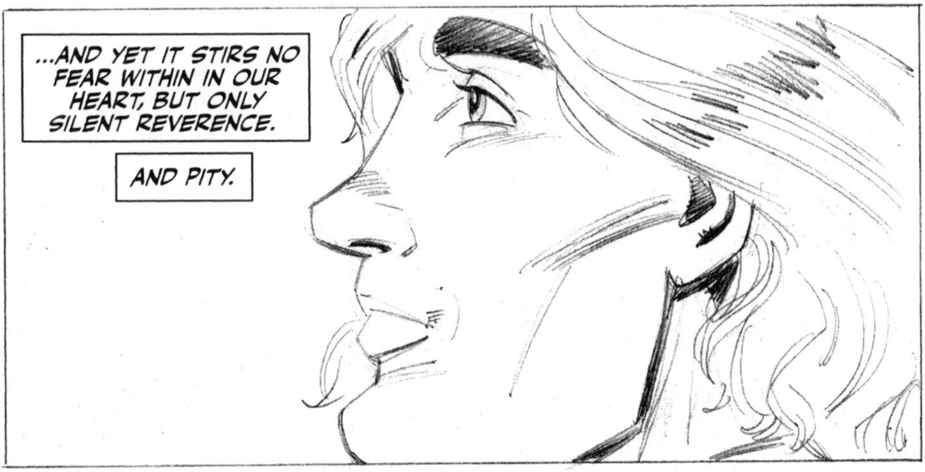
...AND YET IT STIRS NO FEAR WITHIN IN OUR HEART, BUT ONLY SILENT REVERENCE.
AND PITY.

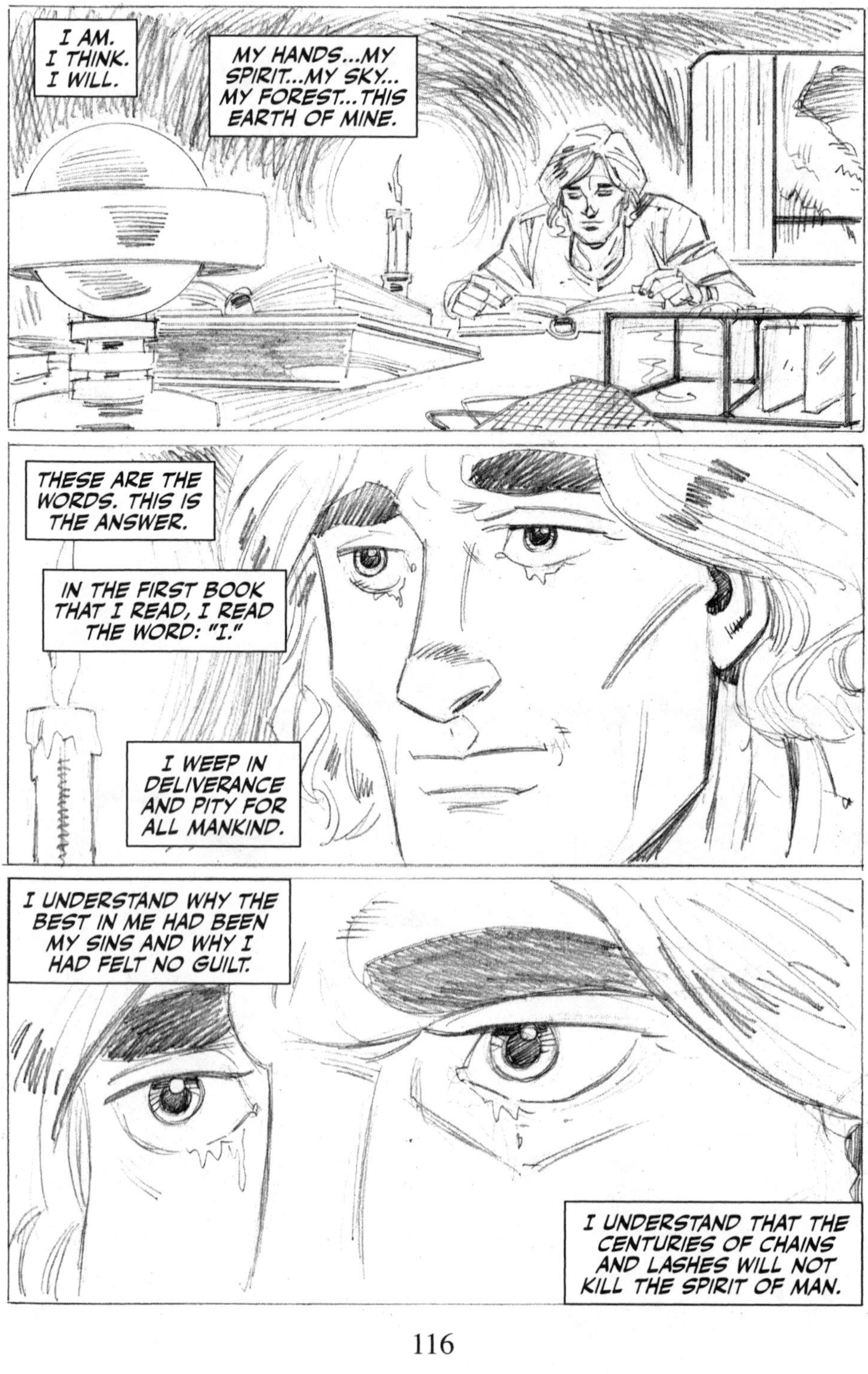
I AM.
I THINK.
I WILL.
MY HANDS...MY SPIRIT...MY SKY... MY FOREST...THIS EARTH OF MINE.
THESE ARE THE WORDS. THIS IS THE ANSWER.
IN THE FIRST BOOK THAT I READ, I READ THE WORD: "I."
I WEEP IN DELIVERANCE AND PITY FOR ALL MANKIND.
I UNDERSTAND WHY THE BEST IN ME HAD BEEN MY SINS AND WHY I HAD FELT NO GUILT.
I UNDERSTAND THAT THE CENTURIES OF CHAINS AND LASHES WILL NOT KILL THE SPIRIT OF MAN.

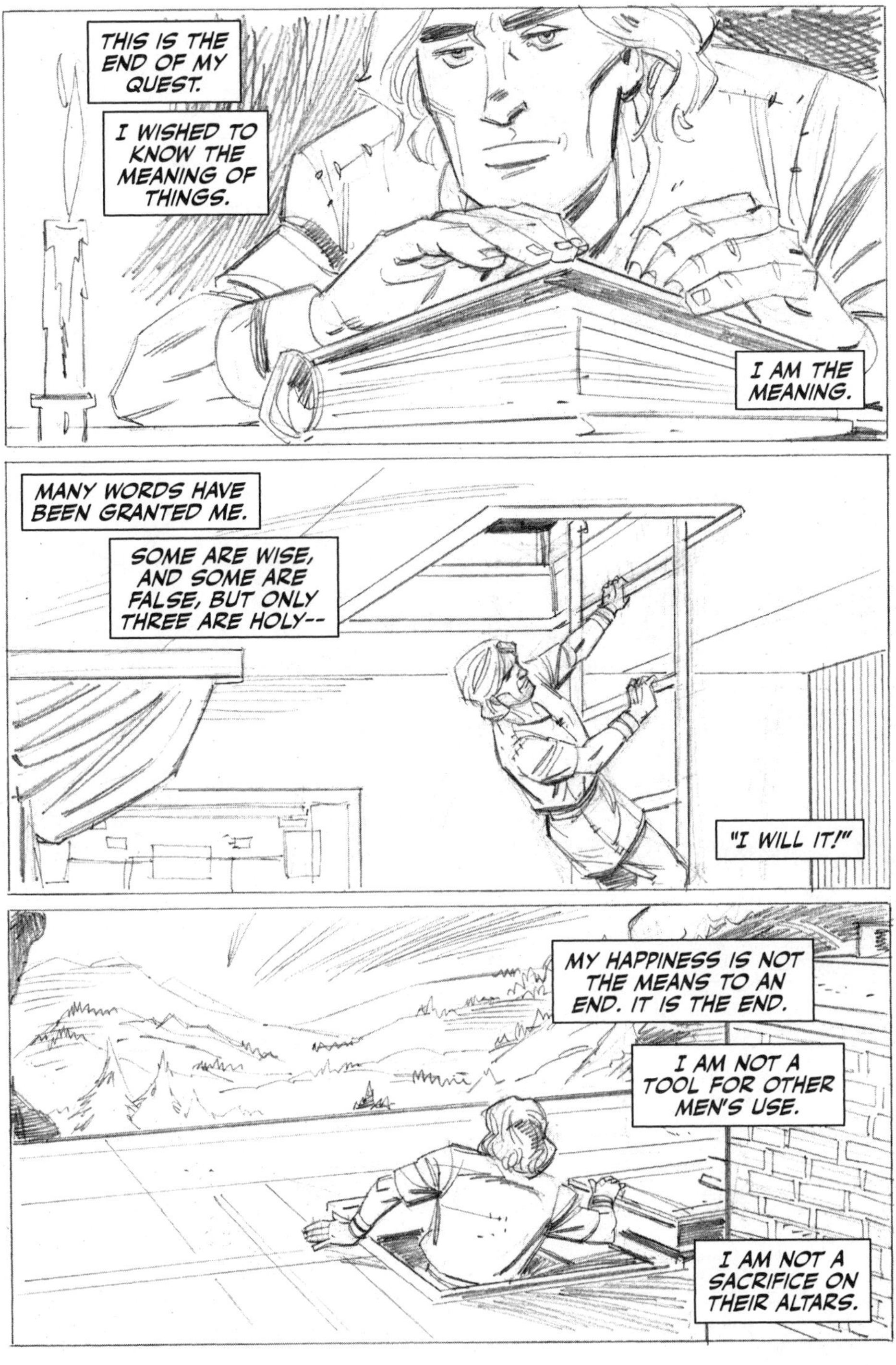
THIS IS THE END OF MY QUEST.
I WISHED TO KNOW THE MEANING OF THINGS.
I AM THE MEANING.
MANY WORDS HAVE BEEN GRANTED ME.
SOME ARE WISE, AND SOME ARE FALSE, BUT ONLY THREE ARE HOLY--
"I WILL IT!"
MY HAPPINESS IS NOT THE MEANS TO AN END. IT IS THE END.
I AM NOT A TOOL FOR OTHER MEN'S USE.
I AM NOT A SACRIFICE ON THEIR ALTARS.

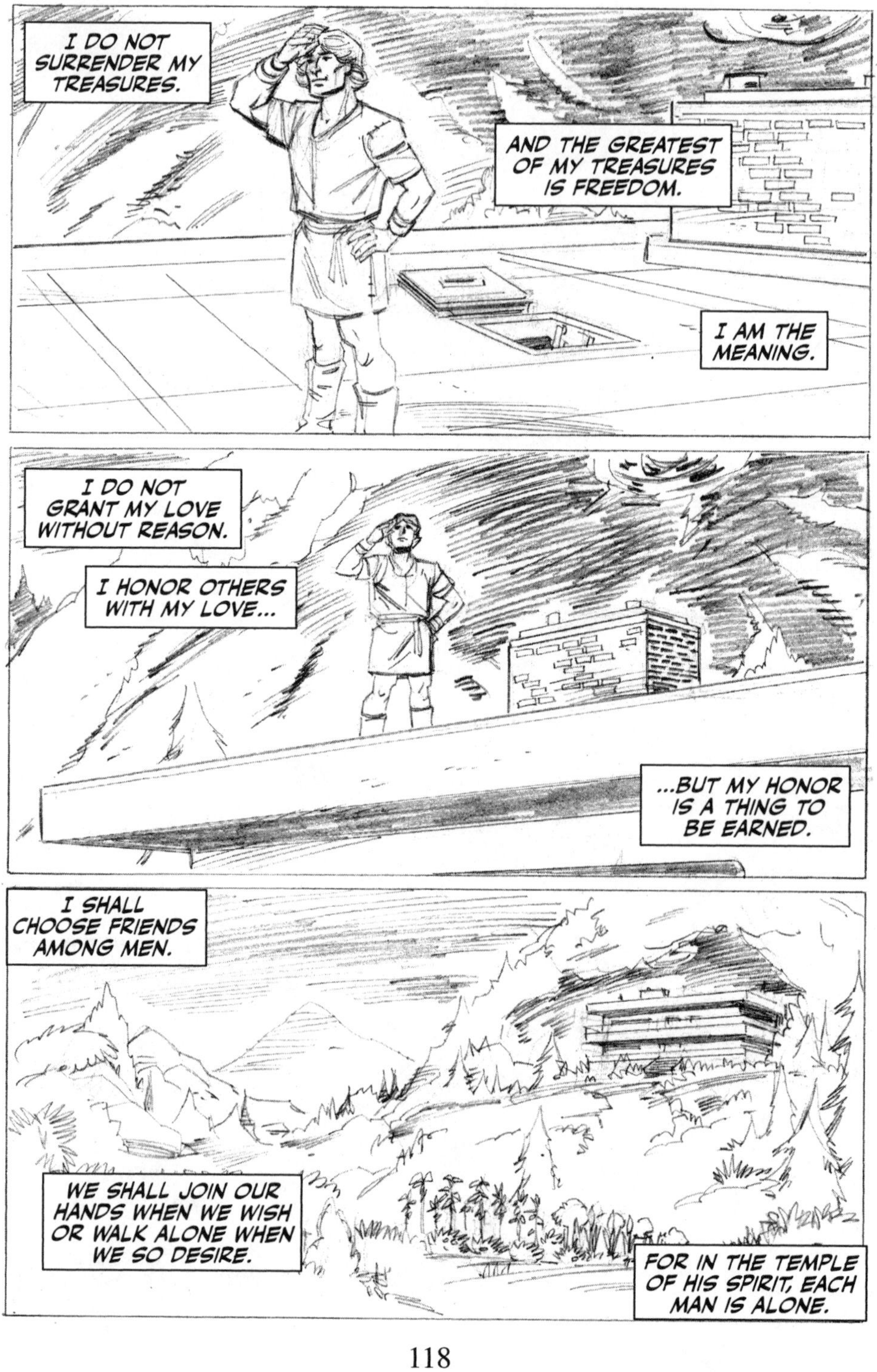
I DO NOT SURRENDER MY TREASURES.
AND THE GREATEST OF MY TREASURES IS FREEDOM.
I AM THE MEANING.
I DO NOT GRANT MY LOVE WITHOUT REASON.
I HONOR OTHERS WITH MY LOVE...
...BUT MY HONOR IS A THING TO BE EARNED.
I SHALL CHOOSE FRIENDS AMONG MEN.
WE SHALL JOIN OUR HANDS WHEN WE WISH OR WALK ALONE WHEN WE SO DESIRE.
FOR IN THE TEMPLE OF HIS SPIRIT, EACH MAN IS ALONE.

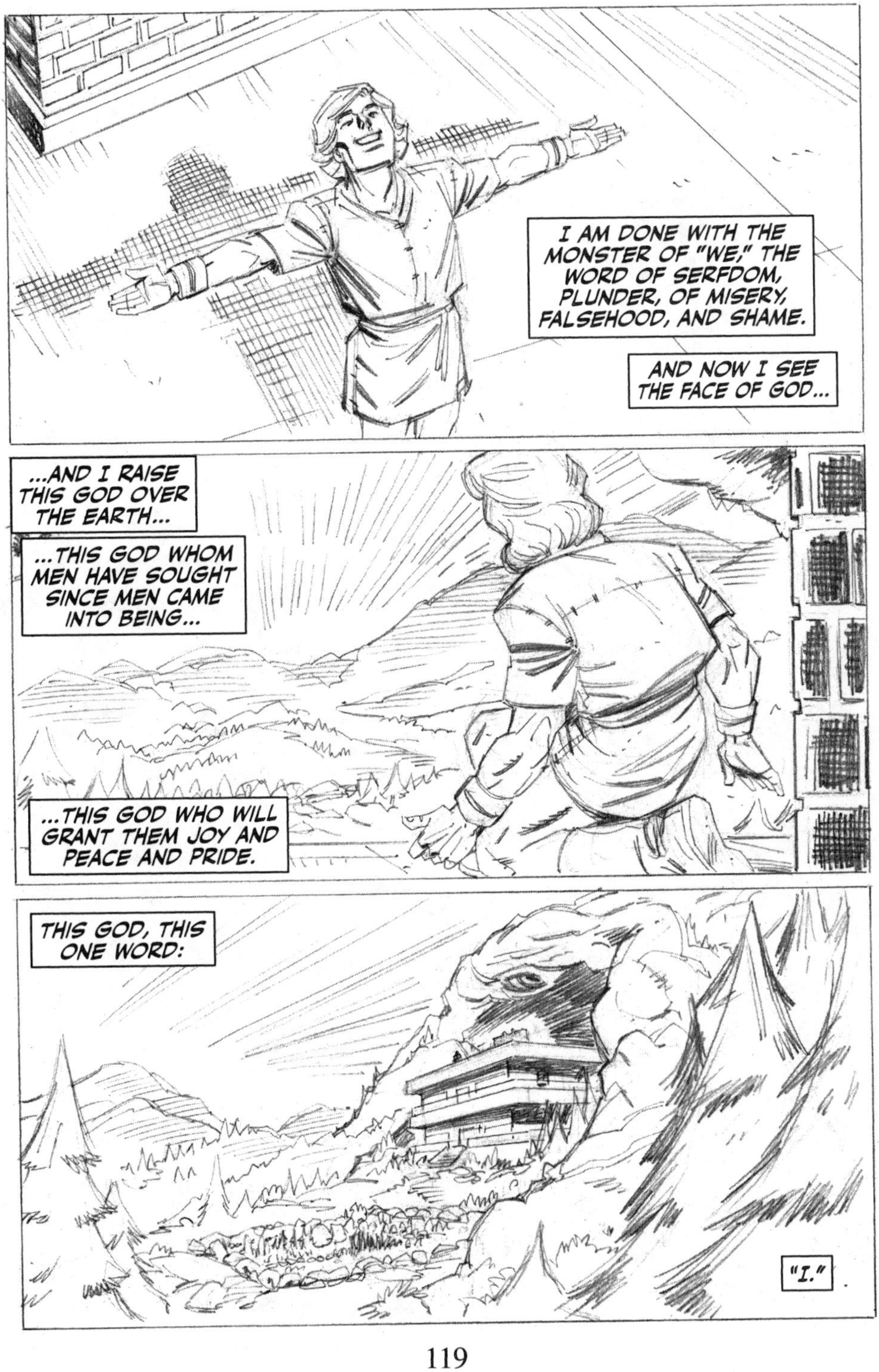
I AM DONE WITH THE MONSTER OF "WE," THE WORD OF SERFDOM, PLUNDER, OF MISERY, FALSEHOOD, AND SHAME.
AND NOW I SEE THE FACE OF GOD...
...AND I RAISE THIS GOD OVER THE EARTH...
...THIS GOD WHOM MEN HAVE SOUGHT SINCE MEN CAME INTO BEING...
...THIS GOD WHO WILL GRANT THEM JOY AND PEACE AND PRIDE.
THIS GOD, THIS ONE WORD:
"I."

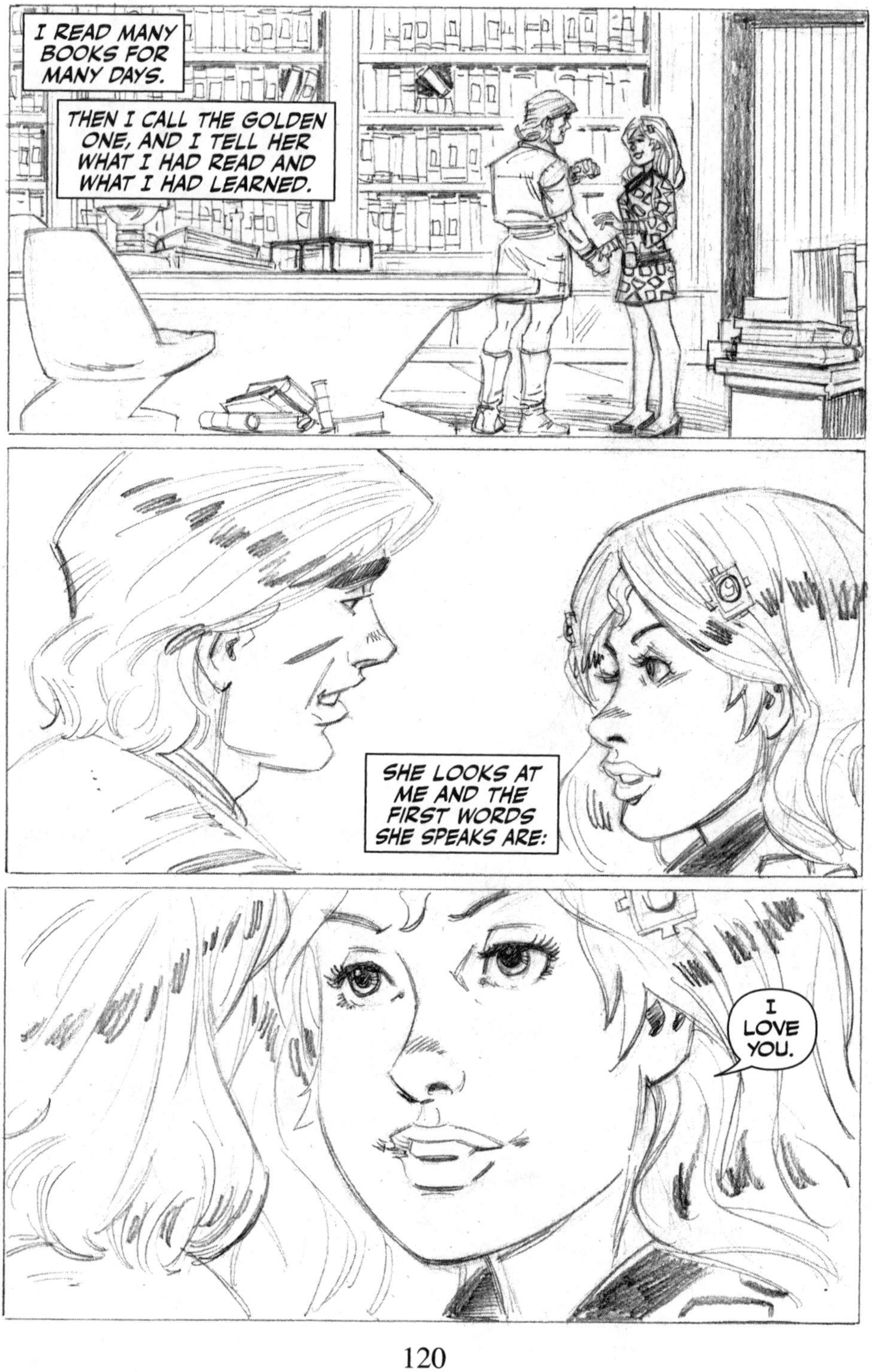
I READ MANY BOOKS FOR MANY DAYS.
THEN I CALL THE GOLDEN ONE, AND I TELL HER WHAT I HAD READ AND WHAT I HAD LEARNED.
SHE LOOKS AT ME AND THE FIRST WORDS SHE SPEAKS ARE:
I LOVE YOU.

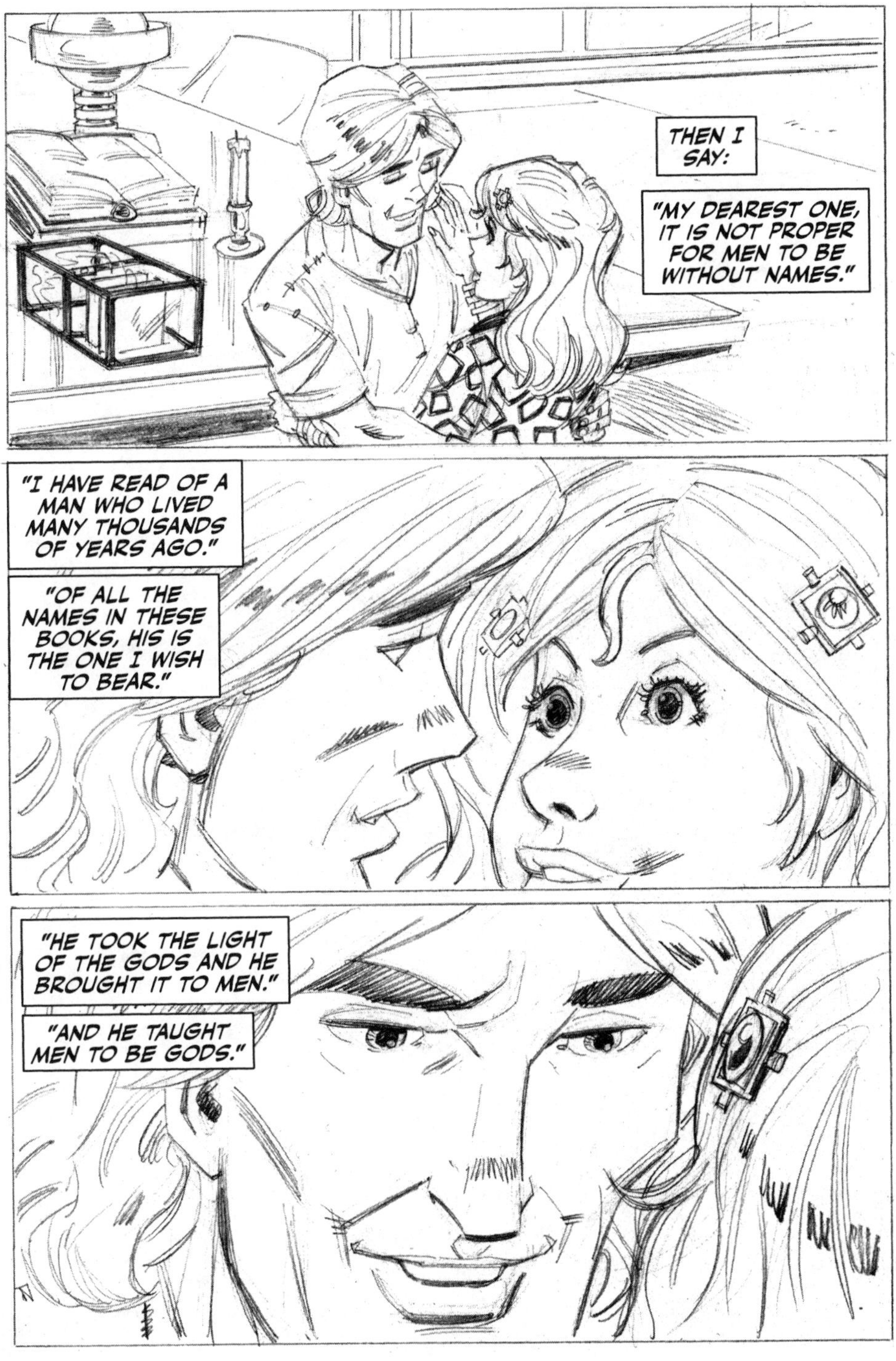
THEN I SAY:
"MY DEAREST ONE, IT IS NOT PROPER FOR MEN TO BE WITHOUT NAMES."
"I HAVE READ OF A MAN WHO LIVED MANY THOUSANDS OF YEARS AGO."
"OF ALL THE NAMES IN THESE BOOKS, HIS IS THE ONE I WISH TO BEAR."
"HE TOOK THE LIGHT OF THE GODS AND HE BROUGHT IT TO MEN."
"AND HE TAUGHT MEN TO BE GODS."

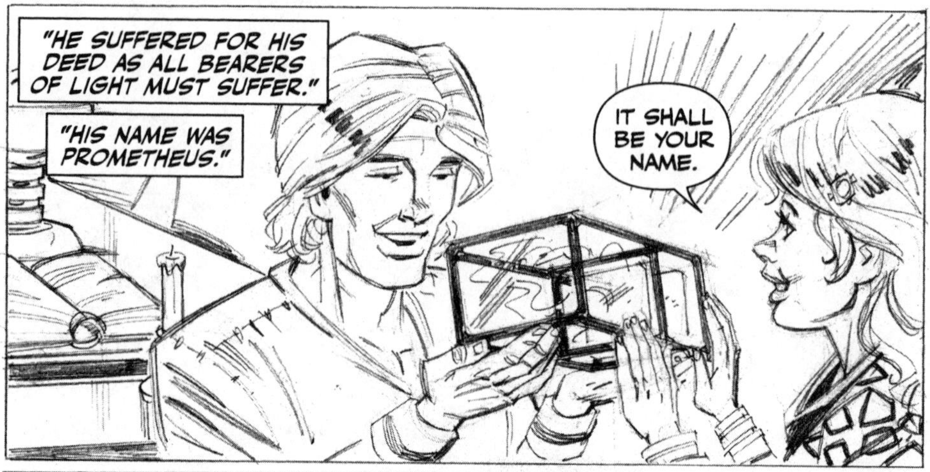
"HE SUFFERED FOR HIS DEED AS ALL BEARERS OF LIGHT MUST SUFFER."
"HIS NAME WAS PROMETHEUS."
IT SHALL BE YOUR NAME.

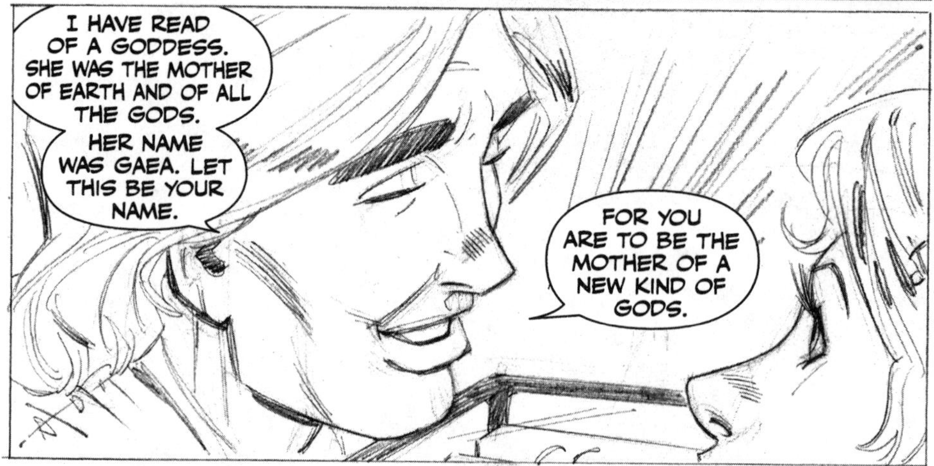
I HAVE READ OF A GODDESS. SHE WAS THE MOTHER OF EARTH AND OF ALL THE GODS.
HER NAME WAS GAEA. LET THIS BE YOUR NAME.
FOR YOU ARE TO BE THE MOTHER OF A NEW KIND OF GODS.

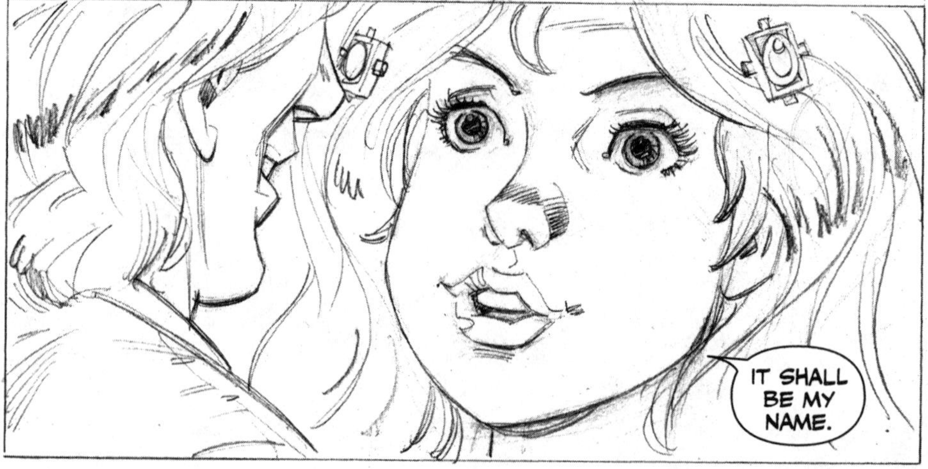
IT SHALL BE MY NAME.

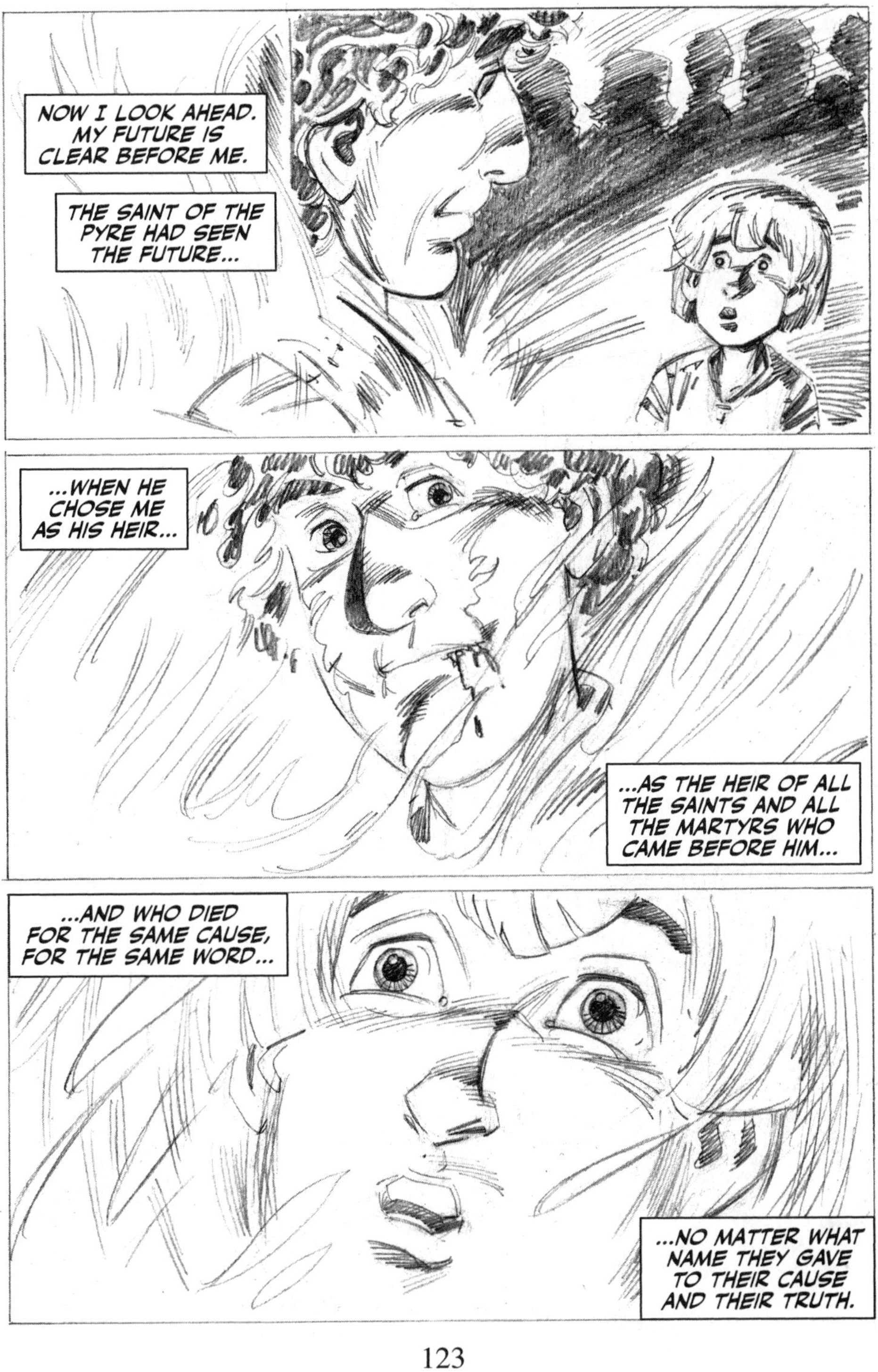
NOW I LOOK AHEAD. MY FUTURE IS CLEAR BEFORE ME.
THE SAINT OF THE PYRE HAD SEEN THE FUTURE...
...WHEN HE CHOSE ME AS HIS HEIR...
...AS THE HEIR OF ALL THE SAINTS AND ALL THE MARTYRS WHO CAME BEFORE HIM...
...AND WHO DIED FOR THE SAME CAUSE, FOR THE SAME WORD...
...NO MATTER WHAT NAME THEY GAVE TO THEIR CAUSE AND THEIR TRUTH.

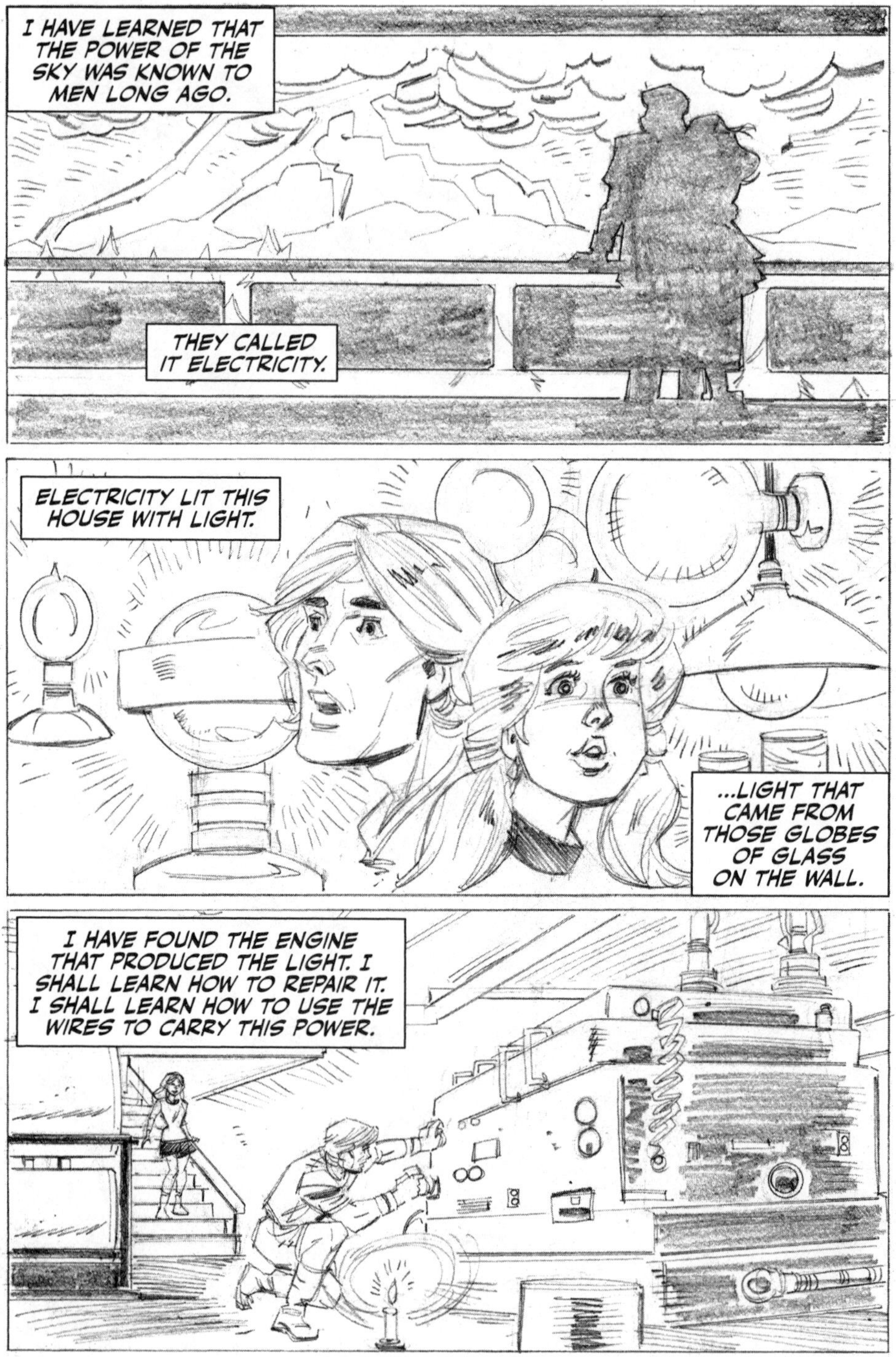
I HAVE LEARNED THAT THE POWER OF THE SKY WAS KNOWN TO MEN LONG AGO.
THEY CALLED IT ELECTRICITY.
ELECTRICITY LIT THIS HOUSE WITH LIGHT.
...LIGHT THAT CAME FROM THOSE GLOBES OF GLASS ON THE WALL.
I HAVE FOUND THE ENGINE THAT PRODUCED THE LIGHT. I SHALL LEARN HOW TO REPAIR IT. I SHALL LEARN HOW TO USE THE WIRES TO CARRY THIS POWER.

I SHALL BUILD A BARRIER OF WIRES AROUND MY HOME AND ACROSS THE PATHS THAT LEAD TO MY HOME.
A BARRIER LIGHT AS A COBWEB, MORE IMPASSABLE THAN A WALL OF GRANITE.
A BARRIER MY BROTHERS WILL NEVER BE ABLE TO CROSS...
...FOR THEY HAVE NOTHING TO FIGHT ME WITH, SAVE THE BRUTE FORCE OF THEIR NUMBERS.
I HAVE MY MIND. I SHALL LIVE MY OWN TRUTH.

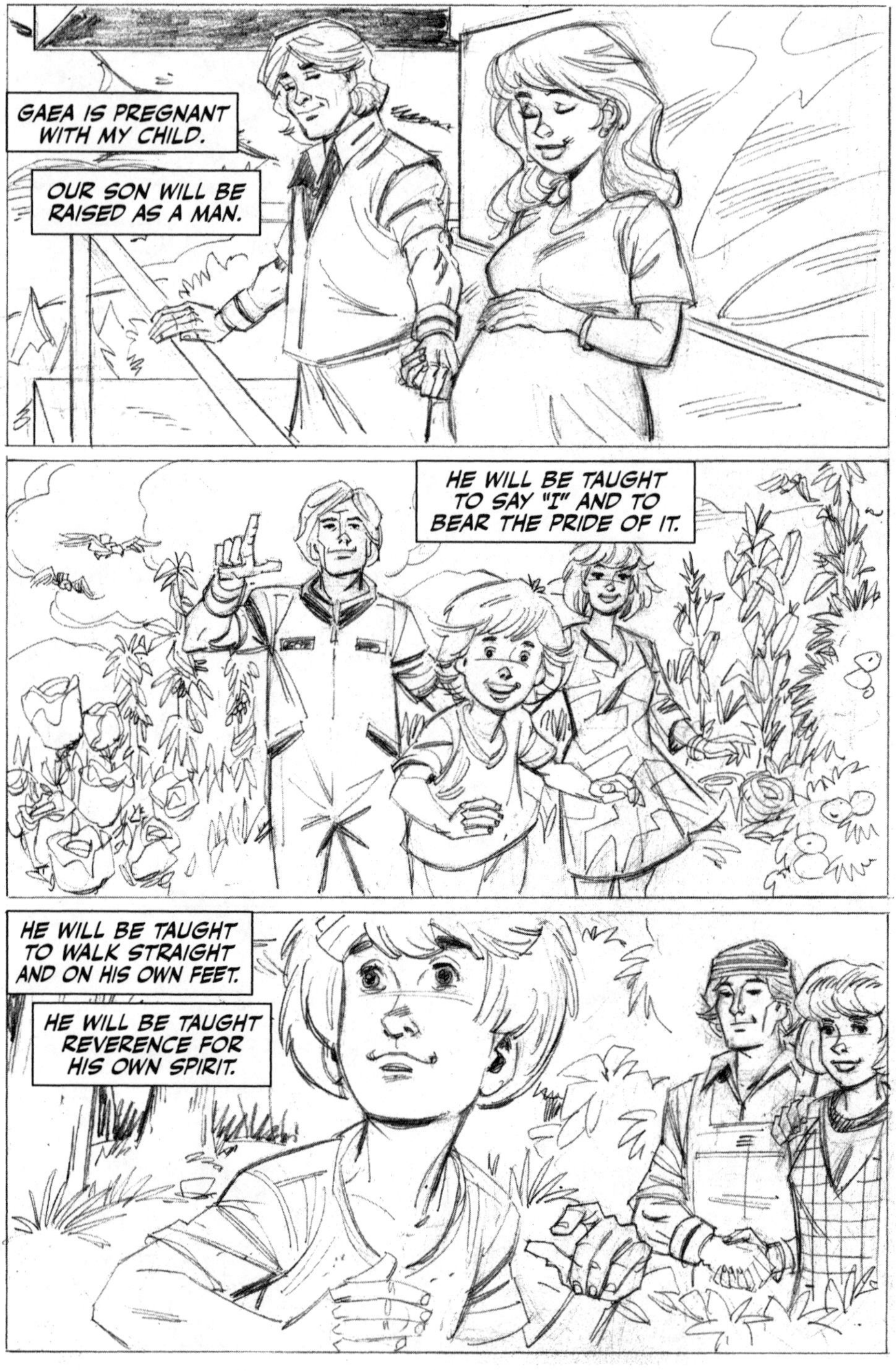
GAEA IS PREGNANT WITH MY CHILD.
OUR SON WILL BE RAISED AS A MAN.
HE WILL BE TAUGHT TO SAY "I" AND TO BEAR THE PRIDE OF IT.
HE WILL BE TAUGHT TO WALK STRAIGHT AND ON HIS OWN FEET.
HE WILL BE TAUGHT REVERENCE FOR HIS OWN SPIRIT.

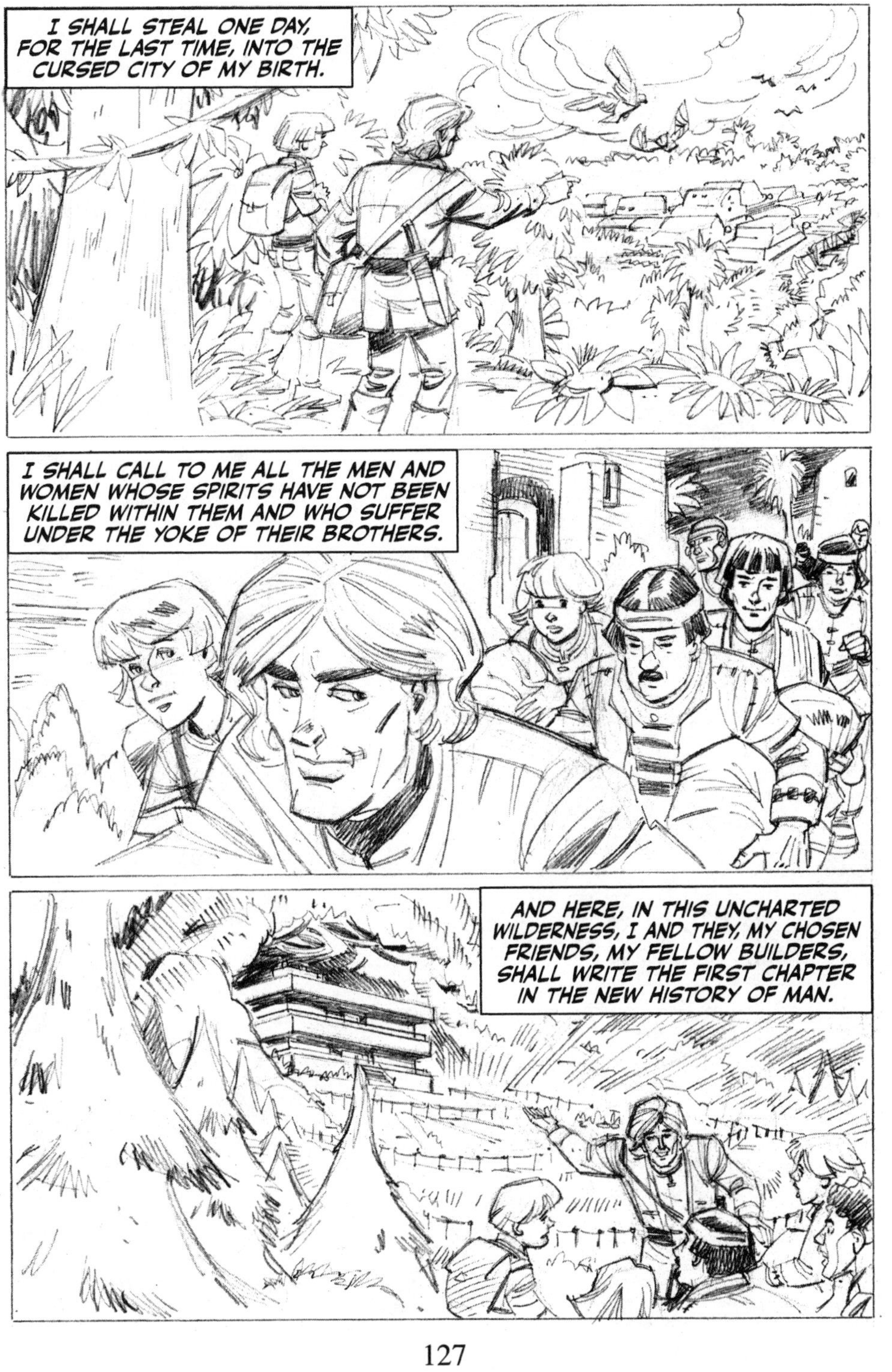
I SHALL STEAL ONE DAY, FOR THE LAST TIME, INTO THE CURSED CITY OF MY BIRTH.
I SHALL CALL TO ME ALL THE MEN AND WOMEN WHOSE SPIRITS HAVE NOT BEEN KILLED WITHIN THEM AND WHO SUFFER UNDER THE YOKE OF THEIR BROTHERS.
AND HERE, IN THIS UNCHARTED WILDERNESS, I AND THEY, MY CHOSEN FRIENDS, MY FELLOW BUILDERS, SHALL WRITE THE FIRST CHAPTER IN THE NEW HISTORY OF MAN.

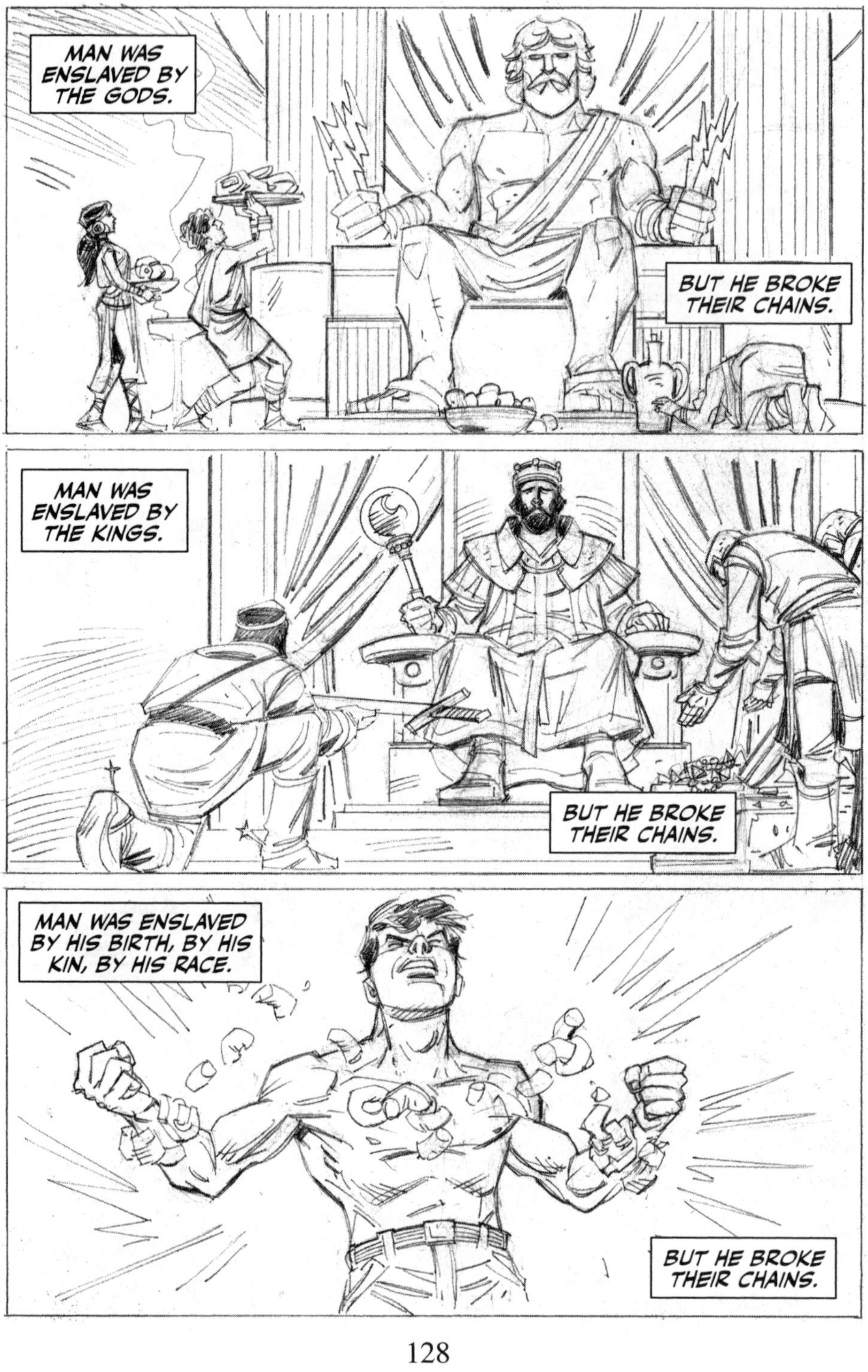
MAN WAS ENSLAVED BY THE GODS.
BUT HE BROKE THEIR CHAINS.
MAN WAS ENSLAVED BY THE KINGS.
BUT HE BROKE THEIR CHAINS.
MAN WAS ENSLAVED BY HIS BIRTH, BY HIS KIN, BY HIS RACE.
BUT HE BROKE THEIR CHAINS.

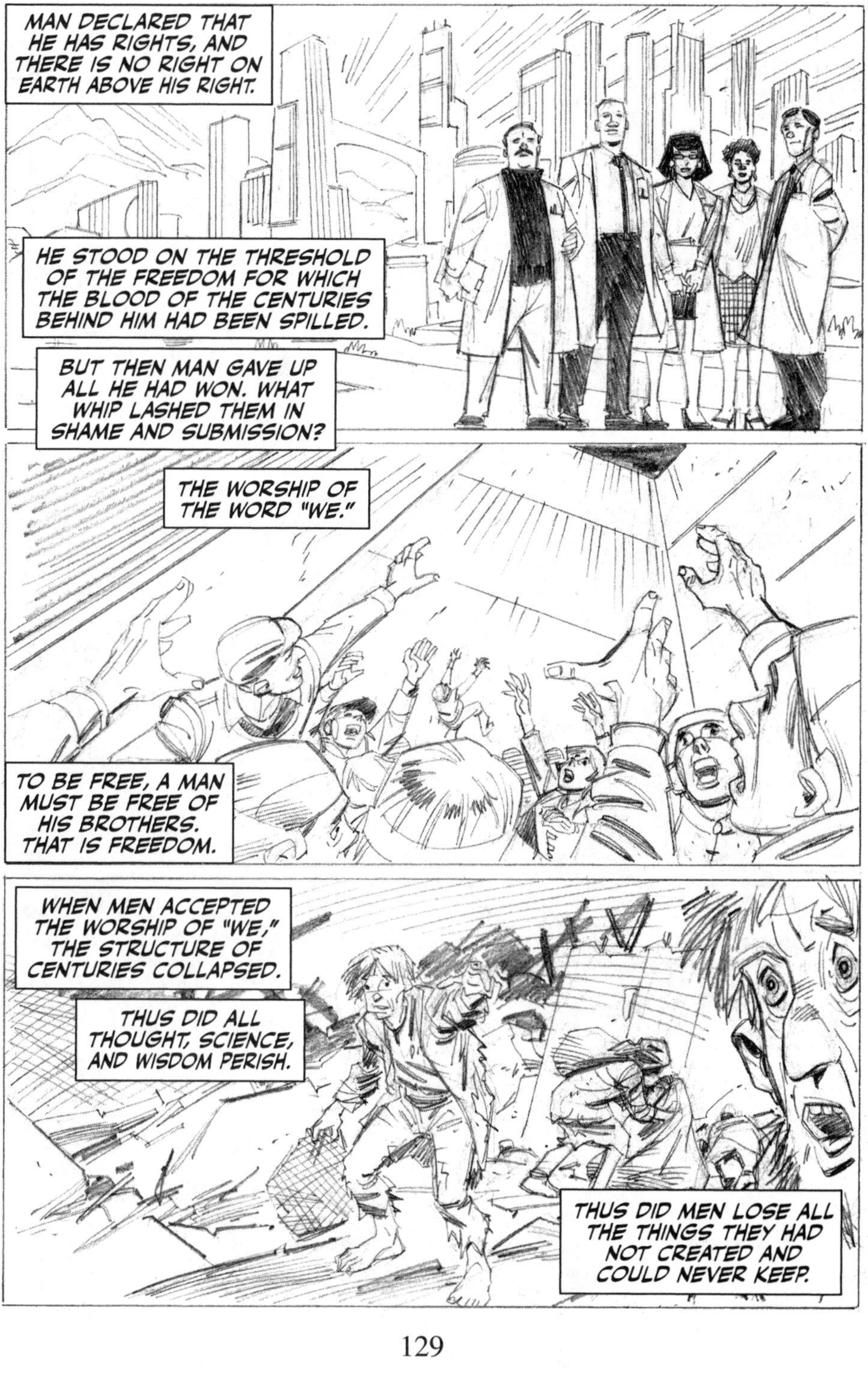
MAN DECLARED THAT HE HAS RIGHTS, AND THERE IS NO RIGHT ON EARTH ABOVE HIS RIGHT.
HE STOOD ON THE THRESHOLD OF THE FREEDOM FOR WHICH THE BLOOD OF THE CENTURIES BEHIND HIM HAD BEEN SPILLED.
BUT THEN MAN GAVE UP ALL HE HAD WON. WHAT WHIP LASHED THEM IN SHAME AND SUBMISSION?
THE WORSHIP OF THE WORD "WE."
TO BE FREE, A MAN MUST BE FREE OF HIS BROTHERS. THAT IS FREEDOM.
WHEN MEN ACCEPTED THE WORSHIP OF "WE," THE STRUCTURE OF CENTURIES COLLAPSED.
THUS DID ALL THOUGHT, SCIENCE, AND WISDOM PERISH.
THUS DID MEN LOSE ALL THE THINGS THEY HAD NOT CREATED AND COULD NEVER KEEP.

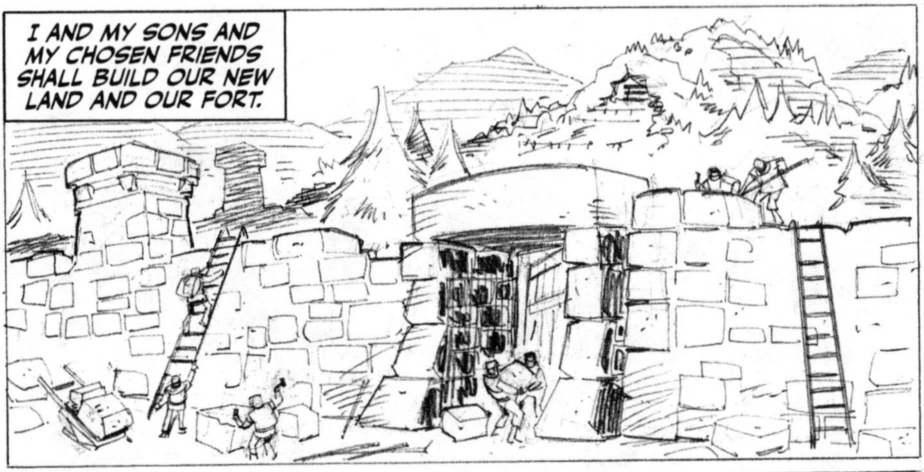
I AND MY SONS AND MY CHOSEN FRIENDS SHALL BUILD OUR NEW LAND AND OUR FORT.

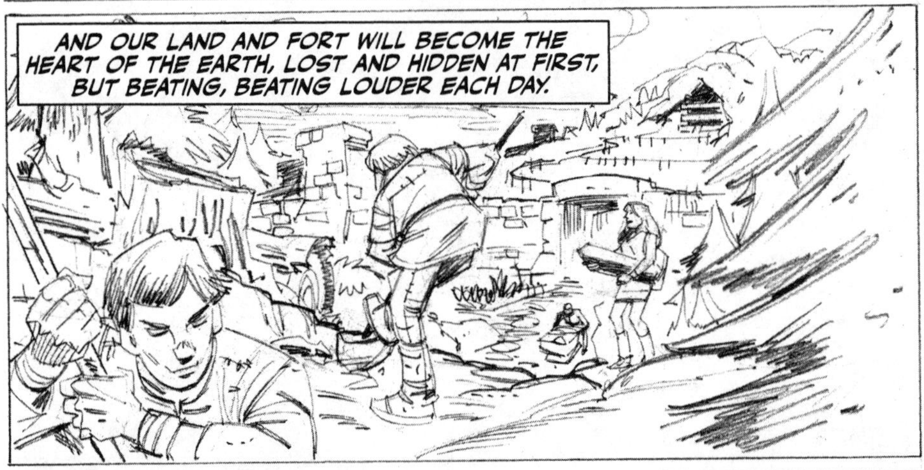
AND OUR LAND AND FORT WILL BECOME THE HEART OF THE EARTH, LOST AND HIDDEN AT FIRST, BUT BEATING, BEATING LOUDER EACH DAY.

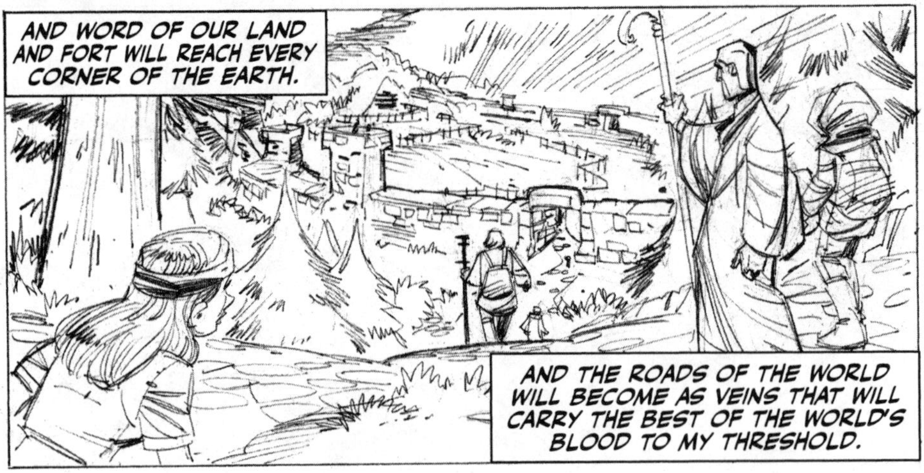
AND WORD OF OUR LAND AND FORT WILL REACH EVERY CORNER OF THE EARTH.
AND THE ROADS OF THE WORLD WILL BECOME AS VEINS THAT WILL CARRY THE BEST OF THE WORLD'S BLOOD TO MY THRESHOLD.

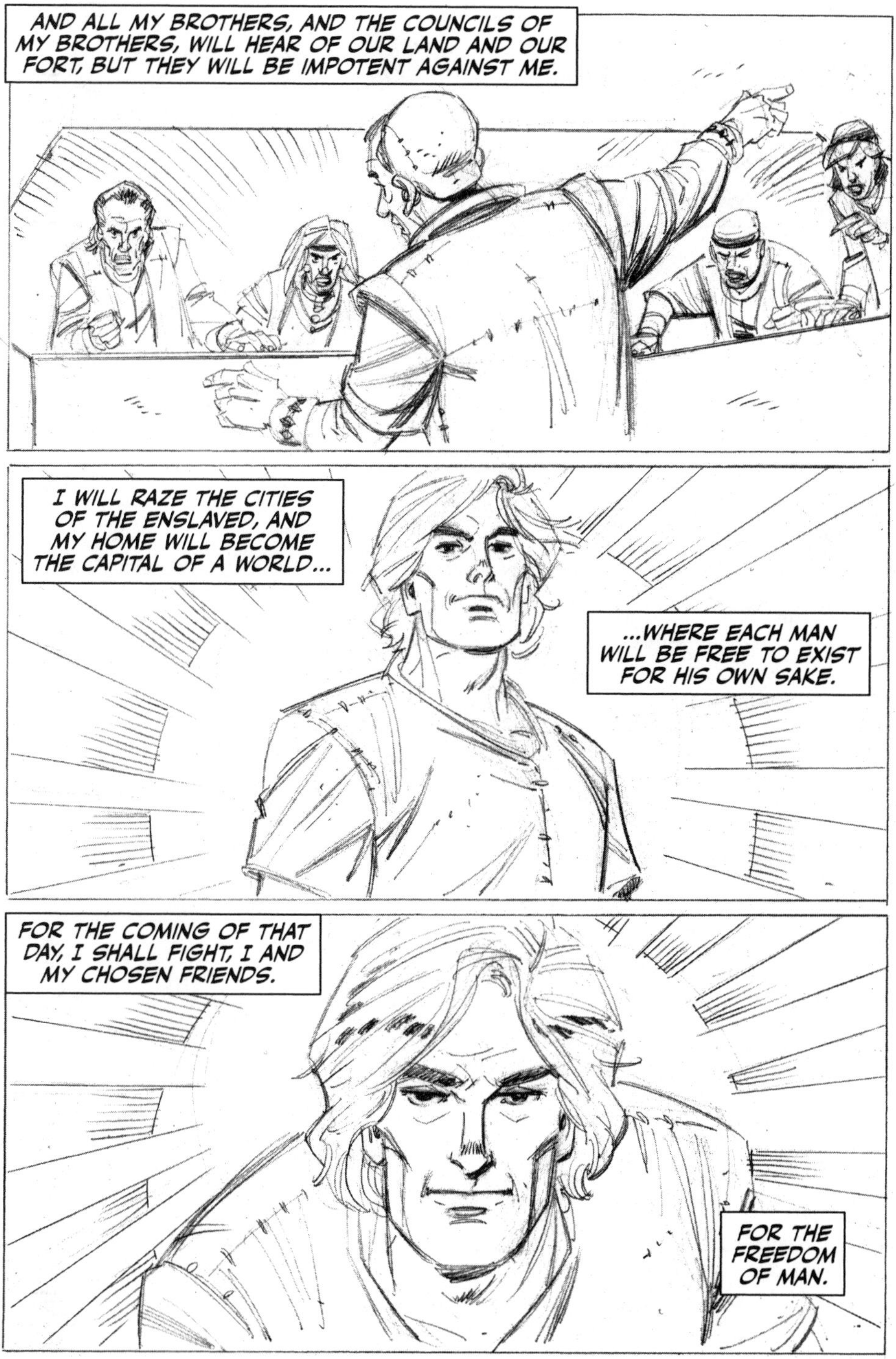
AND ALL MY BROTHERS, AND THE COUNCILS OF MY BROTHERS, WILL HEAR OF OUR LAND AND OUR FORT, BUT THEY WILL BE IMPOTENT AGAINST ME.
I WILL RAZE THE CITIES OF THE ENSLAVED, AND MY HOME WILL BECOME THE CAPITAL OF A WORLD...
...WHERE EACH MAN WILL BE FREE TO EXIST FOR HIS OWN SAKE.
FOR THE COMING OF THAT DAY, I SHALL FIGHT, I AND MY CHOSEN FRIENDS.
FOR THE FREEDOM OF MAN.

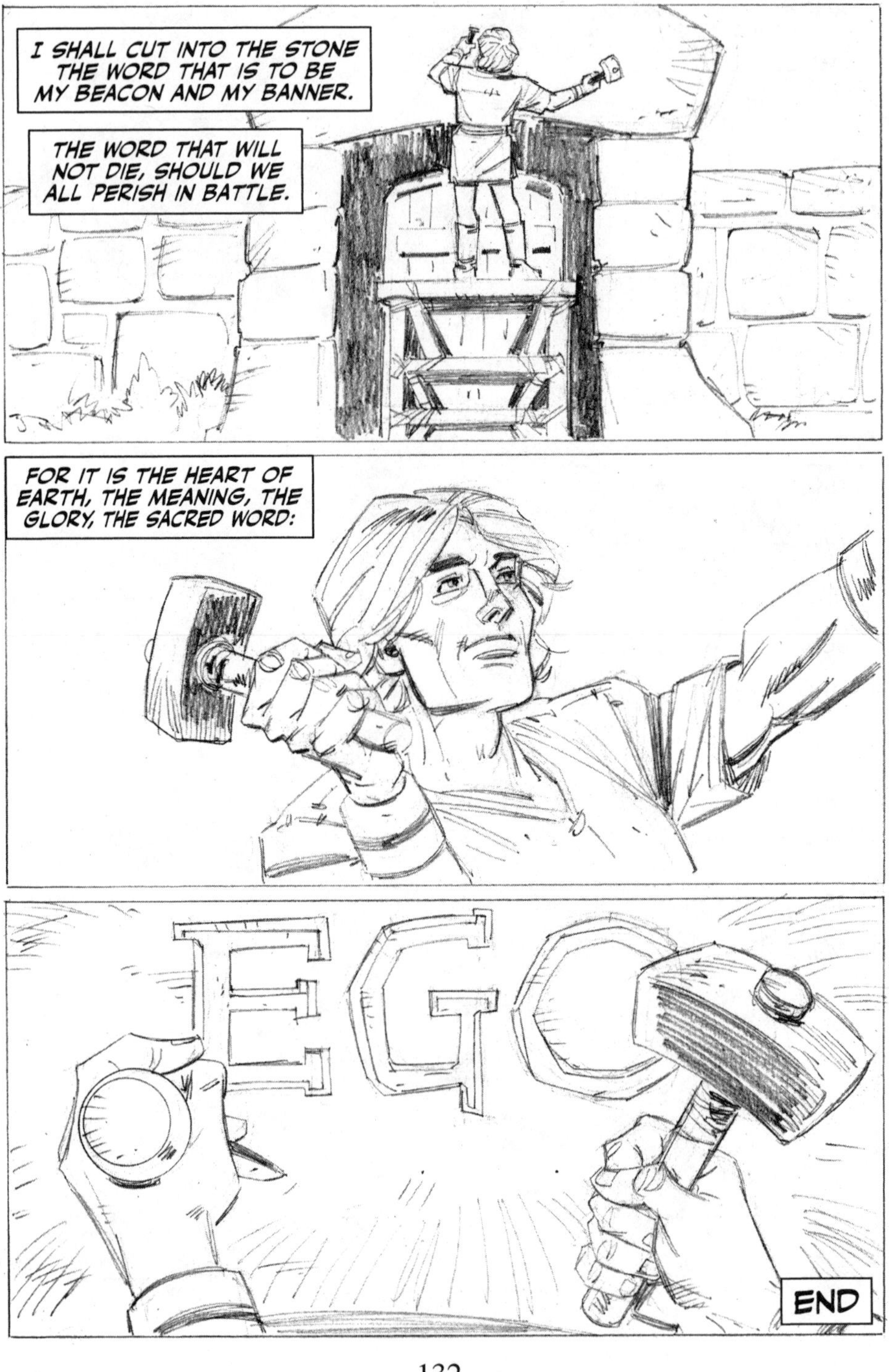
I SHALL CUT INTO THE STONE THE WORD THAT IS TO BE MY BEACON AND MY BANNER.
THE WORD THAT WILL NOT DIE, SHOULD WE ALL PERISH IN BATTLE.
FOR IT IS THE HEART OF EARTH, THE MEANING, THE GLORY, THE SACRED WORD:
EGO
END

ABOUT THE AUTHOR

Born February 2, 1905, **Ayn Rand** published her first novel, *We the Living*, in 1936. *Anthem* followed in 1938. It was with the publication of *The Fountainhead* (1943) and *Atlas Shrugged* (1957) that she achieved her spectacular success. Ms. Rand's unique philosophy, Objectivism, has gained a worldwide audience. The fundamentals of her philosophy are put forth in three nonfiction books, *Introduction to Objectivist Epistemology, The Virtue of Selfishness,* and *Capitalism: The Unknown Ideal.* They are all available in NAL and Signet editions, as is the magnificent statement of her artistic credo, *The Romantic Manifesto.*